1001
AFTERNOONS
IN CHICAGO

A THOUSAND

AFTERNOONS IN

DESIGN·AND
ILLUSTRATIONS
BY·HERMAN
ROSSE

BEN

AND ONE

CHICAGO

THE
UNIVERSITY
OF CHICAGO
PRESS

Chicago & London

WITH AN INTRODUCTION BY BILL SAVAGE

HECHT

The University of Chicago Press, Chicago 60637
The University of Chicago Press, Ltd., London

© 1922, 1927 Pascal Covici, Publisher, Inc.
Introduction © 2009 by the University of Chicago
All rights reserved. Originally published 1922
University of Chicago Press edition 2009
Printed in the United States of America

18 17 16 15 14 13 12 11 10 09   1 2 3 4 5

ISBN-13: 978-0-226-32274-2 (paper)
ISBN-10: 0-226-32274-2 (paper)

Library of Congress Cataloging-in-Publication Data

Hecht, Ben, 1893–1964.
  A thousand and one afternoons in Chicago / Ben Hecht ; design and
illustrations by Herman Rosse ; with an introduction by Bill Savage.
      p. cm.
  Includes bibliographical references.
  ISBN-13: 978-0-226-32274-2 (pbk. : alk. paper)
  ISBN-10: 0-226-32274-2 (pbk. : alk. paper) I. Chicago (Ill.)—Description
and travel. 2. Chicago (Ill.)—Social life and customs—20th century. I.
Rosse, Herman, 1887–1965. II. Savage, Bill. III. Title.
  PS3515.EI8A6 2009
  977.3'II—dc22

                                                        2008047127

⊚The paper used in this publication meets the minimum requirements of the
American National Standard for Information Sciences—Permanence of Paper
for Printed Library Materials, ANSI Z39.48-1992.

INTRODUCTION

If you picked up the *Chicago Daily News* on the afternoon of Thursday, the twenty-third of June, 1921, you would have been greeted by the headline "'All Lies' Orthwein Testimony Called." This sensational murder case topped the news that day, right alongside the box scores of the White Sox 6–0 victory over Cleveland, and the Cubs 6–3 loss to Cincinnati. In international news, Lenin advised the Soviet Republics in the Caucasus region that trade with the United States would be acceptable, the Irish political situation remained unstable, and Lloyd George was proving to be a popular prime minister in Britain. Closer to home, Mayor William "Big Bill" Thompson asked the state of Illinois to require streetcars to reduce their fares back to five cents, and two "colored gunmen" were shot in a battle with police at east 38th Street and Grand Boulevard, which also left the two policemen critically wounded. A few pages into the paper, news of Japanese battles with the Soviets in eastern Siberia appeared next to a photo of William and Mary Lahoda, orphaned when their father shot and killed their mother and himself. As an ironic counterpoint to this grim domestic violence, deeper in the paper appeared another chapter of the serial "Without Mercy: A Tale of Love and Romance." Letters to the editor decried the municipal ban on the daring new one-piece bathing suit and complained about overcrowding on public transportation. "Help for Housekeepers" offered domestic advice, as well as a column by actress Lillian Gish on writing scenarios for the movies. In the sports section, the upcoming Dempsey-Carpentier heavyweight boxing match dominated, along with rumors that Man O' War might be brought out of retirement to race a mile.

There were also ads to catch your eye. At Lane Bryant, summer dresses were $7.95, $9.85, and $12.45; ladies could also get corsets from Mandel Brothers for $2.48, and low shoes from Carson, Pirie, and Scott for $8.50. Men could find union suits—long underwear—at Henry C. Lytton and Sons for $1.35, to wear beneath their $50 suits from Marshall Field and Co. In the agate-type pages at the back of the paper, help wanted ads specified positions such as "Janitor—White. Union. 18 apts, Indiana Av, $75–$80 month and flat: state age, exp. and nationality." Or, "Boy—Loop—office. Age 16. Gentile. Grammar school graduate; want boy not going back to school." Women might find work as typists, waitresses, cashiers, or packers in factories. If you needed an apartment to rent, hundreds were advertised; and if the apartment wasn't entirely vermin free, you could consider the virtues of Stearns' Electric Paste, guaranteed to kill roaches.

Finally, on the back page, "Mutt and Jeff," along with now-forgotten comic strips like "Snoodles," "Petey Dink," and "Somebody's Stenog" occupied their usual spot. But that day, a new feature appeared: "Around the Town: A Thousand and One Afternoons in Chicago." It would run in the *Daily News* every day the paper published for the next year and more. In this column, Ben Hecht began to tell stories of Chicago that today might seem as fabulous (in the original sense) as the world classic his title echoes, the *1001 Arabian Nights*. There, the sultan's wife Scheherazade told stories to save her life; reporter Ben Hecht just told stories to make a living.

But Hecht, along with his editor, Henry Justin Smith, thought that journalism could be literature. In his preface to the columns collected here, Smith describes Hecht's endeavor as "the Big Idea,"

> that just under edge of the news as commonly understood, the news often flatly and unimaginatively told, lay life; that in this urban life there dwelt the stuff of literature . . . he was going to be its interpreter.

Hecht expressed his Big Idea in the paper, now consigned to library microfilm, and in the volume you hold in your hands, first published in 1922.

Hecht arrived in Chicago from Racine, Wisconsin, in 1910 at the age of sixteen, choosing the city over the University of Wisconsin. Chicago at the time was a chaotic place, with smoky industries spread throughout a city transected by railroad lines, a working population dominated by Catholic and Jewish immigrants and their children, with an elite class composed of Protestant old "American" stock. The city, for all its accomplishments in business, finance, architecture, and the arts, was riven by labor conflict, racial and ethnic division, and crime. While the elite attempted to enact the Burnham Plan of 1909 to create "the City Beautiful," organized crime flourished in the Levee District, anticipating the all-out gang warfare that would forever link Chicago's image to Al Capone and the Outfit, and corrupt politicians lined their pockets with boodle for municipal franchises.

It was a great time to be an enterprising young man.

In the era before radio, newspapers were everyone's source of information. Besides the scores of foreign-language and local papers, more than half a dozen English-language papers competed for the attention, and the money, of Chicagoans: the *Tribune*, the *Daily News*, the *Evening Post*, the *Record-Herald*, the *Inter-Ocean*, the *Evening American*, the *Journal*. Hecht got work on this last paper through family. Newspapers were a deadly serious business, cutthroat in more than a metaphorical sense. During circulation wars, papers hired thugs to intimidate or attack anyone delivering, selling—or even reading—rival newspapers. One historian estimates that twenty-seven people died between 1913 and 1917 as men who would go on to become legendary Chicago gangsters, like Dean O'Banion, beat, stabbed, and shot the distributors or readers of competing newspapers.[1] As depicted in Hecht's classic play, *The Front Page* (cowritten with his friend and colleague Charles MacArthur), reporters were hard-bitten, cynical, prone to drink and gambling and the bitterness of thwarted ambition. By the time Hecht began to write "A Thousand and One Afternoons," the Levee vice district had been shut down, but Chicago remained a wide-open town, with the Outfit slaking the thirst of citizens not convinced of the

---

1. Lesy, *Murder City*, 305.

wisdom of Prohibition. Reporters saw the entire city, from Gold Coast penthouse to slum tenement, and knew what was really going on behind the facades of respectable homes and in speakeasies. Hecht later wrote that "I once wore all the windows of Chicago and all its doorways on a key ring. Saloons, mansions, alleys, courtrooms, depots, factories, hotels, police cells, the lake front, the roof tops and the sidewalks were my haberdashery."[2] The reporter's job was to know and depict the city, to go everywhere and talk to anyone.

Hecht took to this culture like an alley cat to a fishmonger's trashcan. He started out as a picture stealer. In the days before reliable and portable photographic equipment, newspapers had to illustrate their circulation-raising stories of urban mayhem with photographs that had already been taken. So when a murder, a suicide, or a sex scandal developed, editors had to obtain family portraits of the dead or disgraced, even though grieving or ashamed families for one craven reason or another might resist sharing such images with their fellow Chicagoans. This trade required its practitioners to be smooth as a con artist and bold as a second-story man, to talk the family out of that formal portrait taken in happier times, or to just steal the damn thing and flee on foot while the mourners were distracted by the minister praying over the deceased.

Hecht's success in this ghoulish form of breaking and entering eventually led to work as a reporter. In one of his autobiographies, Hecht claims that he began his journalistic career by simply making up stories; the reliability of this account cannot be confirmed, since one of the things Hecht consistently made up was details of his own past. Journalistic standards were different then. Papers would have explicit political positions that would shape both reporting and editorials. The idea of the "objective" journalist—telling just the facts, with opinions segregated to the columnists and op-ed pages—had not yet evolved. What mattered was selling papers. Tell a good story, sell the paper, move on to the next story. Hecht

---

2. Hecht, *Child of the Century*, 149–50.

moved from story to story like a shark around a bloody shipwreck. But the culture of Chicago journalism depicted in *The Front Page*—and its later romantic comedy version, *His Girl Friday*—obscures the fact that the Chicago journalists didn't just want to scoop their rivals and sell more papers. They had literary ambitions as well. Hecht famously said that his editor considered the paper a novel composed daily by a score of Balzacs, and in Chicago, that was more than just a conceit. Fiction writers and poets like George Ade, Theodore Dreiser, Eugene Field, and Carl Sandburg all got their start writing for Chicago newspapers. After the World's Fair in 1893, and especially through the Teens and early Twenties, a critical mass of journalists, poets, playwrights, actors, directors, filmmakers, novelists, artists, architects, editors, publishers, patrons of the arts, impresarios, singers, musicians, and audiences all together created the Chicago Renaissance, and Hecht was a key player in this cultural moment.

On the near north side, then called Towertown after the Water Tower at Chicago and Michigan, Chicago culture simmered and boiled. Socialites slummed among the political radicals advocating anarchism, communism, socialism, and other isms long forgotten. In public spaces like Washington Square Park, better known then and now as Bughouse Square, all manner of soapbox speakers worked the crowds that gathered to listen to the freelance orators. In more intimate venues like the nearby Dil Pickle Club, original dramas by Hecht and other playwrights debuted before audiences of ardent Wobblies and green undergraduates, prostitutes and professors, spiritualists and con men.

Hecht's circle at that time included fellow *Daily News* reporter Carl Sandburg, who besides writing *Chicago Poems* was also busy inventing the genre of the film review for the paper. Edgar Lee Masters wrote his *Spoon River Anthology* while working with law partner Clarence Darrow. Sherwood Anderson wrote *Winesburg, Ohio* amid the tumult of Chicago. Hecht wrote two novels, *Erik Dorn* and *Gargoyles*, while also writing "A Thousand and One Afternoons." This creative explosion led H. L. Mencken to assert, "Find a writer who has something American to say and nine times out of ten you will find he has some connection with the gargantuan abattoir by Lake Michigan" and "there is not a single novelist [. . .] deserving of the civilized reader's notice—who has not sprung from the Middle Empire that has Chicago for its capital." Chicago provided Hecht and others a dual critical mass: the energy of a throng of creative individuals emerged in a city that also provided institutional support for the arts. A dozen geniuses could prowl the north Clark Street Red Light district, but without the magazines and newspapers that would publish their work, their words would never be read. Margaret Anderson's *Little Review*, Harriet Monroe's *Poetry*, Hecht's own *Chicago Literary Times*—all provided platforms for artists, fiction writers, and poets. The Chicago Renaissance was the cultural context in which an avowedly literary column like "A Thousand and One Afternoons in Chicago" could appear in a daily newspaper, and then be collected and published in book form by Pascal Covici and William McGee, proprietors of a bookstore that Hecht frequented, another of the institutions that helped the Chicago Renaissance happen.

This flowering of talent has its better-known parallels in the London of the Romantic Poets, the Dublin of the Irish Renaissance, the Paris and New York of the Lost Generation, the New York and San Francisco of the Beats. But soon enough, or all too soon, the Chicago Renaissance dissipated. Publishers and poets alike decamped for New York and, later, Hollywood. The accomplishments of the Modernists—some of whom were first published in Monroe's *Poetry*—soon overshadowed the Chicago Renaissance, and later developments in literary taste would dismiss Sandburg's plain language poetry for highly wrought modernist poetry, and Dreiser's realism for, well, highly wrought modernist fiction. Hecht, fired from the *Daily News* after a scandal caused by his own willful confrontation with literary censorship, would go to both New York and Los Angeles, becoming a Broadway playwright, and perhaps the most accomplished screenwriter and script doctor in movie history. He won the first Academy Award for screenwriting, won a second with his partner MacArthur, and was nominated five other times.

Hecht's accomplishments go beyond the world of storytelling: during the Second World War, Hecht worked to publicize the plight of European Jews facing the Holocaust, and his early support for an independent Jewish state in Palestine later got his films blacklisted in Great Britain. A ship that ran postwar British blockades to bring Holocaust survivors—and arms—to Israel was named the S. S. Ben Hecht. In 2004, the city of Chicago named the section of West Walton Street that forms the northern boundary of Bughouse Square Honorary Ben Hecht Way, not for his writing about Chicago, but for his activism in the fight against the Holocaust.

But while his novels may be unread and his many film credits obscure, for a short time in Chicago in the early 1920s Hecht wrote a series of minor-key masterpieces, some of which are collected here. In these stories, he captured fragments of Chicago when the city was still the exemplar of American industrial urbanism, and when the Chicago Renaissance had not yet faded. The work endures as more than just a period piece, more than another nostalgic window back at the good-old bad-old days. *1001 Afternoons in Chicago* still speaks to anyone interested in urban history, in urban aesthetics, or in good storytelling.

Here, Hecht engages in the quintessential act of urban imagination: he imagines what it might be like to be someone else. Cities, by definition, are crowded with people who are strangers to one another, divided by race, class, ethnicity, gender, language, politics, geography, history. To live in a city is to live among others and Others. Hecht, the bookish Jewish boy from Racine, Wisconsin, had transformed himself into the cosmopolitan urban explorer, going everywhere and talking with anyone in the course of his job. In these stories, he does not deny or efface his own identity—genteelly indicated as "the newspaperman." But in telling of his encounters with others, he imagines what it would be like to be someone else grappling with the physical, cultural, and legal structures of the city. He works to get at the inner life of the young woman who's turned to prostitution ("Fanny"), the Chinese laundryman who writes poetry about the Asian landscape he left behind ("The Soul of Sing

Lee"), the cop who plays cards with condemned prisoners before their execution ("Sociable Gamblers"), Terrible Tommy O'Connor, the cop killer on the run after his escape from County jail on the eve of his own execution ("The Man Hunt"), the passengers and operators of a late-night streetcar ("Clocks and Owl Cars"). The young woman adrift in the city, the countless sisters of Sister Carrie, appear throughout this work. Hecht doesn't impose either the conventional morality of the day or take the easy exit of "free love," but instead tries to imagine and depict what it must be like to be her, as out of place as "an ear of ripe corn dropped in the middle of State and Madison Streets."

This literary attention to the mundane and everyday is part, of course, of the general development of realism, the idea that regular people and routine events are worthy of literary representation. But Hecht goes further, asserting not just the value of such lives in their own terms, but in relation to the broader dominant culture. For instance, in the context of attitudes, then and now, about race, Hecht's assertion that African American comedian, actor, and singer Bert Williams will spend the afterlife in the same artistic Valhalla as classical composers and opera divas is simply astounding ("To Bert Williams"). Williams and other performers in this genre, whether black or white in blackface, were thought the basest exemplars of popular bad taste. But Hecht, when it came to music, was an urban omnivore, devouring classical music and opera along with contemporary blues, jazz, and everything in between. He sought art in all its forms, and these stories make that art alive again for us. Hecht saw beyond the artificial divisions between "high" and "low" culture, an attitude borne out of his newspaper career, where neither high nor low mattered so much as a good story. Bert Williams, Hecht believed and asserted, made great art regardless of the medium in which he worked, just as Hecht himself strove to elevate journalism to the level of literature.

This volume also shows how visual aspects of book design can rise to the level of fine art. Hecht wrote that "the most beautiful-looking book I have ever seen was my own *1001 Afternoons in Chicago*, designed and illustrated by Rosse. True, it contained some hundred and five typographical errors, including the printing of whole paragraphs upside down, but it was nonetheless a book of wonders to behold."[3] As is so often the case, Hecht exaggerates: while there are typographical errors and at least one omitted line, his publishers managed to get all of the paragraphs right side up. But his key point stands: the power of the stories Hecht tells is amplified by Dutch-born artist Herman Rosse's evocative illustrations. Rosse, who was teaching at the Art Institute during this period, depicts in his ink drawings still-recognizable iconic Chicago places and spaces, along with elaborate decorative elements incorporating aspects of art deco architectural design. The masques that accompany so many stories echo the comedy and tragedy icons, and throughout he balances abstraction and realism. Rosse, Hecht wrote, "set a standard for book illustrating never to be surpassed in my time. Tall, black-haired and with a curious medieval look to him, Rosse, the Dutchman, had come from quests in China, Java and Bali to fall in love with the skyscrapers, crowds and bridges of our town."[4] Rosse treated the city—thought by so many to be brutally ugly, beyond the power of art to make beautiful or literature to adequately represent—as a compendium of forms and movement as beautiful as anything in the repertoire of classic fine art. Rosse's eye for detail—how you can see through the corners of windows of a skyscraper towering over lower buildings, how the bridges over the river loom when opened, the harsh lines of back porches and yards softened by laundry on the line, the surging, curvaceous mass of crowds of people in the street or industrial smoke in the sky—parallels Hecht's own focus and precision. And each story is accompanied by a title panel, in which the illustration captures Hecht's mood and subject matter without ever giving away too much of the story to come.

Hecht's stories also grapple with another fundamental issue, the relationship between the built urban environment and the natural world.

---

3. Ibid., 339.
4. Ibid.

This relationship is especially prominent in Chicago, where the great expanse of Lake Michigan sits as a physical—and even, in Hecht's account, metaphysical—counterweight to the architectural pretensions of the city and its builders. Whatever Chicago's accomplishments in skyscrapers and boulevards and parks, the lake cannot be paved over. At best, we fill in the slimmest of edges, poke out some piers, pipe the water in. The mistake many writers make is to take this nature versus the city distinction as a given. Instead, Hecht, as poet and fiction writer Stuart Dybek will do two generations later, asserts that the natural and the urban are inextricably woven together. We perceive the lake from the train or Lake Shore Drive or a landfill beach or a high-rise vista. Buildings and pavement cannot eliminate the power of rain or snow or fog to reshape the world through which you walk, obscuring your vision of the crowded streets and looming buildings. In pieces like "Fog Patterns" and "The Lake" Hecht sees Chicago and the natural world as one thing.

Finally, Hecht saw the physical form of Chicago itself as a text to be interpreted, an aesthetic form and language to be engaged for its own sake and on its own terms. In "Night Diary," he depicts the landscape of Chicago in relation to both the natural world (the moon, which cannot compete with the bright lights of advertising, the river framed in reflections of buildings and bridges) and the mythic world of high culture (distant castles and cathedrals), which seem so far from, if not opposite to, the reality of industrial Chicago and its cityscape. The shapes of windows, fire escapes, and bridges demand their own aesthetic expression. He writes, "look again at the fire escapes that are stamped like letter Z's against the mysterious rectangles; at the rhythmic flight of windows whose black and silver wings are tipped with the yellow winking of the corset and ice cream signs. The windows over the dark river are like an alphabet, like the keyboard of a typewriter." Hecht here imagines the cityscape itself as a machine with which to compose the city, an alphabet with which to write Chicago.

And write Chicago Hecht did. *1001 Afternoons in Chicago* preserves, in language both idiosyncratically Hechtian and broadly Chicagoese, the city of its day and ours. Hecht's Chicago has been utterly transformed—built, broken, rebuilt—as the towers that scraped the sky in the 1920s huddle around the knees of the glass-and-steel ambitions of later generations. And Hecht's Chicago persists, as immigrants still come here, corrupt politicians line their pockets yet, cops and crooks continue to dance their *pas de deux*, and writers still struggle to find the language and form in which to express this place.

BILL SAVAGE
Northwestern University

BIBLIOGRAPHY

Beck, Frank O. *Hobohemia: Emma Goldman, Lucy Parsons, Ben Reitman & Other Agitators & Outsiders in 1920s/30s Chicago*. Chicago: Charles H. Kerr Press, 2000.

Fetherling, Doug. *The Five Lives of Ben Hecht*. New York: Zoetrope, 1977.

Franklin, Rosemont, ed. *The Rise & Fall of the Dil Pickle: Jazz-Age Chicago's Wildest and Most Outrageously Creative Hobohemian Nightspot*. Chicago: Charles H. Kerr Press, 2004.

Grossman, James R., Ann Durkin Keating, and Janice L. Reiff, eds. *The Encyclopedia of Chicago*. Chicago: The University of Chicago Press, 2004.

Hecht, Ben. *A Child of the Century*. New York: Simon and Schuster, 1954.

Lesy, Michael. *Murder City: The Bloody History of Chicago in the Twenties*. New York: W. W. Norton and Company, 2007.

MacAdams, William. *Ben Hecht: The Man Behind the Legend, A Biography*. New York: Charles Scribner's Sons, 1990.

PREFACE

It was a day in the spring of 1921. Dismal shadows, really Hechtian shadows, filled the editorial "coop" in *The Chicago Daily News* building. Outside the rain was slanting down in the way that Hecht's own rain always slants. In walked Hecht. He had been divorced from our staff for some weeks, and had married an overdressed, blatant creature called Publicity. Well, and how did he like Publicity? The answer was written in his sullen eyes; it was written on his furrowed brow, and in the savage way he stabbed the costly furniture with his cane. The alliance with Publicity was an unhappy one. Good pay? Oh yes, preposterous pay. Luncheons with prominent persons? Limitless luncheons. Easy work, short hours, plenteous taxis, hustling associates, glittering results. But—but he couldn't stand it, that was all. He just unaccountably, illogically, and damnably couldn't stand it. If he had to attend another luncheon and eat sweet-breads and peach melba and listen to some orator pronounce a speech he, Hecht, had written, and hear some Magnate outline a campaign which he, Hecht, had invented. . . . and that wasn't all, either. . . . Gentlemen, he just couldn't stand it.

Well, the old job was open.

Ben shuddered. It wasn't the old job that he was thinking about. He had a new idea. Something different. Maybe impossible.

And here followed specifications for "One Thousand and One Afternoons." The title, I believe, came later, along with details like the salary. Hang the salary! I doubt if Ben even heard the figure that was named. He merely said "Uh-huh!" and proceeded to embellish his dream—his dream of a department more brilliant, more artistic, truer (I think he said truer), broader and better than anything in the American press; a literary thriller, a knock-out. . . . and so on.

So much for the mercenary spirit in which "One Thousand and One Afternoons" was conceived.

A week or so later Ben came in again, bringing actual manuscript for eight or ten stories. He was haggard but very happy. It was clear that he had sat up nights with those stories. He thumbed them over as though he hated to let them go. They were the first fruits of his Big Idea—the idea that just under the edge of the news as commonly understood, the news often flatly and unimaginatively told, lay life; that in this urban life there dwelt the stuff of literature, not hidden in remote places, either, but walking the downtown streets, peering from the windows of sky scrapers, sunning itself in parks and boulevards. He was going to be its interpreter. His was to be the lens throwing city life into new colors, his the microscope revealing its contortions in life and death. It was no newspaper dream at all, in fact. It was an artist's dream. And it had begun to come true. Here were the stories. . . . Hoped I'd like 'em.

"One Thousand and One Afternoons" were launched in June, 1921. They were presented to the public as journalism extraordinary; journalism that invaded the realm of literature, where in large part, journalism really dwells. They went out backed by confidence in the genius of Ben Hecht. This, if you please, took place three months before the publication of "Erik Dorn," when not a few critics "discovered" Hecht. It is not too much to say that the first full release of Hecht's literary powers was in "One Thousand and One Afternoons." The sketches themselves reveal his creative delight in them; they ring with the happiness of a spirit at last free to tell what it feels; they teem with thought and impressions long treasured; they are a recital of songs echoing the voices of Ben's own city and performed with a virtuosity granted to him alone. They announced to a Chicago audience which only half understood them the arrival of a prodigy whose precise significance is still unmeasured.

"Erik Dorn" was published. "Gargoyles" took form. Hecht wrote a play in eight days. He experimented with a long manuscript to be begun and finished within eighteen hours. "One Thousand and One Afternoons" continued to pour out of him. His letter-box became too small for his mail. He was bombarded with eulogies, complaints, arguments, "tips," and solicitations. His clipping bureau rained upon him violent reviews of "Dorn." His publishers submerged him with appeals for manuscript. Syndicates wired him, with "name your own terms." New York editors tried to steal him. He continued to write "One Thousand and One Afternoons." He became weary, nervous and bilious; he spent four days in bed, and gave up tobacco. Nothing stopped "One Thousand and One Afternoons." One a day, one a day! Did the flesh fail, and topics give out, and the typewriter became an enemy? No matter. The venturesome undertaking of writing good newspaper sketches, one per diem, had to be carried out. We wondered how he did it. We saw him in moods when he almost surrendered, when the strain of juggling with novels, plays and with contracts, revises, ad-blurbs, sketches, nearly finished "One Thousand and One Afternoon." But a year went by, and through all that year there had not been an issue of *The Chicago Daily News* without a Ben Hecht sketch. And still the manuscripts dropped down regularly on the editor's desk. Comedies, dialogues, homilies, one-act tragedies, storiettes, sepia panels, word-etchings, satires, tone-poems, fuges, bourrees,—something different every day. Rarely anything hopelessly out of key. Stories seemingly born out of nothing, and written—to judge by the typing—in ten minutes, but in reality, as a rule, based upon actual incident, developed by a period of soaking in the peculiar chemicals of Ben's nature, and written with much sophistication in the choice of words. There were dramatic studies often intensely subjective, lit with the moods of Ben himself, not of the things dramatized. There were self-revelations characteristically frank and provokingly debonaire. There was comment upon everything under the sun; assaults upon all the idols of antiquity, of mediaevalism, of neo-boob-ism. There were raw chunks of philosophy, delivered with gusto and sometimes with inaccuracy. There were subtle jabs at well-established Babbitry. And besides, of the thousand and one Hechts visible in the sketches, there were several that appear rarely, if at all, in his novels: The whimsi-cal Hecht, sailing jocosely on the surface of life; the witty Hecht, flinging out novel word-combinations, slang and snappy endings; Hecht the child-lover and animal-lover, with a spe-cial tenderness for dogs; Hecht the sympathetic, betraying his pity for the aged, the forgotten, the forlorn. In the novels he is one of his selves, in the sketches he is many of them. Perhaps this is why he officially spoke slightingly of them at times, why he walked in some days, flung down a manuscript, and said: "Here's a rotten story." Yet it must be that he found pleasure in playing the whole scale, in hopping from the G-string to the E-, in surprising his public each day with a new whim or a recently discovered broken image. I suspect, any-how, that he delighted in making his editor stare and fumble in the Dictionary of Taboos.

Ben will deny most of this. He denies everything. It doesn't matter. It doesn't even matter much, Ben, that your typing was sometimes so blind or that your spelling was occa-sionally atrocious, or that it took three proof-readers and a Library of Universal Knowledge to check up your historical allusions.

✳   ✳   ✳   ✳

The preface is proving horribly inadequate. It is not at all what Ben wants. It does not seem possible to support his theory that "One Thousand and One Afternoons," springing from a literary passion so authentic and continuing so long with a fervor and variety unmatched in newspaper writing, are hack-work, done for a meal ticket. They must have had the momentum of a strictly artistic inspiration and gained fur-ther momentum from the need of expression, from pride in the subtle use of words, from an ardent interest in the city and its human types. Yes, they are newspaper work; they are the writings of a reporter emancipated from the assignment book and the copy-desk; a reporter gone to the heaven of reporters, where they write what they jolly well please and get it printed too! But the sketches are also literature of which I think Ben cannot be altogether ashamed; else why does he print them in a book, and how could Mr. Rosse be moved to make the striking designs with which the book is embellished?

Quite enough has been said. The author, the newspaper editor, the proof-readers and revisers have done their utmost with "One Thousand and One Afternoons." The prefacer confesses failure. It is the turn of the reader. He may welcome the sketches in book form; he may turn scornfully from them and leave them to moulder in the stock-room of Messrs. Covici-McGee. To paraphrase an old comic opera lyric:

"You never can tell about a reader;
Perhaps that's why we think them all so nice.
You never find two alike at any one time
And you never find one alike twice.
You're never very certain that they read you,
And you're often very certain that they don't.
Though an author fancy still that he has the strongest will
It's the reader has the strongest won't.

Yet I think that the book will succeed. It may succeed so far that Mr. Hecht will hear some brazen idiots remarking: "I like it better than 'Dorn' or 'Gargoyles'." Yes, just that ruinous thing may happen. But if it does Ben cannot blame his editor.

HENRY JUSTIN SMITH.

Chicago, July 1, 1922

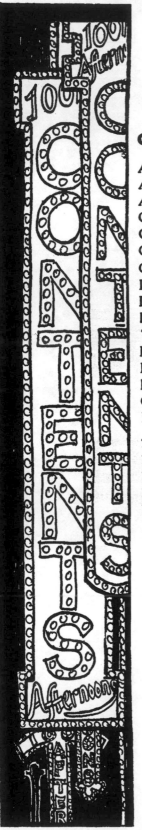

CONTENTS

CONTENTS

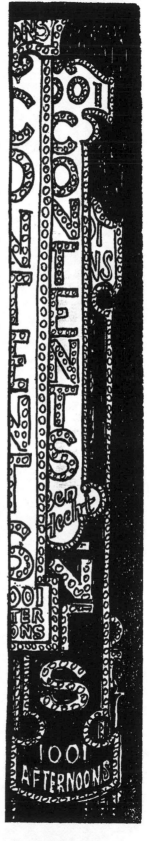

A·THOUSAND AND·ONE AFTERNOONS IN·CHICAGO

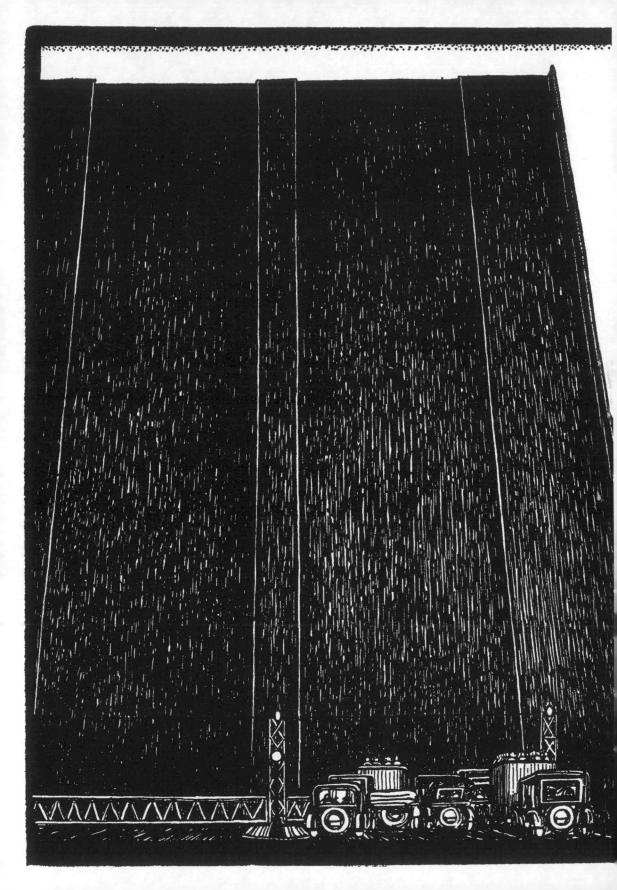

FANNY

Why did Fanny do this? The judge would like to know. The judge would like to help her. The judge says: "Now, Fanny, tell me all about it."

All about it, all about it! Fanny's stoical face stares at the floor. If Fanny had words. But Fanny has no words. Something heavy in her heart, something vague and heavy in her thought—these are all that Fanny has.

Let the policewoman's records show. Three years ago Fanny came to Chicago from a place called Plano. Red-cheeked and black-haired, vivid-eyed and like an ear of ripe corn dropped in the middle of State and Madison streets, Fanny came to the city.

Ah, the lonely city, with its crowds and its lonely lights. The lonely buildings busy with a thousand lonelinesses. People laughing and hurrying along, people eager-eyed for something; summer parks and streets white with snow, the city moon like a distant window, pretty gewgaws in the stores—these are a part of Fanny's story.

The judge wants to know. Fanny's eyes look up. A dog takes a kick like this, with eyes like this, large, dumb and brimming with pathos. The dog's master is a mysterious and inexplicable dispenser of joys and sorrows. His caresses and his beatings are alike mysterious; their reasons seldom to be discerned, never fully understood.

Sometimes in this court where the sinners are haled, where "poised and prim and particular, society stately sits," his honor has a moment of confusion. Eyes lift themselves to him, eyes dumb and brimming with pathos. Eyes stare out of sordid faces, evil faces, wasted faces and say something not admissible as evidence. Eyes say: "I don't know, I don't know. What is it all about?"

These are not to be confused with the eyes that plead shrewdly for mercy, with eyes that feign dramatic naïvetés and offer themselves like primping little penitents to his honor.

19

His honor knows them fairly well. And understands them. They are eyes still bargaining with life.

But Fanny's eyes. Yes, the judge would like to know. A vagueness comes into his precise mind. He half-hears the familiar accusation that the policeman drones, a terribly matter-of-fact drone.

Another raid on a suspected flat. Routine, routine. Evil has its eternal root in the cities. A tireless Satan, bored with the monotony of his rôle; a tireless Justice, bored with the routine of tears and pleadings, lies and guilt.

There is no story in all this. Once his honor, walking home from a banquet, looked up and noticed the stars. Meaningless, immutable stars. There was nothing to be seen by looking at them. They were mysteries to be dismissed. Like the mystery of Fanny's eyes. Meaningless, immutable eyes. They do not bargain. Yet the world stares out of them. The face looks dumbly up at a judge.

No defense. The policeman's drone has ended and Fanny says nothing. This is difficult. Because his honor knows suddenly there is a defense. A monstrous defense. Since there are always two sides to everything. Yes, what is the other side? His honor would like to know. Tell it, Fanny. About the crowds, streets, buildings, lights, about the whirligig of loneliness, about the humpty-dumpty clutter of longings. And then explain about the summer parks and the white snow and the moon window in the sky. Throw in a poignantly ironical dissertation on life, on its uncharted aimlessness, and speak like Sherwood Anderson about the desires that stir in the heart. Speak like Remy de Gourmont and Dostoevsky and Stevie Crane, like Schopenhauer and Dreiser and Isaiah; speak like all the great questioners whose tongues have wagged and whose hearts have burned with questions. His honor will listen bewilderedly and, perhaps, only perhaps, understand for a moment the dumb pathos of your eyes.

20

As it is, you were found, as the copper who reads the newspapers puts it, in a suspected flat. A violation of section 2012 of the City Code. Thirty days in the Bastile, Fanny. Unless his honor is feeling good.

These eyes lifted to him will ask him questions on his way home from a banquet some night.

"How old are you?"

"Twenty."

"Make it twenty-two," his honor smiles. "And you have nothing to say? About how you happened to get into this sort of thing? You look like a good girl. Although looks are often deceiving."

"I went there with him," says Fanny. And she points to a beetle-browed citizen with an unshaven face. A quaint Don Juan, indeed.

"Ever see him before?"

A shake of the head. Plain case. And yet his honor hesitates. His honor feels something expand in his breast. Perhaps he would like to rise and holding forth his hand utter a famous plagiarism — "Go and sin no more." He chews a pen and sighs, instead.

"I'll give you another chance," he says. "The next time it'll be jail. Keep this in mind. If you're brought in again, no excuses will go. Call the next case."

Now one can follow Fanny. She walks out of the court-room. The street swallows her. Nobody in the crowds knows what has happened. Fanny is anybody now. Still, one may follow. Perhaps something will reveal itself, something will add an illuminating touch to the incident of the courtroom.

There is only this. Fanny pauses in front of a drug-store window. The crowds clutter by. Fanny stands looking, without interest, into the window. There is a little mirror inside. The city tumbles by. The city is interested in something vastly complicated.

Staring into the little mirror, Fanny sighs and—powders her nose.

THE AUCTIONEER'S WIFE

An auctioneer must have a compelling manner. He must be gabby and stentorian, witheringly sarcastic and plaintively cajoling. He must be able to detect the faintest symptoms of avarice and desire in the blink of an eyelid, in the tilt of a head. Behind his sing-song of patter as he knocks down a piece of useless bric-a-brac he must be able to remain cool, remain calculating, remain like a hawk prepared to pounce upon his prey. Passion for him must be no more than a mask; anger, sorrow, despair, ecstasy no more than the devices of salesmanship.

But more than all this, an auctioneer must know the magic password into the heart of the professional or amateur collector. He must know the glittering phrases that are the keys to their hobbies. The words that bring a gleam to the eye of the Oriental rug collector. The words that fire the china collector. The stamp collector. The period furniture collector. The tapestry enthusiast. The first edition fan. And so on.

"Ladies and gentlemen, I desire your expert attention for a moment. I have here a curious little thing of exquisite workmanship said to be from the famous collection of Count Valentino of Florence. This delicately molded, beautifully painted candelabra has illuminated the feasts of the old Florentines, twinkled amid the gay, courtly rioting of a time that is no more. Before the bidding for this priceless souvenir is opened I desire, ladies and gentlemen, to state briefly———"

Nathan Ludlow is an auctioneer who knows all the things an auctioneer must know. His eye is piercing. His tongue can roll and rattle for twelve hours at a stretch. His voice is the voice of the tempter, myriad-toned and irresistible.

It was evening. An auspicious evening. It was the evening of Mr. Ludlow's divorce. And Mr. Ludlow sat in his room at the Morrison Hotel, a decanter of juniper juice at his elbow. And while he sat he talked. The subjects varied. There were tales of Ming vases and Satsuma bargains, of porcelains and rugs. And finally Mr. Ludlow arrived at the subject of audiences. And from this subject he progressed with the aid of the juniper juice to the subject of wives. And from the subject of wives he stepped casually into the sad story of his life.

"I'll tell you," said Mr. Ludlow. "Tonight I'm a free man. Judge Pam gave me, or gave her, rather, the divorce. I guess he did well. Maybe she was entitled to it. Desertion and cruelty were the charges. But they don't mean anything. The chief complaint she had against me was that I was an auctioneer."

Mr. Ludlow sighed and ran his long, artist's fingers over his eagle features and brushed back a Byronic lock of hair from his forehead.

"It was four years ago we met," he resumed, " in the Wabash Avenue place. I noticed her when the bidding on a rocking chair started. A pretty girl. And as is often the case among women who attend auctions—a bug, a fan, a fish. You know, the kind that stiffen up when they get excited. The kind that hang on your words and breathe hard while you cut loose with the patter, and lose their heads when you swing into the going-going-gone finale.

"Well, she didn't get the rocking chair. But she was game and came back on a Chinese rug. I began to notice her considerably. My words seemed to have an unusual effect on her. Then I could see that she was not only the kind of fish that lose their heads at auctions, but the terrible kind that believe everything the auctioneer says. You know, they believe that the Oriental rugs really came from the harem of the caliph and that the antique bed really was the one in which DuBarry slept and that the Elizabethan tablecloth really was an Elizabethan tablecloth. They are kind of goofily romantic and they fall hard for everything and they spend their last

23

penny on a lot of truck, you know. Not bad stuff and probably a good deal more useful and lasting than the originals would have been."

Mr. Ludlow smiled a bit apologetically. "I'm not confessing anything you don't know, I hope," he said. "Well, to go on about the missus. I knew I had her from that first day. I wasn't vitally interested, but when she returned six days in succession it got kind of flattering. And the way she looked at me and listened to me when I pulled my stuff—say, I could have knocked down a bouquet of paper roses for the original wreath worn by Venus, I felt so good. That's how I began to think that she was an inspiration to me and how I figured that if I could have somebody like her around I'd soon have them all pocketed as auctioneers.

"I forget just how it was we met, but we did. And I swear, the way she flattered me would have been enough to turn the head of a guy ten times smarter than me and forty times as old. So we got married. That's skipping a lot. But, you know, what's it all amount to, the courting and the things you say and do before you get married? So we got married and then the fun started.

"At first I could hardly believe what the drift of it was. But I hope to die if she wasn't sincere in her ideas about me as an auctioneer. I didn't get it, as I say, and that's where I made my big mistake. I let her come to the auctions and told her not to bid. But when I'd start my patter on some useless piece of 5- and 10-cent store bric-a-brac and give it an identity and hint at Count Rudolph's collection and so on, she was off like a two-year-old down a morning track.

"I didn't know how to fix it or how to head her out of it. For a month I didn't have the heart to disillusion her. I let her buy. Damn it, I never saw such an absolute boob as she was. She'd pick out the most worthless junk I was knocking down and go mad over it and buy it with my good money. It got so that I realized I was slipping. I'd get a

24

promise from her that she wouldn't come into the auction, but I never could be sure. And if I felt like cutting loose on some piece of junk and knocking it down with a lot of flourishes I knew sure as fate that the missus would be there and that she would be the fish that caught fire first and most and that I'd be selling the thing to myself.

"Well, after the first two months of my married life I realized that I'd have to talk turkey to the missus. She was costing me my last nickel at these auctions and the better auctioneer I was the more money I lost, on account of her being so susceptible to my line of stuff. It sounds funny, but it's a fact. So I told her. I made a clean breast. I told her what a liar I was and how all the stuff I pulled from the auction stand was the bunk and how she was a boob for falling for it. And so on and so on. Say, I sold myself to her as the world's greatest, all around, low down, hideous liar that ever walked in shoe leather. And that's how it started. This divorce today is kind of an anti-climax. We ain't had much to do with each other ever since that confession."

Mr. Ludlow stared sorrowfully into the remains of a glass of juniper juice.

"I'll never marry again," he moaned. "I ain't the kind that makes a good husband. A good husband is a man who is just an ordinary liar. And me? Well, I'm an auctioneer."

FOG PATTERNS

The fog tiptoes into the streets. It walks like a great cat through the air and slowly devours the city.

The office buildings vanish, leaving behind thin pencil lines and smoke blurs. The pavements become isolated, low-roofed corridors. Overhead the electric signs whisper enigmatically and the window lights dissolve.

The fog thickens till the city disappears. High up, where the mists thin into a dark, sulphurous glow, roof bubbles float. The great cat's work is done. It stands balancing itself on the heads of people and arches its back against the vanished buildings.

I walk along thinking about the way the streets look and arranging adjectives in my mind. In the heavy mist people appear detached. They no longer seem to belong to a pursuit in common. Usually the busy part of the city is like the exposed mechanism of some monstrous clock. And people scurry about losing themselves in cogs and springs and levers.

But now the monstrous clock is almost hidden. The stores and offices and factories that form the mechanism of this clock are buried behind the fog. The cat has eaten them up. Hidden within the mist the cogs still turn and the springs unwind. But for the moment they seem non-existent. And the people drifting hurriedly by in the fog seem as if they were not going and coming from stores, offices and factories. As if they were solitaries hunting something in the labyrinths of the fog.

Yes, we are all lost and wandering in the thick mists. We have no destinations. The city is without outlines. And the drift of figures is a meaningless thing. Figures that are going nowhere and coming from nowhere. A swarm of supernumeraries who are not in the play. Who saunter, dash, scurry, hesitate in search of a part in the play.

27

This is a curious illusion. I stop and listen to music. Overhead a piano is playing and a voice singing. A song-boosting shop above Monroe and State streets. A ballad of the cheap cabarets. Yet, because it is music, it has a mystery in it.

The fog pictures grow charming. There is an idea in them now. People are detached little decorations etched upon a mist. The cat has eaten up the monstrous clock and people have rid themselves of their routine, which was to tumble and scurry among its cogs and levers. They are done with life, with buying and selling and with the perpetual errand. And they have become a swarm of little ornaments. Men and women denuded of the city. Their outlines posture quaintly in the mist. Their little faces say, "The clock is gone. There is nothing any more to make us alive. So we have become our unconnected selves."

Beside me in the fog a man stands next to a tall paper rack. I remember that this is the rack where the out-of-town papers are on sale. The papers are rolled up and thrust like rows of little white dolls in the rack. I wonder that this should be a newspaper stand. It looks like almost anything else in the fog.

A pretty girl emerges from the background of fog. She talks to the man next to the rack.

"Have you a Des Moines newspaper?" she asks.

The man is very businesslike. He fishes out a news-paper and sells it. At the sight of its headlines the girl's eyes light up. It is as if she had met a very close friend. She will walk along feeling comforted now. Chicago is a stranger. Its fog-hidden buildings and streets are strangers and its crowds criss-crossing everywhere are worse than strangers. But now she has Des Moines under her arm. Des Moines is a companion that will make the fog seem less lonely. Later she will sit down in a hotel room and read of what has hap-pened in Des Moines buildings and Des Moines streets. These will seem like real happenings, whereas the happenings that the Chicago papers print seem like unrealities.

This is Dearborn Street now. Dark and cozy. People are no longer decorations but intimate friends. When it is light and one can see the cogs of the monstrous clock go round and the springs unwind one thinks of people as a part of this mechanism. And so people grow vague in one's mind and unhuman or only half-human.

But now that the mechanism is gone, people stand out with an insistent humanness. People sitting on lunch-counter stools, leaning over coffee cups. People standing behind store counters. People buying cigars and people walking in and out of office buildings. They are very friendly. Their tired faces smile, or at least look somewhat amused and interested. They are interested in the fog and in the fact that one cannot see three feet ahead. And their faces say to each other, "Here we are, all alike. The city is only a make-believe. It can go away but we still remain. We are much more important than the big buildings."

I hear an odd tapping sound on the pavement. It is faint but growing nearer. In another moment a man tapping on the pavement with a cane passes. A blind man. And I think of a plot for a fiction story. If a terrible murder were committed in a marvelous fog that hid everything the chief of police would summon a blind man. And the blind man could track the murderer down in the fog because he alone would be able to move in the thick, obliterating mists. And so the blind man, with his cane tapping, tapping over the pavements and able by long practice to move without sight, would slowly close in on the murderer hemmed in by darkness.

A newsboy cries from the depth of nowhere: "Paper here. Trains crash in fog. Paper."

A friend and I sat in an office. He has been dictating letters, but he stops and stares out of the window. His eyes grow speculative. He says:

"Wouldn't it be odd if it were always like this? I think I'd like it better, wouldn't you? But I suppose they'd invent lights able to penetrate mist and the town would be as garish as ever in a few years. But I like the fog because it slows things up. Things are too damn fast to suit me. I like 'em slow. Like they used to be a century ago."

We talk and my friend becomes reminiscent on the subject of stage coaches and prairie schooners and the days before there were railroads, telephones, electricity and crowds. He has never known such a time, but from what he has read and imagined about it—yes, it would be better.

When I come out it is mid-afternoon. The fog has gone. The city has popped back and sprawls triumphantly into space. For a moment it seems as if the city had sprung up in an hour. Then its sturdy walls and business windows begin to mock at the memory of the fog in my mind. "Fogs do not devour us," they say. "We are the ones who do the devouring. We devour fogs and people and days." Marvelous buildings.

Overhead the sky floats like a gray and white balloon, as if it were a toy belonging to the city.

DON QUIXOTE AND HIS LAST WINDMILL

Sherwood Anderson, the writer, and I were eating lunch in the back room of a saloon. Against the opposite wall sat a red-faced little man with an elaborate mustache and a bald head and a happy grin. He sat alone at a tilted round table and played with a plate of soup.

"Say, that old boy over there is trying to wigwag me," said Anderson. "He keeps winking and making signs. Do you know him?"

I looked and said no. The waiter appeared with a box of cigars.

"Mr. Sklarz presents his compliments," said the waiter, smiling.

"Who's Sklarz?" Anderson asked, helping himself to a cigar. The waiter indicated the red-faced little man. "Him," he whispered.

We continued our meal. Both of us watched Mr. Sklarz casually. He seemed to have lost interest in his soup. He sat beaming happily at the walls, a contagious elation about him. We smiled and nodded our thanks for the cigars. Whereupon after a short lapse, the waiter appeared again.

"What'll you have to drink, gentlemen?" the waiter inquired.

"Nothing," said Anderson, knowing I was broke. The waiter raised his continental eyebrows understandingly.

"Mr. Sklarz invites you, gentlemen, to drink his health— at his expense."

"Two glasses," Anderson ordered. They were brought. We raised them in silent toast to the little red-faced man. He arose and bowed as we drank.

"We'll probably have him on our hands now for an hour," Anderson frowned. I feared the same. But Mr. Sklarz reseated himself and, with many head bowings in our direction, returned to his soup.

"What do you make of our magnanimous friend?" I asked. Anderson shrugged his shoulders.

"He's probably celebrating something," he said. "A queer old boy, isn't he?"

The waiter appeared a third time.

"What'll it be, gentlemen?" he inquired, smiling. "Mr. Sklarz is buying for the house."

For the house. There were some fifteen men eating in the place. Then our friend, despite his unassuming appearance, was evidently a creature of wealth! Well, this was growing interesting. We ordered wine again.

"Ask Mr. Sklarz if he will favor us by joining us at our table for this drink," I told the waiter. The message was delivered. Mr. Sklarz arose and bowed, but sat down again. Anderson and I beckoned in pantomime. Mr. Sklarz arose once more, bowed and hesitated. Then he came over.

As he approached a veritable carnival spirit seemed to deepen around us. The face of this little man with the elaborate black mustache was violent with suppressed good will and mirth. He beamed, bowed, shook hands and sat down. We drank one another's health and, as politely as we could, pressed him to tell us the cause for his celebration and good spirits. He began to talk.

He was a Russian Jew. His name was Sklarz. He had been in the Russian army years ago. In Persia. From a mountain in Persia you could see three great countries. In Turkey he had fought with baggy-trousered soldiers and at night joined them when they played their flutes outside the coffee-houses and sang songs about women and war. Then he had come to America and opened a box factory. He was very prosperous and the factory in which he made boxes grew too small.

So what did he do but take a walk one day to look for a larger factory. And he found a beautiful building just as he wanted. But the building was too beautiful to use for a

32

factory. It should be used for something much nicer. So what did he do then but decide to open a dance-hall, a magnificent dance-hall, where young men and women of refined, fun-loving temperaments could come to dance and have fun.

"When does this dance-hall open?" Anderson asked. Ah, in a little while. There were fittings to buy and put up first. But he would send us special invitations to the opening. In the meantime would we drink his health again? Mr. Sklarz chuckled. The amazing thing was that he wasn't drunk. He was sober.

"So you're celebrating," I said. Yes, he was celebrating. He laughed and leaned over the table toward us. His eyes danced and his elaborate mustache made a grotesque halo for his smile. He didn't want to intrude on us with his story, but in Persia and Turkey and the Urals he had found life very nice. And here in Chicago he had found life also very nice. Life was very nice wherever you went. And Anderson quoted, rather imperfectly, I thought:

> Oh, but life went gayly, gayly
>   In the house of Idah Dally;
> There were always throats to sing
>   Down the river bank with spring.

Mr. Sklarz beamed.

"Yes, yes," he said, "down the river benk mit spring." And he stood up and bowed and summoned the waiter. "See vat all the gentlemen vant," he ordered, "and give them vat they vant mit my compliments." He laughed, or, rather, chuckled. "I must be going. Excuse me," he exclaimed with a quick little bow. "I have other places to call on. Good-by. Remember me—Sam Sklarz. Be good—and don't forget Sam Sklarz when there are throats to zing down the river benk mit spring."

We watched him walk out. His shoulders seemed to dance, his short legs moved with a sprightly lift.

"A queer old boy," said Anderson.   We talked about him for a half hour and then left the place.

Anderson called me up the next morning to ask if I had read about it in the paper.   I told him I had.   A clipping on the desk in front of me ran:

"Sam Sklarz, 46 years old and owner of a box factory on the West Side, committed suicide early this morning by jumping into the drainage canal.   Financial reverses are believed to have caused him to end his life.   According to friends he was on the verge of bankruptcy.   His liabilities were $8,000.   Yesterday morning Sklarz cashed a check for $700, which represented the remains of his bank account, and disappeared.   It is believed that he used the money to pay a few personal debts and then wandered around in a daze until the end.   He left no word of explanation behind."

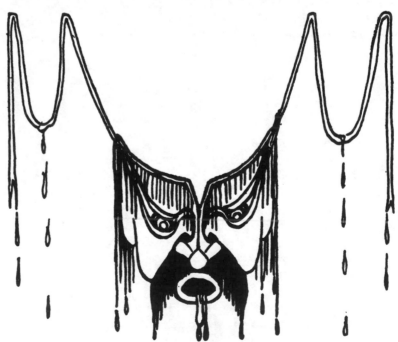

THE MAN HUNT

They were hunting him. Squads of coppers with rifles, detectives, stool pigeons were hunting him. And the people who had read the story in the newspapers and looked at his picture, they too, were hunting him.

Tommy O'Connor looked out of the smeared window of the room in which he sat and stared at the snow. A drift of snow across the roofs. A scribble of snow over the pavement.

There were automobiles racing through the streets loaded with armed men. There were crowds looking for a telltale face in their own midst. Guards, deputies, coppers were surrounding houses and peering into alleys, raiding saloons, ringing doorbells. The whole city was on his heels. The city was like a pack of dogs sniffing wildly for his trail. And when they found it they would come whooping toward him for a leap at his throat.

Well, here he was—waiting. It was snowing outside. There was no noise in the street. A man was passing. One of the pack? No. Just a man. The man looked up. Tommy O'Connor took his face slowly away from the window. He had a gun in his pocket and his hand was holding it. But the man was walking away. Huh! If the guy knew that Lucky Tommy O'Connor was watching him from a window he'd walk a little faster. If the guy knew that Lucky O'Connor, who had busted his way out of jail and was being hunted by a million people with guns, was sitting up here behind the window, he'd throw a fit. But he didn't know. He was like the walls and the windows and the snow outside—quiet and peaceful.

"Nice boy," grinned Tommy O'Connor. Then he began to fidget. He ought to go out and buy a paper. See what was doing. See what became of Mac and the rest of the boys. Maybe they'd all been nabbed. But they couldn't

THE
MAN
HUNT

do him harm. On account nobody knew where he was. No pal. No dame. Nobody knew he was sitting here in the room looking at the snow and just thinking. The papers were probably full of cock-and-bull stories about his racing across the country and hiding in haystacks and behind barns. Kid stuff. Maybe he should ought to of left town. But it felt better in town. Some rube was always sure to pick out a stranger beating it down a empty road. And there was no place to hide. Long, empty stretches, where anybody could see you for a mile.

Better in town. Lots of walls, alleys, roofs. Lots of things like that. No hare-and-hounds effect like in the country. But the papers were probably full of a lot of bunk. He'd take a walk later and buy a few. Better sit still now. There was nothing harder to find than a man sitting still.

Tommy O'Connor yawned. Not much sleep the night before. Well, he'd sleep tonight. Worrying wasn't going to help matters. What if they did come? Let them come. Fill up the street and begin their damn shooting. They didn't think Lucky Tommy was sucker enough to let them march him up on a scaffold and break his neck on the end of a rope. Fat chance. Not him. That sort of stuff happened to other guys, not to Lucky Tommy.

Snowing outside. And quiet. Everybody at work. Funny about that. Tommy O'Connor was the only free man in the city. There was nobody felt like him right now— nobody. Where would he be exactly this time a week from now? If he could only look ahead and see himself at four o'clock next Monday afternoon. But he was free now. No breaking his neck on the end of a rope. If worst came to worst—if worst came to worst—O'Connor's fingers took a grip on the gun in his pocket. They were hunting him. Up and down the streets everywhere. Racing around in taxis, with rifles sticking out of the windows. Well, why didn't they come into this street? All they had to do was figure out: Here's the street Tommy O'Connor is hiding in. And that looks like the house. And then somebody would yell out: "There he is! Behind that window! That's him!" Why didn't this happen?

Christmas, maybe, he'd call on the folks. No. Rube stuff. A million coppers would be watching the house. But he might drop them a letter. Too bad he didn't have any paper, or he might write a lot of letters. To the chief of police and all the head hunters. Some more rube stuff, that. They could tell by the postmark what part of the city he was hiding in and they'd be on him with a whoop.

Funny how he had landed in this room. No plans, no place in particular to head for. That was the best way. Like he'd figured it out and it turned out perfect. Grab the first auto and ride like hell and keep on changing autos and riding around and around in the streets and crawling deeper into the city until the trail was all twisted and he was buried. But he ought to shave his mustache off. Hell. What for? If they came whooping into the street they'd find him, mustache or no mustache. But what if he wanted to buy some papers?

It was getting darker now. The snow was letting up. Just dribbling. Better if it would snow a lot. Then he could sit and have something to watch—snow falling on the street and turning things white. That was on account of his head-ache he was thinking that way. Eats might help, but he wasn't hungry. Scared? No. Just waiting. Hunters winding in and out like the snow that was falling. People were funny. They got a big thrill out of hunting a live man who was free in the streets.

He'd be walking some day. Strolling around the streets free as any of them. Maybe not in town. Some other town. Take a walk down State Street. Drop in at a movie. Kid stuff. Walk over to Mac's saloon and kind of casually say "Hello, fellows." And walk out again. God, they'd never hang him. If the worst came to the worst—if the worst came to the worst—but they'd never hang him.

Dark now. But the guys hunting him weren't going to sleep. Lights were going on in the windows. Better light up the room. People might notice a dark window. But a lighted one would look all right. It was not snowing any more. Just cold.

Well, he'd go out in a while. Stretch his legs and buy the papers and give them a reading. And then take a walk. Just walk around and take in the streets and see if there was anybody he knew. No. Rube stuff, that. Better stick where he was.

Lucky Tommy walked around in the room. The drawn window blind held his eye. Wagons were passing. What for? Yes, and there was a noise. Like people coming. Turn out the light, then. He'd take a look.

Tommy O'Connor peeled back the blind carefully. Dark. Lights in windows. Some guys on the corner. Hunting him? Sure. And they were coming his way. Straight down the street. They were looking up. What for? A gun crept out of Tommy O'Connor's pocket. He pressed himself carefully against the wall. He waited. The minutes grew long. But this was the hunt closing in. They were coming. Black figures of men floating casually down the street. All right—let them come.

Lucky Tommy O'Connor's eyes stared rigidly out of the smeared window at a vague flurry of figures that seemed to be coming, coming his way.

MR. WINKELBERG

There was never a man as irritating as Winkelberg. He was an encyclopedia of misfortune. Everything which can happen to a man had happened to him. He had lost his family, his money and his health. He was, in short, a man completely broken—tall, thin, with a cadaverous face, out of which shone two huge, lusterless eyes. He walked with an angular crawl that reminded one of the emaciated flies one sees at the beginning of winter dragging themselves perversely along as if struggling across an illimitable expanse of flypaper.

It was one of Winkelberg's worst habits to appear at unexpected moments. But perhaps any appearances poor Winkelberg might have made would have had this irritating quality of unexpectedness. One was never looking forward to Winkelberg, and thus the sight of his wan, determined smile, his lusterless eyes and his tenacious crawl was invariably an uncomfortable surprise.

I will be frank. It was Winkelberg's misfortune which first attracted me. I listened to his story avidly. He talked in slow words and there was intelligence in the man. He was able to perceive himself not only as a pain-racked, starving human, but he glimpsed with his large, tired eyes his relation to things outside himself. I remember he said, and without emotion: "There is nobody to blame. Not even myself. And if I cannot blame myself how can I blame the world? The city is like that. I am no good. I am done. Something worn out and useless. People try to take care of the useless ones and they would like to. There are institutions. I was kicked out of two of them. They said I was a faker. Somehow I don't appeal to charitably inclined people."

Later I understood why. It was because of the man's smile—a feeble, tenacious grimace that seemed to be offering a sardonic reproof. It could never have been mistaken for a

39

courageous smile. The secret of its aggravating quality was this: In it Winkelberg accused himself of his uselessness, his feebleness, his poverty. It was as if he were regarding himself continually through the annoyed eyes of others and addressing himself with the words of others: "You, Winkelberg, get out of here. You're a nuisance. You make me uncomfortable because you're poor and diseased and full of gloom. Get out. I don't want you around. Why the devil don't you die?"

And the aggravating thing was that people looked at Winkelberg's smile as into a mirror. They saw in it a reflection of their own attitude toward the man. They felt that Winkelberg understood what they thought of him. And they didn't like that. They didn't like to feel that Winkelberg was aware that deep inside their minds they were always asking: "Why doesn't this Winkelberg die and have it over with?" Because that made them out as cruel, heartless people, not much different in their attitude toward their fellow men from predatory animals in their attitude toward fellow predatory animals. And somehow, although they really felt that way toward Winkelberg, they preferred not to believe it. But Winkelberg's smile was a mirror which would not let them escape this truth. And eventually Winkelberg's smile became for them one of those curious mirrors which exaggerate images grotesquely. Charitably inclined people, as well as all other kinds of inclined people, prefer their Winkelbergs more egoistic. They prefer that unfortunate ones be engrossed in their misfortunes and not go around wearing sardonic, philosophical smiles.

Winkelberg dragged along for a year. He was past fifty. Each time I saw him I was certain I would never see him again. I was certain he would die—drop dead while crawling across his flypaper. But he would appear. I would pretend to be vastly busy. He would sit and wait. He never asked alms. I would have been relieved if he had. Instead

40

he sat and smiled, and his smile said: "You are afraid I am going to ask you for money. Don't worry. I won't ask you for money. I won't bother you at all. Yes, I agree with you, I ought to be dead. It would be better for everybody."

We would talk little. He would throw out a hint now and then that perhaps I could use some of his misfortunes for material. For instance, the time his two children had been burned to death. Or the time he had fallen off the street car while in a sick daze and injured his spine for life, and how he had settled with the street car company for $500 and how he had been robbed on the way to the bank with the money two weeks later.

I refused consistently this offer of "material." This offended Winkelberg. He would shake his head and then he would nod his head understandingly and his smile would say:

"Yes, yes. I understand. You don't want to get involved with me. Because you don't want me to have any more claims on your sympathy than I've got. I'm sorry."

Toward the end Winkelberg's visits grew more frequent. And he became suddenly garrulous. He wished to discuss things. The city. The various institutions. Politics. Art. This phase of Winkelberg was the most unbearable. He was willing to admit himself a social outcast. He was reconciled to the fact that he would starve to death and that everybody who had ever seen him would feel it had been a good thing that he had finally died. But this final plea came from him. He wanted nothing except to talk and hear words in order to relieve the loneliness of his days. He would like abstract discussions that had nothing to do with Winkelberg and the Winkelberg misfortunes. His smile now said: "I am useless, worn out and better off dead. But never mind me. My mind is still alive. It still thinks. I wish it didn't. I wish it crawled around like my body. But seeing that it does, talk to me as if it were a mind belonging to somebody else and not to the insufferable Winkelberg."

I grew suspicious finally. I began to think there was something vitally spurious about this whole Winkelberg business. And I said to myself: "The man's a downright fake. If anybody were as pathetic and impossible and useless as this Winkelberg is he would shoot himself. Winkelberg doesn't shoot himself. So he becomes illogical. Unreal."

A woman I know belongs to the type that becomes charitable around Christmas time. She makes a glowing pretense of aiding the poor. As a matter of fact, she really does aid them, although she regards the poor as a sort of social and spiritual asset. They afford her the double opportunity of appearing in the eyes of her neighbors as a magnanimous soul and of doing something which reflects great credit upon her character. But, anyway, she "does good," and we'll let it go at that.

I told this woman about Winkelberg. I became poignant and moving on the subject of Winkelberg's misfortunes, his trials, sufferings and, above all, his Spartan stoicism. It pleased me to do this. I felt that I was making some amends and that the thing reflected credit upon my character.

So she went to the room on the South Side where Winkelberg sleeps. And they told her there that Winkelberg was dead. He had died last week. She was upset when she told me about it. She had come too late. She might have saved him.

It was a curious thing—but when she told me that Winkelberg was dead I felt combatively that it was untrue. And now since I know certainly that Winkelberg is dead and buried I have developed a curious state of mind. I look up from my desk every once in a while expecting to see him. In the streets I sometimes find myself actually thinking: "I'll bump into him when I turn the corner."

I have managed to discover the secret of this feeling. It is Winkelberg's smile. Winkelberg's smile was the interpretation of the world's attitude toward him, including my own. And thus whenever his name comes to mind his smile appears as if it were the thought in my head. And in Winkelberg's smile I hear myself saying: "He is better off dead."

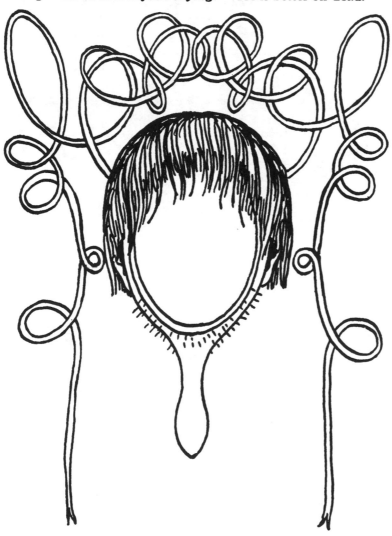

A SELF-MADE MAN

"Over there," said Judge Sabath, "is a man who has been a juror in criminal cases at least a dozen times."

His honor pointed to a short, thin man with a derby on the back of his head and a startling mustache, concealing almost half of his wizened face. The man was sitting a bit childishly on a window ledge in the hall of the Criminal Court building swinging his legs and chewing rhythmically on a plug of tobacco.

"They let him go this morning while picking a jury for a robbery case before me," said the judge. "He tried to stay on, but neither side wanted him. You might get a story out of him. I think he's broken-hearted."

The short, thin man with the derby, swinging his legs from the window ledge said his name was Martin.

"That's true," he said, "what the judge said. I been a juror fourteen times. I was on five murders and four big robberies and then I was on five different assorted kinds of crimes."

"How do you like being a juror, Mr. Martin?"

"Well, sir, I like it a lot. I can say that out of the fourteen times I been a juror I never lost a case."

Mr. Martin aimed at the new cuspidor—and missed.

"There's some jurors as loses nearly every case they're on. They give in first crack. But take the Whitely murder trial I was on. That was as near as I ever come to losing a case. But I managed to hang the jury and the verdict was one of disagreement. Whitely was innocent. Anybody could have told that with half an eye."

"How long have you been serving on juries, Mr. Martin?"

"Going nigh on twenty-three years. I had my first case when I was a young man. It was a minor case—a robbery. I won that despite my youth and inexperience. In those days

44

the cases were much harder than now on account of the lawyers. The old-fashioned lawyer was the talkingest kind of a nuisance I ever had to deal with. He always reminded me of somebody talking at a mark for two dollars a week.

"I don't refer to the orators. I mean the ones who talk during the case itself and who slow things up generally by bothering the witnesses to death with a lot of unnecessary questions. Although the orators are pretty bad, too. There's many a lawyer who has lost out with me on account of the way he made faces in the windup. One of my rules as a juror, a successful one, I might say, is, 'Always mistrust a lawyer who talks too fancy.' "

"Judge Sabath just said that they let you go in his court this morning."

"H'm," snorted Mr. Martin. "That was the lawyer. He's mad at me because he lost a case two years ago that I was on. I won it and he holds a grudge. That's like some lawyers. They don't like the man who licks them.

"But you were asking about the qualifications of an all-around juryman. I'll give 'em to you. First and foremost you want a man of wide experience in human nature. I spend most of my time in the courts when I ain't serving as juror studyin' human nature. You might say that all human nature is the same. But it's my experience that some is more so than others.

"Well, when you know human nature the next step is to figure out about lawyers. Lawyers as a whole is the hardest nut the juror has to crack. To begin with, they're deceivin', and if you let them they'll take advantage of your credulity. There's Mr. Erbstein, for instance, the criminal lawyer. He's a pretty smart one, but I won a case from him only four years ago and he's never forgiven me. I was juror in a manslaughter trial he was trying to run. He thought himself pretty foxy, but when it came to a showdown I put it all over him. There was a guy who was foreman of the jury that time who said I had it all over Mr. Erbstein as an argufier and that my arguments made his look like ten cents. I won easily on five ballots and Mr. Erbstein has never forgave me.

"But I'll go on about the qualifications. First of all, I never read newspapers. Never. No juror should ought to know anything about anything that's going on. I found that out in my youth when I first started in. The first question they ask you is, 'What have you heard about this case and what have you read or said about it?' That's the first one. Well, the right answer is 'nothing.'

"If you can say nothing and prove you're right they'll gobble you up as a juror. For that reason I avoid all newspapers, and right now I don't know what big crimes or cases have been committed at all. I have a clean, unprejudiced mind and I keep it that way.

"Nextly," said Mr. Martin, trying a new sight on the cuspidor, "I don't belong to any lodges whatsoever. They're a handicap. Because if the defendant is a Mason and you are a Elk he would rather have a brother Mason be juror than a strange Elk. So I don't belong to any of them and I don't go to church. I also have no convictions whatsoever about politics and have no favorites of any kind in the matter of authors or statesmen or anything. What I try to do is to keep my mind clean and unprejudiced on all subjects."

"Why do you like serving as a juror?"

Mr. Martin stared.

"Why?" he repeated. "Because it's every man's duty, naturally. And besides," he went on, narrowing his eyes into shrewd slits, "I've just been luckier than most people. Most people only get called a few times during their life. But I get called regularly every year and sometimes twice a year and sometimes four and five times a year for service. Of course, I ain't boasting, but the city has recognized my merits,

46

no doubt, as a juror, knowing all the cases I've won, and it perhaps shows a little partiality to me for that reason. But I feel that I have earned it and I would like nothing said about it or any scandal started."

"What do you think of this Taylor death mystery in Los Angeles, Mr. Martin?"

"Ha, ha," said Mr. Martin, "there you're tryin' to catch me. You thought you could put that over on me without my seein' through it, didn't you? That's just the way the lawyers try to trap me when I'm sittin' on one of my cases. I ain't ever heard of this Taylor death mystery, not reading the papers, you see."

"That's too bad, Mr. Martin. It's quite a story." Mr. Martin sighed and slipped from the window ledge, shaking down his wrinkled, high-water pants.

"Yes," he sighed, a sudden wistfulness coming into his rheumy eyes. "Things have been pretty slow around here. Chicago used to be the place for a juror—none better. But I been thinkin' of going west. Not that I heard anything, mind you, about any of these cases." Mr. Martin glowered virtuously. "I never read the papers, sir, and have no prejudices whatsoever.

"But I've just been feelin' lately that there are wider opportunities in the west for a man of my experience and record than are left around here."

TO BERT WILLIAMS

"Well," said Mr. Bert Williams, in his best "Under the Bamboo Tree" dialect, "If you like mah singin' and actin' so much, how come, you bein' a writer, you don't write somethin' about youah convictions on this subjeck? Oh! It's not youah depahtment! Hm! Tha's jes' mah luck. I was always the mos' unluckiest puhson who ever trifled with misfohtune. Not his depahtment! Tha'—tha's jes' it. I never seems to fall jes' exactly in the ri-right depahtment.

"May I ask, without meanin' to be puhsonal, jes' what is your depahtment? Murder! Oh, you is the one who writes about murders and murderuhs foh the paper! Nothin' else? Is tha' so? Jes' murders and murderuhs and—and things like tha'? Well, tha' jes' shows how deceivin' looks is, fo' when you came in heah I says to mahself, I says, 'this gen'leman is a critic of the drama.' And when I sees you have on a pair o' gloves I added quickly to mahself, 'Yes, suh, chances are he is not only a critic of the drama, but likewise even possuhbly a musical critic.' Yes, suh, all mah life I have had the desire to be interviewed by a musical critic, but no matter how hard I sing or how frequently, no musical critic has yet taken cognizance o' me. No, suh, I get no cognizance whatsoever.

"Not meanin' to disparage you, suh, or your valuable depahtment. Foh if you is in charge o' the murder and murderuh's depahtment o' yo' paper possuhbly some time you may refer to me lightly between stabbin's or shootin's in such wise as to say, foh instance, 'the doomed man was listenin' to Mr. Williams' latest song on the phonograph when he received the bullet wound. Death was instantaneous, the doomed man dyin' with a smile on his lips. Mr. Williams' singin' makes death easy—an' desirable.'

"What, suh? You is! Sam, fetch the gen'leman some o' the firewater, the non-company brand, Sam. All right, say when. Aw, shucks, that ain't enough to wet a cat's whiskers. Say when again. There, tha's better. Here, Sam. You got to help drink this. It's important. The gen'leman says if I will wait a little while, jes' a little while, he is goin' to alter his depahtment on the newspaper. Wasn't that it? Oh, I see. In the magazine. Very well. Here's to what you says about me some day in the magazine. An' when you writes it don't forget to mention somewhere along in it how when I was playin' in San Francisco and Sarah Bernhardt was playin' there, and this was years ago, don' forget to mention along with what you write about mah singin' and actin' that I come to mah dressing room one evenin', in Frisco, and there's the hugest box o' flowers you ever saw with mah name on it. An' I open it up and, boy! There plain as the nose on your face is a card among the flowers readin', 'to a fellow artist, from Sarah Bernhardt.' And—whilst we are, so to speak, on the subjeck—you can put in likewise what Eleanora Duse said o' me. You know who she is, I suppose, the very most superlative genius o' the stage, suh. Yes, suh, the very most. An' she says o' me when she went back to Italy, how I was the best artist on the American stage.

"Artist! Tha' always makes Sam laugh, don't it, Sam, when he heahs me refuhed to as artist. An'—have another beaker o' firewater, suh. It's strictly non-company brand. An' here's how again to tha' day you speak of when you write this article about me. An', boy, make it soon, 'cause this life, this sinful theat'ical life, is killin' me fast. But I'll try an' wait. Here's howdy."

He didn't wait. And today a lazy, crooked grin and a dolorous-eyed black face drift among the shades in the Valhalla where the Great Actors sit reading their press notices to one another. The Great Actors who have died since the day of Euripides—they sit around in their favorite make-ups in the Valhalla reserved for all good and glorious Thespians.

49

A company of ladies and gentlemen that would make
Mr. Belasco's heart stop beating! The Booths and Barretts
from antiquity down, the Mrs. Siddonses and Pattis, the
Cyranos, Hamlets, buffoons and heroes. All of them in their
favorite make-ups, in their favorite cap and bells, their favorite
swords, their favorite doublet and hose—all of them sit around
in the special Valhalla of the Great Actors reading their press
notices to one another and listening to the hosannas of such
critics as have managed to pry into the anterior heaven.

And today Bert Williams makes his entrance. Yes, suh,
it took that long to find just the right make-up. To get just
the right kind of ill-fitting white gloves and floppy shoes and
nondescript pants. But it's an important entrance. The lazy
crooked grin is a bit nervous. The dolorous eyes peer sadly
through the opening door of this new theater.

Lawdy, man, this is got a Broadway first night backed
off the boards. Rejane, Caruso, Coquelin, Garrick and a
thousand others sittin' against the towering walls, sittin' with
their eyes on the huge door within' to see who's a-comin' in
now.

All right, professor, jes' a little music. Nothin' much.
Anything kind o' sad and fidgetylike. Tha's it, that-a-boy.
There's no use worryin'—much. 'Member what Duse said as
I was the greatest artist, an' 'member how Sarah Bernhardt
sent me roses in Frisco an' says, 'To a fellow artist'? Yes,
suh, they can't do mo' than walk out on me. An' ah's been
walked out on befo'.

All right, professor. Tha's it. Now I'll stick my hand
inside the door and wiggle mah fingers kind o' slow like.
Jes' like that. An' I'll come on slow. Nothin' to worry about
—much.

A wrinkled white-gloved hand moving slowly inside the
door of the Valhalla. Sad, fidgety music. Silence in the
great hall. This is another one coming on—another entrance.

50

A lazy, crooked grin and a dolorous-eyed black face. Floppy shoes and woebegone pants.

Bravo, Mr. Williams! The great hall rings with hand-clapping. The great hall begins to fill with chuckles. There it is——the same curious grin, the lugubrious apology of a grin, the weary, pessimistic child of a grin.

The Great Actors, eager-eyed and silent, sit back on their thrones. The door of the Valhalla of Great Actors swings slowly shut. No Flo Ziegfeld lighting this time, but a great shoot of sunshine for a "garden." And the music different, easier to sing to, somehow. Music of harps and flutes. And a deep voice rises.

Yes, I would have liked to have been there in the Valhalla of the Great Actors, when Bert Williams came shuffling through the towering doors and stood singing his entrance song to the silent, eager-eyed throng of Rejanes, Barretts and Coquelins——

> Ah ain't ever done nothin' to nobody,
> Ah ain't ever got nothin' from nobody——no time, nohow.
> Ah ain't ever goin' t' do nothin' for nobody——
> Till somebody——

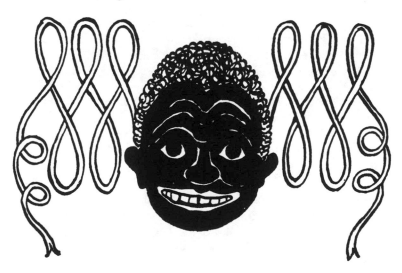

MICHIGAN AVENUE

This is a deplorable street, a luxurious couch of a street in which the afternoon lolls like a gaudy sybarite. Overhead the sky stretches itself like a holiday awning. The sun lays harlequin stripes across the building faces. The smoke plumes from the I. C. engines scribble gray, white and lavender fantasies against the shining air.

A deplorable street—a cement and plate glass Circe. We walk—a long procession of us. It is curious to note how we adjust ourselves to backgrounds. In other streets we are hurried, flurried, worried. We summon portentous frowns to our faces. Our arms swinging at our sides proclaim, "Make way, make way! We are launched upon activities vital to the commonwealth!"

But here—the sun bursts a shower of little golden balloons from the high windows. The green of a park makes a cool salaam to the beetle-topped traffic of automobiles. Rubber tires roll down the wide avenue and make a sound like the drawn-out striking of a match. Marble columns, fountains, incompleted architectural elegancies, two sculptured lions and the baffling effulgence of a cinder-veiled museum offer themselves like pensively anonymous guests. And we walk like Pierrots and Pierrettes, like John Drews and Jack Barrymores and Leo Ditrichsteins; like Nazimovas, Patricia Collinges and Messalinas on parole.

I have squandered an afternoon seduced from labors by this Pied Piper of a street. And not only I but everybody I ever knew or heard of was in this street, strutting up and down as if there were no vital projects demanding their attention, as if life were not a stern and productive routine. And where was the Rotary Club? Not a sign of the Rotary Club. One billboard would have saved me; the admonitions that "work is man's duty to his nation," that my country needed me as much in peace as in war, would have scattered the insidious spell of this street and sent me back to the typewriter with at least a story of some waiter in a loop beanery who was once a reigning prince of Patagonia.

But there was no sign, no billboard to inspire me with a sense of duty. So we strutted—the long procession of us— a masquerade of leisure and complacency. Here was a street in which a shave and a haircut, a shine and a clean collar exhilarated a man with a feeling of power and virtue. As if there were nothing else to the day than to decorate himself for the amusement of others.

There were beggars in the street but they only add by way of contrast to the effulgence of our procession. And, besides, are they beggars? Augustus Caesar attired himself in beggar's clothes one day each year and asked alms in the highways of Rome.

I begin to notice something. An expression in our faces as we drift by the fastidious ballyhoos of the shop windows. We are waiting for something—actors walking up and down in the wings waiting for their cues to go on. This is intelligible. This magician of a street has created the illusion in our heads that there are adventure and romance around us.

Fauns, Pierrots, Launcelots, Leanders—we walk, expectantly waiting for our scenes to materialize. Here the little steno in the green tam is Laïs of Corinth, the dowager alighting from the electric is Zenobia. Illusions dress the entire procession. Semiramis, Leda, and tailored nymphs; dryad eyes gleam from powder-white masks. Or, if the classics bore you, Watteau and the rococo pertness of the Grand Monarch. And there are Gothic noses, Moorish eyebrows, Byzantine slippers. Take your pick, walk up and down and wait for your cue.

There are two lives that people lead. One is the real life of business, mating, plans, bankruptcies and gas bills. The other is an unreal life—a life of secret grandeurs which compensate for the monotony of the days. Sitting at our desks, hanging on to straps in the street cars, waiting for the

53

dentist, eating in silence in our homes—we give ourselves to these secret grandeurs. Day-dreams in which we figure as heroes and Napoleons and Don Juans, in which we triumph sensationally over the stupidities and arrogances of our enemies—we think them out detail by detail. Sometimes we like to be alone because we have a particularly thrilling incident to tell ourselves, and when our friends say good-by we sigh with relief and wrap ourselves with a shiver of delight in the mantles of imagination. And we live for a charming hour through a fascinating fiction in which things are as they should be and we startle the world with our superiorities.

This street, I begin to understand, is consecrated to the unrealities so precious to us. We come here and for a little while allow our dreams to peer timorously at life. In the streets west of here we are what we are—browbeaten, weary-eyed, terribly optimistic units of the boobilariat. Our secret characterizations we hide desperately from the frowns of windows and the squeal of "L" trains.

But here in this Circe of streets the sun warms us, the sky and the spaces of shining air lure us and we step furtively out of ourselves. And give us ten minutes. Observe—a street of heroes and heroines. Actors all. Great and irresistible egoists. Do we want riches? Then we have only to raise our finger. Slaves will attend with sesterces and dinars. A street of joyous Caligulas and Neros, with here and there a Ghengis Khan, an Attila.

The high buildings waver like gray and golden ferns in the sun. The sky stretches itself in a holiday awning over our heads. A breeze coming from the lake brings an odorous spice into our noses. Adventure and romance! Yes—and observe how unnecessary are plots. Here in this Circe of streets are all the plots. All the great triumphs, assassinations, amorous conquests of history unravel themselves within a distance of five blocks. The great moments of the world live themselves over again in a silent make-believe.

54

Here is one who has just swum the Hellespont, one who has subdued Cleopatra; here one whose eyes are just launching a thousand ships. What a street!

The afternoon wanes. Our procession turns toward home. For a few minutes the elation of our make-believes in the Avenue lingers. But the "L" trains crowd up, the street cars crowd up. It is difficult to remain a Caesar or a Don Quixote. So we withdraw and our faces become alike as turtle backs.

And see, the afternoon has been squandered. There were things which should have been done. I blush indignantly at the memory of my thoughts during the shining hours in the Avenue. For I spent the valuable moments conversing with the devil. I imagined him coming for me and for two hours I elaborated a dialogue between him and myself in which I gave him my immortal soul and he in turn promised to write all the stories, novels and plays I wanted. All I would have to do was furnish the paper and leave it in a certain place and call for it the next morning and it would be completed— anything I asked for, a story, novel or play; a poem, a world-shattering manifesto—anything.

Alas, I am still in possession of my immortal soul!

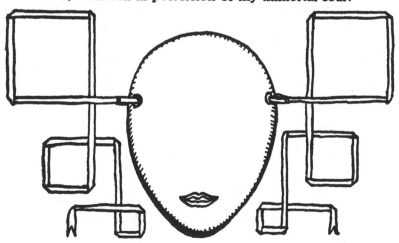

COEUR DE LION AND THE SOUP AND FISH

COEUR DE LION AND THE SOUP AND FISH

For they're hangin' Danny Deever—

The voice of Capt. MacVeigh of the British army rose defiantly in the North La Salle Street hall bedroom. The herculean captain, attired in a tattered bathrobe, underwear, socks and one slipper, patted the bottom of the iron with his finger and then carefully applied it to a trouser leg stretched on an ironing board in front of him.

Again the voice:

> For they're hangin' Danny Deever;
> You can hear the death march play,
> And they're ta ta ta da
> They're taking him away,
> Ta da ta ta—

The captain was on the rocks. *Sic transit gloria mundi.* Or how saith the poet, "The lion and the lizard keep the courts where Jamshid gloried and drank deep." Bust, was the captain. "Dying, Egypt, dying, ebbs the crimson life blood fast." Flatter than a hoecake was the captain.

"Farewell, my bluebell, farewell to thee," sang the captain as the iron crept cautiously over the great trouser leg of his Gargantuan full-dress suit. African mines blown up. Two inheritances shot. A last remittance blah. Rent bills, club bills, grocery bills, tailor bills, gambling bills. "Ho, Britons never will be slaves," sang the intrepid captain. Fought the bloody Boers, fought the Irawadi, fought the bloody Huns, and what was it Lady B. said at the dinner in his honor only two years ago? Ah, yes, here's to our British Tartarin, Capt. MacVeagh. But who the devil was Tartarin?

Never mind. "There's a long, long trail a-windin' and ta da ta ta ta tum," sang Capt. MacVeagh and he took up the other trouser leg. Egad, what a life! Not a sou markee left. Not a thin copper, not a farthing! "Strike me blind, me wife's confined and I'm a blooming father," sang Capt. MacVeagh,

56

"For they're hangin' Danny Deever, you can hear the death march play———"

This was the last phalanx. This thing on the ironing board was Horatius at the bridge holding in check the hordes of false Tarquin. Everything gone but this. Not even a pair of pants or a smoking coat. Not a blooming thing left but this —a full-dress suit beginning to shine a bit in the rear.

"The shades of night were falling fast when through an Alpine village passed"—egad, what a primitive existence. Like an Irunti in the Australian bush. Telling time by the sun. It must be approachin' six, thought the captain as his voice trailed off.

Beautiful thought. "Mabel, little Mabel, with her face against the pane, sits beside the window, looking at the rain." That was Capt. MacVeagh of the British army, prisoner in a La Salle Street hall bedroom. No clothes to wear, nothing but the soup and fish. So he must sit and wait till evening came, till a gentleman could put on his best bib and tucker, and then—*allons!* Freshly shaved, pink jowled, swinging his ebony stick, his pumps gleaming with a new coat of vaseline, off for the British Officers' Club!

All day long the herculean captain sulked in his tent— an Achilles with a sliver in his heel. But come evening, come the gentle shades of darkness, and presto! Like a lily of the field, who spun not nor toiled; like a knight of the boulevards, this servant of the king leaped forth in all his glory. The landlady was beginning to lose her awe of the dress suit, the booming barytone and the large aristocratic pink face of her mysterious boarder. And she was pressing for back rent. But the club was still tolerant.

"A soldier o' the legion lay dyin' in Algiers," chanted the captain, and with his shoulders back he strode into the wide world. A meal at the club, and gadzooks but his stomach was in arms! Not a bite since the last club meal. God bless the club!

"Get a job?" repeated the captain to one of the members, "I would but the devil take it, how can a man go around asking for a job in a dress suit? And I'm so rotten big that none of my friends can loan me a suit. And my credit is gone with at least twelve different tailors. I'm sort o' taboo as a borrower. Barry, old top, if you will chase the blighter after another highball, I'll drink your excellent health."

"There's a job if you want it that you can do in your dress suit," said his friend Barry. "If you don't mind night work."

"Not at all," growled Capt. MacVeagh.

"Well," said the friend, "there's a circus in town and they want a man to drive the chariot in the chariot race. It's only a little circus. And there's only three chariots in the race. You get $10 for driving and $25 a night if you win the race. And they give you a bloomin' toga to put on over your suit, you know, and a ribbon to tie around your head. And there you are."

"Righto!" cried the captain, "and where is this rendez-vous of skill and daring? I'm off. I'll drive that chariot out of breath."

Capt. MacVeagh got the job. Capt. MacVeagh won the first race. Clad in a flapping toga, a ribbon round his fore-head, the hero of the British army went Berserker on the home stretch and, lashing his four ponies into a panic, came glo-riously down the last lap, two lengths ahead and twenty-five marvelous coins of the realm to the good.

That night at the club Capt. MacVeagh stood treat. British wassail and what not. The twenty-five dollars melted pleasantly and the captain fell off in a happy doze as rosy fingered Aurora touched the city roof-tops.

But, alas, the wages of sin! For the captain was not so good when he mounted his chariot the second night. A beehive buzzed in his head and huge, globular disturbances seemed to fill the air. And, standing waveringly on his feet as the giddy chariot bounced down the track, the captain let forth a sudden yell and sailed off into space. The chariot ponies and hero of the British army had gone crashing into the side lines.

"When they brought him to the hospital in the ambulance," explained the captain's friend, "they had taken the toga off him, of course, and the old boy was in his dress clothes. This kind o' knocked their eyes out, so what do they do but give him the most expensive suite in the place and the prettiest nurse and the star surgeon. And they mend and feed him up for two weeks. We all called on him and brought him a few flowers. The lad was surely in clover.

"The hospital authorities had nothing to go on but this dress suit as evidence. And when the nurse asked him what he wanted done with the suit, saying it was a bit torn from the accident, MacVeagh waves his hand and answers, 'Oh, throw the blasted thing out of the window or give it to the janitor.' And she did. I always thought it quite a story."

"But how did it end? What became of the captain when they found out he couldn't pay his bill and all that? And where's he now?"

"You'll have to end the thing to suit yourself," said the captain's friend. "All I know is that after almost forgetting about MacVeagh I got a letter from him from London yesterday. A rather mysterious letter on Lady Somebody's stationery. It read something like this: "The paths of glory lead but to the grave. Thanks for the flowers. And three cheers, me lad, for the British Empire."

THE SYBARITE

They had been poor all their lives. The neighbors said: "It's a wonder how the Sikoras get along."

They lived in a rear flat. Four rooms that were dark and three children that were noisy. The three children used Wabansia Avenue as a playground. Dodging wagons and trucks was a diversion which played havoc with their shoes, but increased their skill in dodging wagons and trucks.

The neighbors said: "Old man Sikora is pretty sick. It's a wonder where they'll get money to pay the doctor."

Then old man Sikora, who wasn't so old (but poverty and hard work with a pick give a man an aged look), was taken to the county hospital. The Sikora children continued to dodge wagons and trucks and Mrs. Sikora went out three days a week to do washing. And the milkman and the grocer came around regularly and explained to Mrs. Sikora that they, too, had to live and she must pay her bills.

Then the neighbors said: "Did you hear about it? Old man Sikora died last night in the hospital. What will poor Mrs. Sikora do now? They ain't got a thing."

And old man Sikora was brought home because his widow insisted upon it. The neighbors came in and looked at the body and wept with Mrs. Sikora, and the children sat around after school and looked uncomfortably at the walls. And some one asked: "How you going to bury him, Mrs. Sikora?"

"Oh," said Mrs. Sikora, "I'm going to have a good funeral."

There was an insurance policy for $500. The Sikoras had kept it up, scraping together the $10 premiums when the time came. Mrs. Sikora took the policy to the husband of a woman whose washing she had done. The husband was in the real estate business.

60

"I need money to bury my man," she said. "He died last night in the hospital."

She was red-eyed and dressed in black and the real estate man said: "What do you want?"

When Mrs. Sikora explained he gave her $400 for the policy and she went to an undertaker. Her eyes were still red with crying. They stared at the luxurious fittings of the undertaker's parlors. There were magnificent palms in magnificent jardinières, and plush chairs and large, inviting sofas and an imposing mahogany desk and a cuspidor of shining brass. Mrs. Sikora felt thrilled at the sight of these luxuries.

Then the undertaker came in and she explained to him.

The neighbors said: "Are you going to Mr. Sikora's funeral? It's going to be a big funeral. I got invited yesterday."

Wabansia Avenue was alive with automobiles. Innumerable relatives of Mr. and Mrs. Sikora arrived in automobiles, their faces staring with surprise out of the limousine windows as if they were seeing the world from a new angle. There were also neighbors. These were dressed even more impressively than the relatives. But everybody, neighbors and relatives, had on their Sunday clothes. And the unlucky ones who hadn't been invited leaned out of the windows of Wabansia Avenue and looked enviously at the entourage.

There was a band—fifteen pieces. And there was one open automobile filled with flowers, filled to overflowing. The band stopped in front of the Sikora flat, or rather in front of the building, for the Sikora flat was in the rear and Mrs. Sikora didn't want the band to stop in the alley. Then the envious ones leaning out of the windows couldn't see the band and that would be a drawback.

The band played, great, sad songs. The cornets and trombones sent a muted shiver through the street. The band stopped playing and the people leaning out of the windows sighed. Ah, it was a nice funeral!

61

Inside the Sikora house four men stood up beside the handsome black coffin and sang. Mrs. Sikora in a voluminous black veil listened with tears running from her face. Never had she heard such beautiful singing before—all in time and all the notes sweet and inspiring. She wept some more and solicitous arms raised her to her feet. Solicitous arms guided her out of the flower-filled room as six men lifted the black coffin and carried it into the street.

Slowly the automobiles rolled away. And behind the open car heaped with flowers rode Mrs. Sikora. The dolorous music of the band filled her with a gentle ecstasy. The flower scents drifted to her and when her eyes glanced furtively out of the back window of the limousine she could see the procession reaching for almost a half block. All black limousines filled with faces staring in surprise at the street.

And in front of the flower car in an ornamental hearse rode Mr. Sikora. The wheels of the hearse were heavily tired. They made no sound and the chauffeur was careful that his precious burden should not be joggled.

Slowly through the loop the procession picked its way. Crowds of people paused to stare back at the staring ones in the automobiles and to listen to the fine music that rose above the clamor of the "L" trains and the street cars and the trucks.

The sun lay over the cemetery. The handsome black coffin went out of sight. The fifteen musicians began to play once more and Mrs. Sikora, weeping anew, allowed solicitous arms to help her back into the limousine and with a sigh she leaned back and closed her eyes and let herself weep while the music played, while the limousine rolled smoothly along. It was like a dream, a strange thing imagined or read about somewhere.

The neighbors sniffed indignantly. "Did you hear about Mrs. Sikora?" they said. These were the same ones who had leaned enviously out of the Wabansia Avenue windows.

"She spent all her insurance money on a crazy funeral," the neighbors said, "and did you hear about it? The Juvenile Court is going to take her children away because she can't support them. The officer was out to see her yesterday and she's got no money to pay her bills. She spent the whole money —it was something like $2,000—on the funeral. Huh!"

Mrs. Sikora, weeping, explained to the Juvenile Court officer.

"My man died," she said, "and—and I spent the money for the funeral. It was not for myself, but for him I spent the money."

It will turn out all right, some day. And in the meantime Mrs. Sikora, when she is washing clothes for someone, will be able when her back aches too much to remember the day she rode in the black limousine and the band played and the air was filled with the smell of flowers.

DAPPER PETE AND THE SUCKER PLAY

Dapper Pete Handley, the veteran con man, shook hands all around with his old friends in the detective bureau and followed his captors into the basement. Another pinch for Dapper Pete; another jam to pry out of. The cell door closed and Pete composed his lean, gambler's face, eyed his mani-cured nails and with a sigh sat down on the wooden cell bench to wait for his lawyer.

"Whether I'm guilty of this or not," said Dapper Pete, "it goes to show what a sucker a guy is—even a smart guy. This ain't no sermon against a life of crime I'm pulling, mind you. I'm too old to do that and my sense of humor is workin' too good. I'm only sayin' what a sucker a guy is—sometimes. Take me."

Dapper Pete registered mock woe.

"Not that I'm guilty, mind you, or anything like that. But on general principles I usually keep out of the way of the coppers. Especially when there's been a misunderstanding concerning some deal or other. Well, how I happen to be here just goes to show what a sucker a guy is—even me."

Pressed for the key to his self-accusation, Dapper Pete continued:

"I come straight here from Grand Island, Neb. I had a deal on in Grand Island and worked it for a couple of months. And after I finished there was trouble and I left. I knew there would be warrants and commotion, the deal having flopped and a lot of prominent citizens feeling as if they had been bilked. You know how them get-rich-quick investors are. If they don't make 3,000 per cent profit over night they raise a squawk right away. And wanna arrest you.

"So I lit out and came to Chicago and when I got here some friends of mine tipped me off that there was considerable hunt for me. Well, I figured that the Nebraska coppers had let out a big holler and I thought it best to lay kind of low and keep out of trouble. That was only last week, you see.

"So I get the bright idea. Layin' around town with nothin' to do but keep out of sight ain't the cinch it sounds. You get so sick and tired of your own company that you're almost ready to throw your arms around the first harness bull you meet.

"But," smiled Dapper Pete, "I restrained myself."

There was time out while Pete discussed the irresponsibility, cruelty and selfishness of policemen in general. After which he continued with his original narrative:

"It was like this," he said. "I made up my mind that I would take in a few of the points of interest in the city I ain't ever got around to. Being a Chicagoan, like most Chicagoans I ain't ever seen any of our natural wonders at all. So first day out I figured that the place no copper would ever look for me would be like the Field Museum and in the zoo and on the beach and like that.

"So, first of all, I join a rubberneck crowd in one of the carryalls with a megaphone guy in charge. And I ride around all day. I got kind of nervous owing to the many coppers we kept passing and exchanging courtesies with. But I stuck all day, knowing that no sleuth was going looking for Dapper Pete on a rubberneck wagon.

"Well, then I spent three days in the Field Museum, eyeing the exhibits. Can you beat it? I walk around and walk around rubbering at mummies and bones and—well, I ain't kiddin', but they was among the three most interesting days I ever put in. And I felt pretty good, too, knowin' that no copper would be thinking of Dapper Pete as being in the museums.

"Then after that I went to the zoo and rubbered at the animals and birds. And I sat in the park and watched comical ball games and golf games and the like. And then I went on some of those boats that run between no place and nowhere —you get on at a pier and ride for a half hour and get off at a pier and have to call a taxi in order to find your way back to anywhere. You get me?

"I'm tellin' you all this," said Dapper Pete cautiously, "with no reference to the charges involved and for which I am pinched and incarcerated for, see? But I thought you might make a story out of the way a guy like me with all my experience dogin' coppers can play himself for a sucker.

"Well, pretty soon I pretty near run out of rube spots to take in. And then I think suddenly of the observation towers like on the Masonic Temple and the Wrigley Building. I headed for them right away, figuring to take a sandwich or so along and spend the day leisurely giving the city the once over from my eerie perch.

"And when I come home that night and told my friends about it they was all excited. They all agreed that I had made the discovery of the age and all claimed to feel sorry they wasn't hiding out from the coppers, just for the sake of bein' able to lay low on top of a loop building. It does sound pretty good, even now.

"I was on my fifth day and was just walking in on the Masonic Temple observation platform when things began to happen. You know how the city looks from high up. Like a lot of toys crawling around. And it's nice and cool and on the whole as good a place to lay low in as you want. And there's always kind of comical company, see? Rubes on their honeymoon and sightseers and old maids and finicky old parties afraid of fallin' off, and gals and their Johns lookin' for some quiet place to spoon.

Dapper Pete sighed in memory.

"I am sitting there nibbling a sandwich," he went on, "when a hick comes along and looks at me."

" 'Hello, pardner,' he says. 'How's the gas mine business?'

"And I look at him and pretend I don't savvy at all. But this terrible looking rube grins and walks up to me, so

66

help me God, and pulls back his lapel and shows me the big star.

" 'You better come along peaceabul,' he says. 'I know you, Pete Handley,' just like that. So I get up and follow this hick down the elevator and he turns me over to a cop on State Street and I am given the ride to the hoosegow. Can you beat it?''

"But who was the party with the star and why the pinch?'' I asked Dapper Pete. That gentleman screwed his lean, gambler's face into a ludicrous frown.

"Him," he sighed, "that was Jim Sloan, constable from Grand Island, Neb. And they sent him here about two weeks ago to find me. See? And all this rube does is ride around in rubberneck wagons and take in the museums and parks, having no idee where I was. He figured merely on enjoyin' himself at Nebraska's expense.

"And he was just on the observation tower lookin' over the city in his rube way when I have to walk into him. Yes, sir, Pete Handley, and there ain't no slicker guy in the country, walkin' like a prize sucker right into the arms of a Grand Island, Neb., constable. It all goes to show," sighed Dapper Pete, "what a small world it is after all."

WATERFRONT FANCIES

Man's capacity for faith is infinite. He is able to believe with passion in things invisible. He can achieve a fantastic confidence in the Unknowable. Here he sits on the breakwater near the Municipal Pier, a fishpole in his hand, staring patiently into the agate-colored water. He can see nothing. The lake is enormous. It contains thousands of square miles of water.

And yet this man is possessed of an unshakable faith that by some mysterious legerdemain of chance a fish, with ten thousand square miles of water to swim in safely, will seek out the little minnow less than an inch in length which he has lowered beside the breakwater. And so, the victim of preposterous conviction, he sits and eyes the tip of his fishpole with unflagging hope.

It is warm. The sun spreads a brightly colored but uncomfortable woolen blanket over their heads. A tepid breeze, reminiscent of cinders, whirls idly over the warm cement. Strung along the pier are a hundred figures, all in identical postures. They sit in defiance of all logic, all mathematics. For it is easy to calculate that if there are a half million fish in Lake Michigan and each fish displaces less than five cubic inches of water there would be only two and a half million cubic inches of fish altogether lost in an expanse containing at least eight hundred billion cubic inches of water. Therefore, the chance of one fish being at any one particular spot are one in four hundred thousand. In other words, the odds against each of these strangely patient men watching the ends of their fishpoles—the odds against their catching a fish —are four hundred thousand to one.

It is therefore somewhat amazing to stand and watch what happens along the sunny breakwater. Every three minutes one of the poles jerks out of the water with a wriggling prize on the hook.

68

"How are they coming?" we ask.

"Oh, so, so," answers one of the fishermen and points mutely to a string of several dozen perch floating under his feet in the water.

Thus does man, by virtue of his faith, rise above the science of mathematics and the barriers of logic. Thus is his fantastic belief in things unseen and easily disproved vindicated. He catches fish where by the law of probabilities there should be no fish. With the whole lake stretching mockingly before him he sits consumed with a preposterous, a fanatical faith in the little half-inch minnow dangling at the end of his line.

The hours pass. The sun grows hotter. The piles of stone and steel along the lake front seem to waver. From the distant streets come faint noises. On a hot day the city is as appealing as a half-cooled cinder patch. Poor devils in factories, poor devils in stores, in offices. One must sigh thinking of them. Life is even vaster than the lake in which these fishermen fish. And happiness is mathematically elusive as the fish for which the fishermen wait. And yet—

An old man with a battered face. A young man with a battered face. Silent, stoical, battered-looking men with fishpoles. A hundred, two hundred, they sit staring into the water of the lake as if they were looking for something. For fish? Incredible. One does not sit like this watching for something to become visible. Why? Because then there would be an air of suspense about the watcher. He would grow nervous after an hour, when the thing remained still invisible, and finally he would fall into hysterics and unquestionably shriek.

And these men grow calmer. Then what are they looking at, hour after hour, under the hot sun? Nothing. They are letting the rhythm of water and sky lull them into a sleep—a surcease from living. This is a very poetical thing for a hundred battered-looking men to attempt. Yet life may be as intimidating to honest, unimaginative ones as to their self-styled superiors.

There are many types fishing. But all of them look soiled. Idlers, workers, unhappy ones—they come to forget, to let the agate eye of the lake stare them into a few hours of oblivion.

But there is something else. Long ago men hunted and fished to keep alive. They fought with animals and sat with empty stomachs staring at the water, not in quest of Nirvanas but of fish. So now, after ages and ages have passed, there is left a vague memory of this in the minds of these fishermen. This memory makes them still feel a certain thrill in the business of pursuit. Even as they sit, stoical and inanimate, forgetful of unpaid bills, unfinished and never-to-be-finished plans ——there comes this curious thrill. A mouth tugs at the little minnow. The pole jerks electrically in the hand. Something alive is on the hook. And the fisherman for an instant recovers his past. He is Ab, fighting with an evening meal off the coast of Wales, two glacial periods ago. His body quivers, his muscles set, his eyes flash.

Zip! The line leaps out of the water. Another monster of the deep, whose conquest is necessary for the survival of the race of man, has been overcome. There he hangs, writhing on a hook! There he swings toward his triumphant foe, and the hand of the fisherman on the municipal breakwater, trembling with mysterious elation, closes about the wet, firm body of an outraged perch.

A make-believe hunt that now bears the name of sport. Yes, but not always. Here is one with a red, battered face and a curiously practical air about him. He is putting his fish in a basket and counting them. Two dozen perch.

"Want to sell them?"

He shakes his head.

"What are you going to do with them?"

He looks up and grins slowly. Then he points to his lips with his fingers and makes signs. This means he is dumb. He places his hand over his stomach and grins again. He is going to eat them. It is time to go home and do this, so he puts up his fishpole and packs his primitive paraphernalia—a tin can, a rusty spike, a bamboo pole.

Here is one, then, who, in the heart of the steel forest called civilization, still seeks out long forgotten ways of keeping life in his body. He hunts for fish.

The sun slides down the sky. The fishermen begin to pack up. They walk with their heads down and bent forward like number 7s. They raise their eyes occasionally to the piles of stone and steel that mark the city front. Back to their troubles and their cinder patch, but—and this is a curious fact—their eyes gleam with hope and curiosity.

THE SNOB

THE SNOB

We happen to be on the same street car. A drizzle softens the windows. She sits with her pasty face and her dull, little eyes looking out at the dripping street. Her cotton suit curls at the lapels. The ends of her shoes curl like a pair of burlesque Oriental slippers. She holds her hands in her lap. Red, thick fingers that whisper tiredly, "We have worked," lie in her lap.

A slavey on her day off. There is no mistaking this. Nineteen or twenty years old, homely as a mud fence; ungraceful, doltish, she sits staring out of the window and her eyes blink at the rain. A peasant from southeastern Europe, a field hand who fell into the steerage of a transatlantic liner and fell out again. Now she has a day off and she goes riding into the country on a street car.

She will get off and slosh with her heavy feet through wet grass. She will walk down the muddied roads and drink in the odor of fields and trees once more. These are romantic conjectures. The car jolts along. It is going west. The rain continues. It runs diagonal dots across the window.

Everybody out. This is the end of the line. I have gone farther than necessary. But there is the slavey. We have been talking. At least I talked. She listened, her doltish face opening its mouth, her little eyes blinking. She has pimples, her skin is muddied. A distressful-looking creature.

Yet there is something. This is her day off—a day free from the sweat of labor—and she goes on a street car into the country. So it would seem that under this blinking, frowzy exterior desire spreads its wings. She has memories, this blousy one. She has dreams.

The drizzle flies softly through the air. The city has disappeared. We walk down an incongruous stretch of pavement. It leads toward a forest or what looks like a forest. There are no houses. The sky asserts itself. I look up, but the shambling one whose clothes become active under water keeps her eyes to the pavement. This is disillusioning! "Here, slavey, is the sky," I think; "it becomes romantic for the moment because to you it is the symbol of lost dreams, or happy hours in fields. To me it is nothing but a sky. I have no interest in skies. But I am looking at it for you and enjoying it through your romantic eyes."

But her romantic eyes are oblivious. They consult the rain-washed pavement before her and nothing else. Very well, there are other and nicer skies in her heart that she contemplates. This is an inferior sky overhead. We walk on.

You see, I have been wrong. It is not green fields that lured the heavy feet of this slavey. She is not a peasant Cinderella. Grief, yes, hidden sorrow, has led her here. This is a cemetery.

It rains over the cemetery. There is silence. The white stones glisten. They stand like beggars asking alms of the winding paths. And this blousy one has come to be close to one of the white stones. Under one of them lies somebody whose image still lives in her heart.

She will kneel in the wet grass and her pasty little face will blink its dull eyes over a grave. Like a little clown in her curling cotton suit, her lumpy shoes, her idiotic hat, she will offer her tears to the pitiless silence of trees, wind, rain and white stones.

"Do you like them there?" She asks. She points to a cluster of fancy headstones.

"Do you?" I ask.

She smiles.

"Oh yes," she says. And she stops. She is admiring the tombstones. We walk on.

It is incredible. This blousy one, this dull-eyed one has come to the cemetery on her day off—to admire the tombstones. Ah, here is drama of a poignant kind. Let us pray God there is nothing pathologic here and that this is an idyl

73

of despair, that the lumpish little slavey sits on the rain-washed bench dreaming of fine tombstones as a flapper might dream of fine dresses.

Yes, at last we are on the track. We talk. These are very pretty, she says. Life is dull. The days are drab. The place where she works is like an oven. There is nothing pretty to look at—even in mirrors there is nothing cool and pretty. Clothes grow lumpy when she puts them on. Boys giggle and call names when she goes out. And so, outcast, she comes here to the cemetery to dream of a day when something cool and pretty will belong to her. A headstone, perhaps a stately one with a figure above it. It will stand over her. She will be dead then and unable to enjoy it. But now she is alive. Now she can think of how pretty the stone will look and thus enjoy it in advance. This, after all, is the technique of all dreams.

We grow confidential. I have asked what sort she likes best, what sort it pleases her most to think about as standing over her grave when she dies. And she has pointed some out. It rains. The trees shake water and the wind hurries past the white stones.

"I will tell you something," she says. "Here, look at this." From one of her curled pockets she removes a piece of paper. It is crumpled. I open it and read:

"In case of Accident please notify Misses Burbley,——Sheridan Road, and have body removed to Home of Parents who are residents of Corliss Wisconsin where they have resided for twenty Years and the diseased is a only Daughter named Clara. Age nineteen and educated in Corliss public Schools where she Graduated as a girl but came to Chicago in serch of employment and in case of accident funeral was held from Home of the Parents, many Frends attending and please Omit flours. . . ."

"I got lot of them writ out," said Clara, blinking. "You wanna read more? Why I write them out? Oh, because,

74

you can't tell, maybe you get run over and in accident and how they going to know who you are or what to do with the diseased if they don't find something?"

Her thick red hands grew excited. She produced further obituaries. From her pocketbook, from her bosom, from her pockets and one from under her hat. I read them. They were all alike, couched in vaguely bombastic terms. We sat in the rain and I thought:

"Alas, Clara is a bounder. A snob. She writes her own obituaries. Alive she can think of herself only as Clara, the slavey at whom the boys giggle and call names. But dead, she is the 'deseased'—the stately corpse commanding unprecedented attention. The prospect stirs a certain snobbishness in her. And she sits and writes her death notices out—using language she tries to remember from reading the funeral accounts of rich and powerful people."

Clara, her hat awry, her doltish body sagging in the rain —shuffled down the dirt road once more. Her outing is over. Cinderella returns to the ashes of life.

THE WAY HOME

He shuffles around in front of the Clinton Street employ-ment agency. The signs say: "Pick men wanted, section hands wanted, farm laborers wanted."

A Mexican stands woodenly against the window front. His eyes are open but asleep. He has the air of one come from a far country who lives upon memories.

There are others—roughly dressed exiles. Their eyes occasionally study the signs, deciphering with difficulty the crudely chalked words on the bulletin boards. Slav, Swede, Pole, Italian, Greek—they read in a language foreign to them that men are wanted on the farms in the Dakotas, in the lumber camps, on the roadbeds in Montana. Hard-handed men with dull, seamed faces and glittering eyes—the spike-haired proletaire from a dozen lands looking for jobs.

But this one who shuffles about in a tattered mackinaw, huge baggy trousers frayed at the feet, this one whose giant's body swings loosely back and forth under the signs, is a more curious exile. His Mexican brother leaning woodenly against the window has a slow dream in his eyes. Life is simple to his thought. It was hard for him in Mexico. And adven-ture and avarice sent him northward in quest of easier ways and more numerous comforts. Now he hunts a job on a chilly spring morning. When the proper job is chalked up on the bulletin board he will go in and ask for it. He stands and waits and thinks how happy he was in the country he aban-doned and what a fool he was to leave the white dust of its roads, its hills and blazing suns. And some day, he thinks, he will go back, although there is nothing to go back for. Yet it is pleasant to stand and dream of a place one has known and whither one may return.

But this one who shuffles, this giant in a tattered mackinaw who slouches along under the bulletin signs asking for section hands and laborers, there is no dream of remembered places in his eyes. Dull, blue eyes that peer bewilderedly out of a

76

powerful and empty face. The forehead is puckered as if in thought. The heavy jaws protrude with a hint of ferocity in their set. There is a reddish cast to his hair and face and the backs of his great hands, hanging limply almost to his knees, are covered with red hair.

The nose of this shuffling one is larger than the noses in the city streets. His fingers are larger, his neck is larger. There is a curious earthy look to this shuffling one seldom to be seen about men in streets. He is a huge creature with great thighs and Laocoön sinews and he towers a head above his brothers in front of the employment office. He is of a different mold from the men in the street. Strength ripples under his tattered mackinaw and his stiff looking hands could break the heads of two men against each other like eggshells while they rained puny blows on his dull face.

And yet of all the men moving about on the pavement in front of the Clinton Street bulletin boards it is this shuffling one who is the most impotent seeming. His figure is the most helpless. It slouches as under a final defeat. His eyes are the dullest.

He stops at the corner and stands waiting, his head lowered, his shoulders hunched in and he looks like a man weighed down by a harness.

A curious exile from whose blood has vanished all memory of the country to which he belongs. A faraway land, ages beyond the sun-warmed roads of which his Mexican brother dreams as he stands under the bulletin boards. A land which the ingenuity of the world has left forever behind. This is a land that once reached over all the seas.

For it was like this that men once looked in an age before the myths of the Persians and Hindus began to fertilize the animal soul of the race. In the forests north of the earliest cities of Greece, along the wild coasts tapering from the Tatar lands to the peninsula of the Basques, men like this shuffling one once ranged alone and in tribes. Huge, powerful men

77

whose foreheads sloped back and whose jaws sloped forward and whose stiff hands reached an inch nearer their knees than today.

This giant in the tattered mackinaw is an exile from this land and there is no dream of it left in his blood. The body of his fathers has returned to him. Their long, loose arms, their thick muscles and heavy pounding veins are his, but their voices are buried too deep to rise again in him. The mutterings of warrior councils, the shouts of terrible hunts are lost somewhere in him and he shuffles along, his sloping forehead in a pucker of thought as if he were trying to remember. But no memories come. Instead a bewilderment. The swarming streets bewilder him. The towering buildings, the noises of traffic and people dull his eyes and bring his shoulders together like the shoulders of some helpless captive.

He returns to the employment office and raises his eyes to the bulletin boards. He reads slowly, his large lips moving as they form words. In another day or another week he will be riding somewhere, his dull eyes gazing out of the train window. They will call him Ole or Pat or Jim in some camp in the Dakotas or along some roadbed in Montana. He will stand with a puny pick handle in his huge hands and his arms will rise and fall mechanically as he hews away along a deserted track. And his forehead will still be puckered in a frown of bewilderment. The thing held in his fists will seem like a strange toy.

"Farm laborers in Kansas," says the bulletin board as the clerk with his piece of chalk re-enters the office. The Mexican slowly removes himself from the window and the contemplation of memories. Kansas lies to the south and to the south is the way home. He goes in and talks to the man behind the long desk.

An hour later the clerk and his piece of chalk emerge. The exiles are still mooching around on the pavement and the shuffling one stands on the curb staring dully at the street under him.

"Section hands, Alberta, Canada, transportation," says the new bulletin. There is no stir among the exiles. This is to the north. It is still cold in the north. But the shuffling one has turned. His eyes again trace the crudely chalked letters of the bulletin board. His lips move as he tells himself what is written.

And then as if unconsciously he moves toward the door. Alberta is to the north and the voices that lie buried deep under the giant's mackinaw whisper darkly that to the north —to the north is the way home.

THE PIG

"Sofie Popapovitch versus Anton Popapovitch," cries the clerk. A number of broken-hearted matrons awaiting their turn before the bar of justice in the Domestic Relations Court find time to giggle at the name Popapovitch.

"Silence," cries the clerk. Very well, silence. Anton steps out. What's the matter with Anton? An indignant face, its chin raised, its eyes marching defiantly to the bar of justice. Sofie too, but weeping. And a lawyer, Sofie's lawyer.

Well, what's up? Why should the Popapovitches take up valuable time. Think of the taxpayers supporting this court and two Popapovitches marching up to have an argument on the taxpayers' money. Well, that's civilization.

Ah, ah! It appears that Anton, the rogue, went to a grand ball and raffle given by his lodge. What's wrong with that? Why must Sofie weep over that? Women are incredible. He went to the grand ball with his wife, as a man should. A very fine citizen, Anton. He belongs to a lodge that gives grand balls and he takes his wife.

Go on, says the judge, what happened? What's the complaint? Time is precious. Let's have it in a nutshell.

This is a good idea. People spend a frightful lot of unnecessary time weeping and mumbling in the courts. Mrs. Popapovitch will please stop weeping and get down to brass tacks. Very well, the complaint is, your honor, that Mr. Popapovitch got drunk at the grand ball. But that wasn't the end of it. There's some more. A paragraph of tears and then, your honor, listen to this: Mr. Popapovitch not only got drunk but he took a chance on the raffle which cost one dollar and he won.

But what did he win! Oh, oh! He won a pig. A live pig. That was the prize. A small, live pig with a ribbon round its neck. And, says Mrs. Popapovitch (there's humor in a long foreign-sounding name because it conjures up visions of bewildered, flat-faced people and bewildered, flat-faced people are always humorous), and, says she, they had been married ten years. Happily married. She washed, scrubbed, tended house. There were no children. Well, what of that? Lots of people had no children.

Anyway, Anton worked, brought home his pay envelope O. K. And then he wins this pig. And what does he do? He takes it home. He won't leave it anywhere.

"What!" he says, "I leave this pig anywhere? Are you crazy? It's my pig. I win him. I take him home with me."

And then? Well, it's midnight, your honor. And Anton carries the pig upstairs into the flat. But there's no place to put him. Where can one put a pig in a flat, your honor? No place. The pig don't like to stand on carpets. And what pig likes to sleep on hard wood floors? A pig's a pig. And what's good for a pig? Aha! a pig pen.

So, your honor, Anton puts him in the bathtub. And he starts down stairs with a basket and all night long he keeps bringing up basketfuls of dirt dug up from the alley. Dirt, cinders, more dirt. And he puts it in the bathtub. And what does the pig do? He squeals, grunts and wants to go home. He fights to get out of the bathtub. There's such a noise nobody can sleep. But Anton says, "Nice little pig. I fix you up fine. Nice little pig."

And so he fills the bathtub up with dirt. Then he turns on the water. And what does he say? He says, "Now, little pig, we have fine mud for you. Nice fine mud." Yes, your honor, a whole bathtub full of mud. And when the pig sees this he gets happy and lies down and goes to sleep. And Anton sits in the bathroom and looks at the pig all night and says, "See. He's asleep. It's like home for him."

But the next day Anton must go to work. All right, he'll go to work. But first, understand everybody, he don't want this pig touched. The pig stays in the bathtub and he must be there when he comes home.

All right. The pig stays in the bathtub, your honor. Anton wants it. Tomorrow the pig will be killed and that'll be an end for the pig.

Anton comes home and he goes in the bathroom and he sits and looks at the pig and complains the mud is dried up and why don't somebody take care of his pig. His damn pig. He brings up more dirt and makes more mud. And the pig tries to climb out and throws mud all over the bathroom.

That's one day. And then there's another day. And finally a third day. Will Anton let anybody kill his pig? Aha! He'll break somebody's neck if he does. But, your honor, Mrs. Popapovitch killed the pig. A terrible thing, isn't it, to kill a pig that keeps squealing in the bathtub and splashing mud all day?

But what does Anton do when he comes home and finds his pig killed? My God! He hits her, your honor. He hits her on the head. His own wife whom he loves and lives with for ten years. He throws her down and hollers, "You killed my little pig! You good for nothing. I'll show you."

What a disgrace for the neighbors! Lucky there are no children, your honor. Married ten years but no children. And it's lucky now. Because the disgrace would have been worse. The neighbors come. They pull him away from his wife. Her eye is black and blue. Her nose is bleeding. That's all, your honor."

A very bad case for Anton Popapovitch. A decidedly bad case. Step forward, Anton Popapovitch, and explain it, if you can. Did you beat her up? Did you do this thing? And are you ashamed and willing to apologize and kiss and make up?

Anton, step forward and tell his honor. But be careful. Mrs. Popapovitch has a lawyer and it will go bad with you if you don't talk carefully.

All right. Here's Anton. He nods and keeps on nodding. What is this? What's he nodding about? Did this happen as your wife says, Anton? Anton blows out his cheeks and rubs his workingman's hand over his mouth. To think that you should beat your wife who has always been good to you, Anton. Who has cooked and been true to you! And there are no children to worry you. Not one. And you beat her. Bah, is that a man? Don't you love your wife? Yes. All right, then why did you do it?

Anton looks up surprised. "Because," says Anton, still surprised, "like she say. She kill my pig. You hear yourself, your honor. She say she kill him. And I put him in the bathtub and give him mud. And she kill him."

But is that a reason to beat your wife and nearly kill her? It is, says Anton. Well, then, why? Tell the judge, why you were so fond of this pig, Anton.

Ah, yes, Anton Popapovitch, tell the judge why you loved this little pig so much and made a home for him with mud in the bathtub. Why you dreamed of him as you stood working in the factory? Why you ran home to him and fed him and sat and looked at him and whispered "Nice little pig?" Why?

God knows. But Anton Popapovitch can't explain it. It must remain one of the mysteries of our city, your honor. Call the next case. Put Anton Popapovitch on parole. Perhaps it was because. . . , well, the matter is ended. Anton Popapovitch sighs and looks with accusing eyes at his wife Sofie, with accusing eyes that hint at evidence unheard.

THE LITTLE FOP

This little caricature of a fop, loitering in the hotel lobby, enthralled by his own fastidiousness, gazing furtively at the glisten of his newly manicured nails and shuddering with awe at the memory of the puckered white silk lining inside his Prince of Wales derby—I've watched him for more than a month now. Here he comes, his pointed button shoes, his razor-edged trousers, his natty tan overcoat with its high waist band and its amazing lapels that stick up over his shoulders like the ears of a jackass, here he comes embroidered and scented and looking like a cross between a soft-shoe dancer and a somnambulist. And here he takes his position, holding his gloves in his hand, his Prince of Wales derby jammed down on his patent-leather hair.

Observe him. This is a pose. He is living up to a fashion illustration in one of the magazines. Or perhaps he is duplicating an attitude of some one studied in a Michigan Avenue club entrance. His right arm is crooked as if he were about to place his hand over his heart and bow. His left arm hangs with a slight curve at his side. His feet should be together, but they shift nervously. His head is turned to the left and slightly raised—like a movie actor posing for a cigarette advertisement.

And there he stands, a dead ringer for one of the waxen dummies to be seen in a Halsted Street Men's Snappy Furnishings Store.

I've watched him for a month, off and on. And his face still says nothing. His eyes are curiously emotionless. They appear suddenly in his face. He is undersized. His nose, despite the recent massage and powder, has a slight oleaginous gleam to it. The cheek bones are a bit high, the mouth a trifle wide and the chin slightly bulbous. As he blinks about him with his small, almost Mongolian eyes he looks like some honest little immigrant from Bohemia or Poland whom

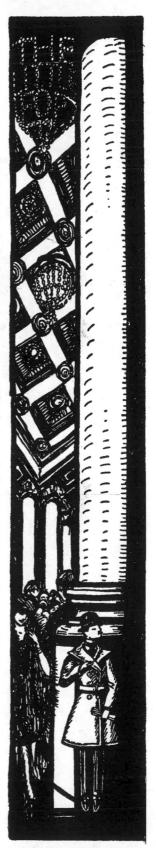

a malignant sorcerer has changed into a caricature fashion plate. This is, indeed, the legend of Cinderella and the fairy godmother with an ending of pathos.

Yet, though his face says nothing, there is a provoking air to this little fop. His studied inanimation, his crudely self-conscious pose, his dull, little, peasant eyes staring at the faces that drift by in the lobby—these ask for translation. Why is he here? What does he want? Why does he come every evening and stand and watch the little hotel parade? Ah, one never sees him in the dining room or on the dance floor. One never meets him between the acts in the theater lobby. And one never sees him talking to anybody. He is always alone. People pass him with a curious glance and think to themselves, "Ah, a young man about town! What a shame to dissipate like that!" They sometimes notice the masterly way in which he sizes up a fur-coated "chicken" stalking thin-leggedly through the lobby and think to themselves: "The scoundrel! He's the kind of creature that makes a big city dangerous. A carefully combed and scented vulture waiting to swoop down from the side lines."

Evening after evening between 6 o'clock and midnight he drifts in and out of the lobby, up and down Randolph Street and takes up his position at various points of vantage where crowds pass, where women pass. I've watched him. No one ever talks to him. There are no salutations. He is unknown and worse. For the women, the rouged and orna-mental ones, know him a bit too well. They know the care-fully counted nickels in his trousers pocket, the transfers he is saving for the three-cent rebate that may come some day, the various newspaper coupons through which he hopes to make a killing.

All this they know and through a sixth sense, a curious instinct of sex divination, they know the necktie counter or information desk behind which he works during the day, the stuffy bedroom to which he will go home to sleep, the vacuity of his mind and gaudy emptiness of his spirit. They know all this and pass him up with never a smile. Yes, even the manicure girls in the barber shop give him the out-and-out sneer and the hat-check girls and even the floor girls—the chambermaids—all of whom he has tried to date up—they all respond with an identical raspberry to his invitations.

But he asks for translation—this determined little caricature of the hotel lobby. A little peasant masquerading as a dazzled moth around the bright lights. Not entirely. There is something else. There is something of a great dream behind the ridiculous pathos of this over-dressed little fool. There is something in him that desires expression, that will never achieve expression, and that will always leave him just such an absurd little clown of a fop.

When the manicure girls read this they will snort. Because they know him too well. "Of all the half-witted dumbbells I ever saw in my life," they will say, "he wins the cement earmuffs. Nobody home, honest to Gawd, he's nothin' but a nasty little fourflusher. We know him and his kind."

Fortunately I don't know him as well as the manicure girls do, so there is room for this speculation as I watch him in the evening now and then. I see him standing under the blaze of lobby lights, in the thick of passing fur coats and dinner jackets, in the midst of laughter, escorts, intrigues, actors, famous names.

He stands perfectly still, with his right arm crooked as if he were going to place his hand over his heart and bow, with his left arm slightly curved at his side. Grace. This is a pose denoting grace. He got it somewhere from an illustration. And he holds it. Here is life. The real stuff. The real thing. Lights and laughter. Glories, coiffures, swell dames, great actors, guys loaded with coin. His little Mongolian eyes blink through his amusing aplomb. Here are gilded pillars and marbled walls, great rugs and marvelous furniture. Here music is playing somewhere and people are eating off gold-edged dishes.

And now you will smile at me, not him. Because watching him of evenings, on and off, a curious notion takes hold of my thoughts. I have noticed the race oddities of his face. the Mongolian eyes, the Slavic cheek bones, the Italian hair. A mixed breed, this little fop. Mixed through a dozen centuries. Fathers and mothers that came from a hundred parts of the earth. But down the centuries they had one thing in common. Servitude. The Carlovingian courts, the courts of the De Medici, the Valois, and long before that, the great houses that lay around the Roman hills. Dragged from their villages, east, west, north and south, they flitted in the trappings of servitude through the vast halls of tyrants, barons, Caesars, sybarites, debauchees. They were the torchbearers, the caitiffs, the varlets, the bathkeepers, the inanimate figures whose faces watched from the shadows the great orgies of Tiberius, the bacchanals of satraps, kings, captains and squires.

And here their little great-great-grandson stands as they stood, the ghost of their servitude in his sluggish blood. He is content with his rôle of watcher as his people were content. These slightly grotesque trappings of his are a disguise. He wishes to disguise the fact that he is of the torchbearers, the varlets, the bathkeepers who produced him. So he imitates servilely what he fancies to be the distinguishing marks of his betters—their clothes, their manners, their aplomb. This accomplished, he is content to yield himself to the mysterious impulses and dreams that move silently through him.

And so he takes his position beside his people—the mixed breeds dragged from their scattered villages—so he stands as they stood through the centuries, their faces watching from the shadows the gorgeousness and tumult of the great aristocrats.

MOTTKA

Since most of the great minds that have weighed the subject have arrived at the opinion that between poverty and crime there is an inevitable affinity, the suspicion with which the eye of Policeman Billings rested upon Mottka, the vender of roasted chestnuts, reflected creditably upon that good officer's grasp of the higher philosophies.

Policeman Billings, sworn to uphold the law and assist in the protection of property, viewed the complications and mysteries of the social system with a simple and penetrating logic. The rich are not dangerous, reasoned Policeman Billings, because they have what they want. But the poor who have not what they want are, despite paradox and precedent, always to be watched closely. A raggedly dressed man walking in a dark, lonely street may be honesty itself. Yet rags, even when worn for virtue's sake, are a dubious assurance of virtue. They are always ominous to one sworn to protect property and uphold the law.

There is a maxim by Chateaubriand, or perhaps it was Stendhal—maxims have a way of leaving home—which claims that the equilibrium of society rests upon the acquiescence of its oppressed and unfortunate.

In passing the battered chestnut roaster of the unfortunate Mottka, Policeman Billings was aware in his own way of the foregoing elements of social philosophy. Mottka had chosen for his little shop an old soapbox which a wastrel providence had deposited in the alley on Twenty-second Street, a few feet west of State Street. Here Mottka sat, nursing the fire of his chestnut roaster with odd bits of refuse which seldom reached the dignity of coal or even wood.

He was an old man and the world had used him poorly. He was, in fact, one of those upon whom the equilibrium of the social system rests. He was unfortunate, oppressed and acquiescent. Arriving early in the forenoon he set up his

89

shop, lighted his fire and took his place on the soapbox. When the lights began to wink out along this highway of evil ghosts Mottka was still to be seen hunched over his chestnut roaster and waiting.

Policeman Billings strolling over his beat was wont to observe Mottka. There were many things demanding the philosophical attention of Policeman Billings. Not so long ago the neighborhood which he policed had been renowned to the four corners of the earth as the rendezvous of more temptations than even St. Anthony enumerated in his interesting brochure on the subject. And Policeman Billings felt the presence of much of this evil lingering in the brick walls, broken windows and sagging pavements of the district.

It was after a number of days on the beat that Policeman Billings began to take Mottka seriously. There was something curious about the chestnut vender, and the eye of the good officer grew narrow with suspicion. "This man," reasoned Policeman Billings, "makes pretense of being a vender of roasted chestnuts. He sits all day in the alley between two saloons. I have never noticed him sell any chestnuts. And come to think of it, I have never seen more than a half-dozen chestnuts on his roasting pan. I begin to suspect that this old man is a fraud and that his roasting chestnuts is a blind. He is very likely a lookout for some bootlegger gang or criminal mob. And I will keep an eye on him."

Mottka remained unaware of Policeman Billing's attention. He continued to sit hunched over his roaster, nursing the little fire under it as best he could—and waiting. But finally Policeman Billings called himself to his attention in no uncertain way.

"What's your name?" asked the good officer, stopping before the chestnut vender.

"Mottka," answered Mottka.

"And what are you doing here?" asked Policeman Billings, frowning.

"I roast chestnuts and sell them," said Mottka.

"Hm!" said Policeman Billings, "you do, eh? Well, we'll see about that. Come along."

Mottka rose without question. One does not ask questions of an officer of the law. Mottka stood up and put the fire out and put the handful of chestnuts in his pocket and picked up his roaster and followed the officer. A half-hour later Mottka stood before the sergeant in the Twenty-second street station.

"What's the trouble?" asked the sergeant.

And Policeman Billings explained.

"He claims to be selling chestnuts and roasting them. But I never see him sell any, much less do I see him roasting any. He's got about a dozen chestnuts altogether and I think he may bear looking into."

"What about it, Mottka?" asked the sergeant.

Mottka shrugged his shoulders, shook his head and smiled deprecatingly.

"Nothing," he said, "I got a chestnut roaster I got from a friend on the West Side. And I try to make business. I got a license."

"But the officer says you never roast any chestnuts and he thinks you're a fake."

"Yes, yes," smiled Mottka; "I don't have so many chestnuts. I can't afford only a little bit at a time. Some time I buy a basket of chestnuts."

"Where do you live, Mottka?"

"Oh, on the West Side. On the West Side."

"And what did you do before you roasted chestnuts?"

"Me? Oh, I was in a business. Yes, in a business. And it failed. So I got the chestnut roaster. I got a license."

"It seems to me I've seen you before, Mottka."

"Yes, yes. A policeman bring me here before when I was on Wabash Avenue with my chestnuts."

"What did he bring you in for?"

"Oh, because he thinks I am a crook, because I don't have enough chestnuts to sell. He says I am a lookout for crooks and he brings me in."

Mottka laughed softly and shrugged his shoulders.

"I am no crook. Only I am too poor to buy more chestnuts."

Policeman Billings frowned, but not at Mottka.

"Here," said the good officer, and he handed Mottka a dollar. Three other upholders of the law were present and they too handed Mottka money.

"Go and buy yourself some chestnuts, Mottka," said the sergeant, "so the officers won't be runnin' you in on suspicion of bein' a criminal."

Now Mottka's chestnut roaster in the alley off State Street is full of chestnuts. A bright fire burns under the pan and Mottka sits watching the chestnuts brown and peel as they roast. And if you were to ask him about things he would say:

"Tell something? What is there to tell? Nothing."

"FA'N TA MIG!"

Avast and belay there! Take in the topgallants, wind up the mizzenmast and reef the cleets! This is Tobias Wooden-Leg plowing his way through a high sea in Grand Avenue.

Aye, what a night, what a night! The devil astride the jib boom, his tail lashing in the wind. "Pokker!" says Tobias, "fa'n ta mig. Hold tight and here we go!"

The boys in the Elite poolroom stand grinning in the doorway. Old Norske Tobias is on a tear again, his red face shining with the memory of Stavanger storms, his beard bristling like a north cat's back. An Odin in caricature.

They watch him pass. Drunker than a fiddler's wench. Drunker than a bootlegger's pal. Drunk as the devil himself and roaring at the top of his voice: "Belay, there! Hold tight and here we go!" Poor Tobias Wooden-Leg, the years keep plucking out his hairs and twisting his fingers into talons. Seventy years have squeezed him. And they have brought him piety and wisdom. They have taught him virtue and holiness.

But the wind suddenly rises and comes blowing out of Stavanger again. The great sea suddenly lifts under his one good leg. And Tobias with his Bibles and his prayer books struggles in the dark of his Grand Avenue bedroom. The devil comes and sits on his window sill, a devil with long locks and bronze wings beside his ears and a three-pronged pitchfork in his hand.

"Ho, ho!" cries this one on the window sill. "What are you doing here, Tobias? With the north wind blowing and the gray seas standing on their heads? Grown old, Tobias, eh? Sitting in a corner and mumbling over litanies."

And it has always been like that since he came to Grand Avenue ten years ago. It has always turned out that Tobias takes off his white shirt and puts on his sailor's black sweater

93

and fastens on his old wooden leg and follows the one on the
window sill.

Avast and belay! The night is still young and a sailor
man's abroad. The sergeant going off duty at the Chicago
Avenue station passes and winks and calls: "Hello, Tobias.
Pretty rough tonight."

"Fa'n ta mig!" roars Tobias. "Hold tight." And he
steers for Clark Street. And now the one on the window sill
is gone and the storm grows quiet. And poor Tobias Wooden-
Leg, the venerable and pious, who has won the grace of God
through a terrific fight, finds himself again lost and strayed.

Of what good were the prayers and the night after night
readings in the old sea captain's Bible stolen forty years ago?
Of what good the promises and tears of repentance, when this
thing that seemed to rise out of forgotten seas could come and
jump up on his window sill and bewitch him as if he were a
heedless boy? When it could sit laughing at him until in its
laugh he heard the sounds of old winds roaring and old seas
standing on their heads, and he put on his black sweater—the
moth-eaten badge of his sinfulness—and he put on his wooden
leg and lifted out the handful of money from under the corner
of the carpet?

What good were the prayers if they couldn't keep him
pious? Yes, that was it. And here the habitués along North
Clark Street grin. For Tobias Wooden-Leg is coming down
the pavement, his head hanging low, his beard no longer
bristling and his soul on a hunt for a new God. A strong
God. A powerful and commanding God, stronger than the
long-locked, bronze-winged one of the window sill.

They grin because this is an old story. Tobias is an old
character. Once every two or three months for ten years
Tobias has come like this with his head lowered searching
for a new and powerful God that would keep him pious and
that would kill the devil that seemed never to die inside his
old Norske soul.

So he had taken them all—a jumble of gods, a patch-
work of religions. Every soapbox apostle in the district had
at one time converted him. Holy Roller, Methodist, Jumper,
Yogi, Swami, Zionite—he had bowed his head before their
and a dozen other varied gods. And the missions in the
district had come to know him as "the convert." He had
been faithful to each of the creeds as long as he remained
sober and as long as he sat in his room of nights reading in
his Bible.

But come a storm out of Stavanger, come a whistling
under the eaves and a thumping of wind on the window pane
and Tobias was off again. "He is not a good God!" Tobias
would cry in his new "repentance." "His religion is too weak.
The devil is stronger than Him. I want a stronger religion.
Pagh, I want somebody big enough to kill this fanden inside
me."

The crowd around the soapbox evangelist is rather slight.
The night is cold. The wind bites and the street has a dismal
air. The evangelist stands around the corner from the old
book store in whose windows thousands of musty volumes
are piled like the bones of hermits. The man who owns this
curious book store is a sun-worshipper. And the evangelist
on the soapbox is a friend of his.

The slight crowd listens. Peace comes from the sun.
The sun is the source of light and of health. It is the eye
of God. Terrible by day and watching by night. It is the
fire of life. The slight crowd grins and the evangelist, his
mind bubbling with a cabalistic jargon remembered out of
musty books, tries to explain something that seems vivid in
his heart but vague to his tongue.

They will drop away soon because the night is cold and
the evangelist a bit too nutty for serious attention. But here
comes Tobias Wooden-Leg and some of the listeners grin and
nudge one another. Tobias, with his voice hoarse and his blue
eyes shining with wrath—wrath at himself and wrath at the

95

God who had abandoned him, unable to cope with the one on the window sill.

Tobias listens. Terrible by day and ever watchful by night. The King of Kings, the Great Majesty and secret symbol of the absolute. Tobias drinks in the jargon of the soapbox man and then shouts: "I'll join, I'll join! I want a strong God!"

So now Tobias Wooden-Leg is a sun-worshipper. The boys in the Elite poolroom will tell you all about it. How he walks the street at dawn with his head raised and bows every seven steps. And how in the evening he is to be seen standing at his window bowing to the sun going down. And how he has been around saying: "Well, I have found the big God at last. No more monkey business for me. Listen to what it says in the book about him." And how he will quote from the sea captain's Bible stolen forty years ago.

But the boys also say: "Just wait."

And they wink, meaning that another storm will blow up out of Stavanger in Norway and old Tobias will come plowing down the street again howling that fa'n ta mig the devil has him and that old Thor leaped on his window sill and tossed the all-powerful sun out of the sky with his hammer.

FANTASTIC LOLLYPOPS

They will never start. No, they will never start. In another two minutes Mr. Prokofieff will go mad. They should have started at eleven. It is now ten minutes after eleven. And they have not yet started. Ah, Mr. Prokofieff has gone mad.

But Mr. Prokofieff is a modernist; so nobody pays much attention. Musicians are all mad. And a modernist musician, du lieber Gott! A Russian modernist musician!

The medieval face of Mr. Boris Anisfeld pops over the rows of empty seats. It is very likely that Mr. Anisfeld will also go mad. For Mr. Anisfeld is, in a way, a collaborator of Mr. Prokofieff. It is the full dress rehearsal of "The Love for Three Oranges." Mr. Prokofieff wrote the words and music. Mr. Anisfeld painted the scenery.

"Mees Garden weel be hear in a meenute," the medieval face of Boris whispers into the Muscovite ears of Serge.

Eleven-fifteen, and Miss Garden has arrived. She is armed, having brought along her heaviest shillalah. Mr. Prokofieff is on his feet. He takes off his coat. The medieval face of Mr. Anisfeld vanishes. Tap, tap, on the conductor's stand. Lights out. A fanfare from the orchestra's right.

Last rehearsal for the world premier of a modernist opera! One winter morning years ago the music critics of Paris sat and laughed themselves green in the face over the incomprehensible banalities of an impossible modernist opera called "Tannhäuser." And who will say that critics have lost their sense of humor. There will unquestionably be laughter before this morning is over.

Music like this has never come from the orchestra pit of the Auditorium. Strange combinations of sounds that seem to come from street pianos, New Year's eve horns, harmonicas and old-fashioned musical beer steins that play when you lift

97

them up. Mr. Prokofieff waves his shirt-sleeved arms and the sounds increase.

There is nothing difficult about this music—that is, unless you are unfortunate enough to be a music critic. But to the untutored ear there is a charming capriciousness about the sounds from the orchestra. Cadenzas pirouette in the treble. Largos toboggan in the bass. It sounds like the picture of a crazy Christmas tree drawn by a happy child. Which is a most peculiar way for music to sound.

But, attention! The curtain is up. Bottle greens and fantastic reds. Here is a scene as if the music Mr. Prokofieff were waving out of the orchestra had come to life. Lines that look like the music sounds. Colors that embrace one another in tender dissonances. Yes, like that.

And here, galubcheck (I think it's galubcheck), are the actors. What is it all about? Ah, Mr. Prokofieff knows and Boris knows and maybe the actors know. But all it is necessary for us to know is that music and color and a quaint, almost gargoylian, caprice are tumbling around in front of our eyes and ears.

And there is M. Jacques Coini. He will not participate in the world premier. Except in spirit. Now M. Coini is present in the flesh. He wears a business suit, spats of tan and a gray fedora. M. Coini is the stage director. He instructs the actors how to act. He tells the choruses where to chorus and what to do with their hands, masks, feet, voices, eyes and noses.

The hobgoblin extravaganza Mr. Prokofieff wrote unfolds itself with rapidity. Theater habitués eavesdropping on the rehearsal mumble in the half-dark that there was never anything like this seen on earth or in heaven. Mr. Anisfeld's scenery explodes like a succession of medieval skyrockets. A phantasmagoria of sound, color and action crowds the startled proscenium. For there is no question but that the proscenium, with the names of Verdi, Bach, Haydn and Beethoven chiseled on it, is considerably startled.

Through this business of skyrockets and crescendos and hobgoblins M. Coini stands out like a lighthouse in a cubist storm. However bewildering the plot, however humpty-dumpty the music, M. Coini is intelligible drama. His brisk little figure in its pressed pants, spats and fedora, bounces around amid the apoplectic disturbances like some busybody Alice in an operatic Wonderland.

The opus mounts. The music mounts. Singers attired as singers were never attired before crawl on, bounce on, tumble on. And M. Coini, as undisturbed as a traffic cop or a loop pigeon, commands his stage. He tells the singers where to stand while they sing, and when they don't sing to suit him he sings himself. He leads the chorus on and tells it where to dance, and when they don't dance to suit him he dances himself. He moves the scenery himself. He fights with Mr. Prokofieff while the music splashes and roars around him. He fights with Boris. He fights with electricians and wigmakers.

It is admirable. M. Coini, in his tan spats and gray fedora, is more fantastic than the entire cast of devils and Christmas trees and lollypops, who seem to be the leading actors in the play. Mr. Prokofieff and Miss Garden have made a mistake. They should have let M. Coini play "The Love for Three Oranges" all by himself. They should have let him be the dream towers and the weird chorus, the enchantress and the melancholy prince. M. Coini is the greatest opera I have ever seen. All he needed was M. Prokofieff's music and the superbly childish visions of the medieval Boris for a background.

The music leaps into a gaudy balloon and sails away in marvelous zigzags, way over the heads of the hobgoblins on the stage and the music critics off the stage. Miss Garden beckons with her shillalah. Mr. Prokofieff arrives panting at her side. He bows, kisses the back of her hand and stands at attention. Also the medieval face of Mr. Anisfeld drifts gently through the gloom and joins the two.

The first act of "The Oranges" is over. Two critics exchanging opinions glower at Mr. Prokofieff. One says: "What a shame! What a shame! Nobody will understand it." The other agrees. But perhaps they only mean that music critics will fail to understand it and that untutored ones like ourselves will find in the hurdy-gurdy rhythms and contortions of Mr. Prokofieff and Mr. Anisfeld a strange delight. As if some one had given us a musical lollypop to suck and rub in our hair.

I have an interview with Mr. Prokofieff to add. The interview came first and doesn't sit well at the end of these notes. Because Mr. Prokofieff, sighing a bit nervously in expectation of the world's premier, said: "I am a classicist. I derive from the classical composers."

This may be true, but the critics will question it. Instead of quoting Mr. Prokofieff at this time, it may be more apropos merely to say that I would rather see and listen to his opera than to the entire repertoire of the company put together. This is not criticism, but a prejudice in favor of fantastic lollypops.

NOTES FOR A TRAGEDY

Jan Pedlowski came home yesterday and found that his wife had run away. There was supper on the table. And under the soup plate was a letter addressed to Jan. It read, in Polish:

"I am sick and tired. You keep on nagging me all the time and I can't stand it any more. You will be better off without me.

Paula."

Jan ate his supper and then put his hat and coat on and went over to see the sergeant at the West Chicago Avenue police station. The sergeant appeared to be busy, so Jan waited. Then he stepped forward and said:

"My wife has run away. I want to catch her."

The sergeant was lacking in sympathy. He told Jan to go home and wait and that the missus would probably come back. And that if she didn't he could get a divorce.

"I don't want a divorce," said Jan. "I want to catch her."

But Jan went home. It was no use running around looking for her and losing sleep. And, besides, he had to be in court tomorrow. The landlord had left a notice that the Pedlowskis must get out of their flat because they didn't pay their rent.

Before coming home Jan had arranged with the foreman at the plating works for two hours off, to be taken out of his pay. He could come to work at seven and work until half-past nine, then go to court and be back, maybe, by half-past eleven.

So Jan went to bed. He put the letter his wife had left in his coat pocket, because he had a vague idea it might be evidence. He might show it to somebody and maybe it would help.

101

It was snowing when Jan left the plating works in the morning to come to court. He arrived at the City Hall and wandered around, confused by the crowd of people pouring in and out of the elevators. But it was growing late and he only had two hours off. So Jan made inquiries. Where was the court where he should go?

"Judge Barasa on the eighth floor," said the starter. Jan went there.

A lot of people were in the court room. Jan sat down among them and looked like them—blank, uninterested, as if waiting for a train in the railroad station.

One thing worried Jan. The two hours off. If they didn't call him he'd be late and the foreman would be mad. He might lose his job, and jobs were hard to get. It took five weeks to get this one. It would take longer now.

But they called Jan Pedlowski and he came forward to where the judge sat. At first Jan had felt confused and frightened. He had worried about coming to court and standing before the judge. Now it seemed all right. Everybody was nice and businesslike. A lawyer said:

"There's almost two months' rent due now. Eighteen dollars for the November rent and $27.50 for December."

"Can you pay the rent?" the judge asked of Jan.

Jan looked and blinked and tried to think of something to say. He could only think of "My wife Paula ran away last night. Here, she wrote this letter left me on the table when I come home last night."

"I see," said the judge. "But what about the rent? If I give you until January 10, do you think you can pay it?"

"I don't know," said Jan, rubbing his eyes. "I got job now, but they going to lay off after new year. If I have job I pay it all. I can pay $10 now."

"Have you got it with you," asked the judge.

"Yes," said Jan. "I was going to buy Christmas present for Paula, but she ran away."

Jan handed over the $10 and listened to the judge explain that he would be allowed to stay where he was until January 10 and have till then to pay his rent. When this was over he walked out, putting his hat on too soon, so that the bailiff cried: "Hats off in the courtroom." Jan grabbed his hat and grew red.

Now he had almost a full hour and a half before going to the factory. It had taken less time than he thought. Jan started to walk. It was cold and the streets were slippery. He walked along with his hands in the frayed pockets of his overcoat and his breath congealing over his walrus mustache.

His eyes were set and his face serious. Jan's thoughts were simple. Rent—Paula—jobs. Christmas, perhaps, too. But he walked along like anybody else in the loop.

Jan wandered as far as Quincy and La Salle streets. Here he stopped and looked around. It was beginning to snow heavier now. He stood still like a man waiting. And having nothing to do he took the letter his wife had left under the soup plate and read it again.

When Jan had folded the letter up and started to walk once more his eyes suddenly lighted up. He turned and started to run and as he ran he cried: "Paula, Paula!" Some of the crowd moving on paused and looked at a stocky man with a heavy mustache running across the street and shouting a woman's name.

The cabs were thick at the moment and it was hard running across. But Jan kept on, his overcoat flapping behind him and his short legs jumping up and down as he moved. A young woman with a cheap fur around her neck had stopped. There were others who paused to watch Jan. But this young woman was one of the few who didn't smile.

She waited as if puzzled for a moment and then started to lose herself in the crowd. She walked swiftly ahead, her eyes anxiously on the corner. And in the meantime Jan came galumphing toward the curbing still crying: "Paula, Paula!" At the curbing, however, Jan came to a full stop. His toe had caught the cement and he shot forward, landing on his hands and chin.

A crowd gathered around Jan and some one helped him to his feet. His chin was bleeding and his hands were scraped from hitting the cold pavement. He made no sign, however, of injury, but stood blinking in the direction the young woman with the cheap fur had gone.

A policeman arrived and inquired sympathetically what was wrong. Jan brushed himself mechanically as the policeman spoke. Then he answered: "Nothing, I fell down." The policeman went away and Jan turned back to catch a Milwaukee Avenue street car.

He stood on the corner waiting and fingering his bruised chin. He seemed to be getting impatient as the car failed to appear. Finally he thrust his hand inside his pocket and drew out the letter again. He held it without reading for an instant and then tore it up.

When the car came Jan was still tearing up the letter, his thick fingers trying vainly to divide it into tinier bits.

CORAL, AMBER AND JADE

There are no gold and scarlet lanterns bobbing like fat little oriental Pierrots over this street. No firecracker colors daub its sad walls. Walk the whole length and not a dragon or a thumbnail balcony or a pigtail will you see.

Instead, a very efficient, very conservative Chinatown and a colony of very efficient and very matter-of-fact Chinamen who have gradually taken possession of a small district around Twenty-second Street and Wentworth Avenue. A rather famous district in its way, where once the city's tenderloin put forth its red shadows.

But now as you walk, the night stares evilly out of wooden ruins. Stretches of sagging, empty buildings, whose windows and doors seem to have been chewed away, an intimidating silence, a graveyard of crumbling little houses—these remain. And you see Venus, grown old and toothless, snoozing amid the débris of another day.

Then the Chinamen begin. Lights twinkle. Clean-looking interiors and carefully washed store windows. Roofs have been hammered back in place, stairways nailed together again. The sagging walls and lopsided cottages have taken a new lease on life. Another of the innumerable little business districts that dot the city has fought its way into evidence.

There are few oddities. Through the glass of the store fronts you see curiously immobile groups, men seated in chairs, smoking long pipes and waiting in silence. Strange fruits, foods, herbs, cloths, trinkets, lie on the orderly shelves around them. The floors look scrubbed and there is an absence of litter. It is all very efficient and very natural except for the immobility of the men in the chairs and the silence that seems to have descended on them.

A Chinese silence. And if you linger in the neighborhood you begin to feel that this is more Chinese than the gaudy dragons and the firecracker daubs and the bobbing paper lanterns of fiction.

This night I am looking for Billy Lee. No. 2209 Wentworth Avenue, says Mr. Lee's card. We are to talk over some matters, one of which has already been made public, others of which may never be.

He sits in his inner office, attired like a very efficient American business man, does Mr. Lee. We say hello and start the talk. In the rooms outside the inner office are a dozen Chinese. But there is no sound. They are sitting in chairs or standing up. All smoking. All silent. A sense of strange preoccupation lies over the place. Yet one feels that the twelve silent men are preoccupied with nothing except, possibly, the fact that they are Chinese.

Mr. Lee himself is none too garrulous. We have been talking for several minutes when he becomes totally silent and after a long pause hands me a cablegram. The cablegram reads: "Hongkong—Ying Yan: Bandits captured Foo Wing and wife. Send $5,000 immediately. Signed: Taichow."

"I just received this," says Mr. Lee. "Ying Yan is my father. Foo Wing is my brother. His American name is Andrew Lee. He went to Hongkong ten months ago and was married. This is terrible. I am worried to death."

Mr. Lee appears to sink into a studious calm. His eyes regard the cablegram stolidly. He remarks at length: "Bad news. This is very bad news."

From outside comes a sudden singsong of Chinese. One of the twelve men has said something. He finishes. Silence resumes. There seems to be no answer. Mr. Lee puts the cablegram back in his pocket and some one knocks on the door.

"Come in," says Mr. Lee. A Chinese youth enters. He carries a bundle.

"Meet Mr. Tang," says Billy Lee. We shake hands and

Mr. Tang begins talking in Chinese. Mr. Lee listens, nods his head and then holds out his hand for the bundle.

"This is a very interesting event," says Mr. Lee in English. "Mr. Tang is just over from the Orient. He comes from north of China, from Wu Chang, where the revolution started, you know. He has with him a very interesting matter."

Mr. Lee unwraps the bundle. He removes a long necklace made of curiously carved wooden beads, large balls of jade and pendants of silk and semi-precious stones.

Next he removes a second necklace somewhat longer than the first. It is made of marvelously matched amber beads, balls of jade and pendants of coral.

"A very interesting matter," says Mr. Lee. "Mr. Tang is son of a formerly very wealthy and high-born mandarin family. But his family has lost everything and Mr. Tang is here seeking an education in modern business. He has left of his family's wealth only these two things here. They are necklaces such as only mandarins could wear when they appeared before the emperor in court in the old days.

"You see these have three pendants, so they show the mandarin was a gentleman of the third class under the emperor. They have been in Mr. Tang's family's possession for generations. You will notice this one of carved beads is made of beads which are formed from the pits of the Chinese olive. There are two hundred beads and on each is carved some figure or scene which in all represent the history of China."

Mr. Lee holds the two necklaces in his hand. Mr. Tang stands by silently. His eyes gaze at the beads.

"Your father wore them at court?" inquires Mr. Lee in the manner of a host.

Mr. Tang nods his head slowly and adds a word in Chinese.

"He says his family wore them for generations," explains Mr. Lee. "Now the family is vanished and all that is left are these insignia of their nobility. And Mr. Tang wishes me to dispose of them for him so he may have money to go to school."

Mr. Lee and Mr. Tang are then both silent. Mr. Lee slips one of the necklaces over his head. It hangs down over his American coat and American silk shirt in a rather incongruous way. But there seems to be nothing incongruous in the matter for Lee and Tang. Billy Lee with the necklace around his neck, the three mandarin pendants against his belt, looks at Mr. Tang and Mr. Tang bows and leaves.

Our matters have been fully discussed and I follow a half-hour later. There are still twelve men in the room. They stand and sit and smoke. None speaks. I notice in the group the immobile figure of Mr. Tang. He is smoking an American cigarette—one of the twelve silently preoccupied residents of Chinatown who have gathered in Billy Lee's place to wait for something.

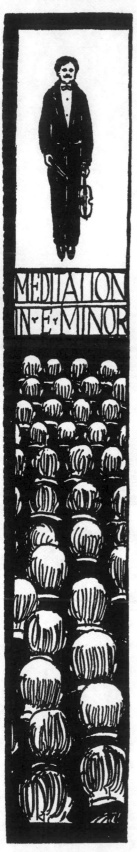

MEDITATION IN E MINOR

Well, well, well. The lady pianist will now oblige with something very refined. When in the name of 750,000 gods of reason will I ever learn enough to stay at home and go to bed instead of searching kittenishly for diversion in neighborhood movie and vaudeville houses?

No. Wrong. The lady is not a pianist. She is merely an accompanist. She is going to accompany something on the piano. A cornet, probably. Or a ukulele. *Parbleu*, what a face! Two hundred and eighty-five years old, if a day.

Aha! His nobs. A fiddler. "Silver Threads Among the Gold," and something fancy from the opera. And all dressed up in his wedding suit. The white tie is a bit soiled and the white vest longs mutely for the laundryman. And if he's going to wear a dress suit, if he insists upon wearing a dress suit, why doesn't he press his pants?

But how did a man with a face like this ever happen to think he could fiddle? An English nobleman. Or maybe a Swedish nobleman. Hm! A very interesting face. A little bit touched with flabbiness. And somewhat soiled, intangibly soiled. Like an English nobleman or a Swedish nobleman who has stayed up all night drinking.

And he holds his fiddle in an odd way. Like what? Well, like a fiddler. Like a marvelous fiddler. It hangs limply from his hand as if it were nonexistent. Kreisler holds his fiddle like that. A close-cropped blond mustache and the beginnings of a paunch. Nevertheless a very refined gentleman, a baron somewhat the worse for a night of bourbon.

The idiotic orchestra, the idiotic orchestra! Did anybody ever hear such an idiotic orchestra? Three violins, one 'cello, one cornet, one flute and a drum all out of tune, all out of time. The prelude. And his nobs grins. Poor fellow. But who taught him how to hold a fiddle like that?

We're off. An E minor chord from our friend at the piano. Hm, something classical. Ho, ho! Viotti. Well,

well, here's a howdeedo. His nobs is going to play the concerto. Good-by, good luck and God bless him. If I was in bed, if I was in bed, I wouldn't have to listen to a refined gentleman with his swell pants unpressed murdering poor Viotti. A swell gentleman with his eyes carefully made up. I didn't notice his eyes before. All set, Paganini. Your turn. Let's go.

Ah, that was a note! Well, well, well, his nobs can play. Hm! A cadenza in double stops! And the E minor scale in harmonics! Listen to the baron in the dirty white vest. The man's a violinist. Observe—calisthenics on the G string and in the second position. A very difficult position and easily faked. And when did Heifetz ever take a run like that? Up, down and the fingers hammering like thoroughbreds on a fast track. Pizzicato with the left hand and obbligato glissando!

Hoopla! The fellow's showing off! And it isn't a Drdla souvenir or a vaudeville Brahms arrangement. But twenty years of practice. Yes, sir, there are twenty years and eight hours a day, every day for twenty years, in these acrobatics. There are twenty years, twenty years, behind this technique. And well-spent years.

But tell me, Cyril, for whom is our baron showing off— for whom? Our baron with the soiled tie and the made-up eyes, fiddling coldly, elaborately for a handful of annoyed flappers, amused shoe clerks and bored home lovers sitting stolidly in the dark, waiting stolidly and defiantly to be diverted?

Bravo! Five of us applaud. No, six. A gentleman in an upper box applauds with some degree of violence. And there is the orchestra leader—a dark-skinned, black-eyed, curly-headed youth, nodding and smiling.

Next on the program? Ah, a ballad. A thing the cabaret ladies sing, "Do You Think of Me?" A faint smile on our baron's face. But the fiddle leaps into position as if for another cold, elaborate attack. It takes twenty years, twenty well-spent years to learn to hold a bow like that. Firmly, casually, indifferently as one holds a pencil between one's fingers.

Admission 33 cents, including war tax. But this is worth —well, it is what the novelists call an illuminating experience. This gentleman of music whose fingers have for twenty years absorbed the souls of Beethoven and Sarasate, Liszt and Moussorgski, this aristocrat of the catgut is posturing sardonically before the three bored fates. He is pouring twenty years, twenty well-spent years, into a tawdry little ballad. Ah, how our baron's fiddle sings! And the darkened faces in front hum to themselves: "When you're flirt-ing with another, do you ever think—of—me."

Yes, my tired-faced baron, there's a question. Do you? We, out front, all have our little underworlds in which we live sometimes while music plays and beautiful things come to our eyes. And yours? This tin-pan alley ballad throbbing liquidly from the strings of your fiddle—"When you're flirt-ing with another do you ever think—of—me?" Of the twenty years, the twenty well-spent years? Of the soul that your fingers captured? Of the dream that took form in your firm wrist?

And now the chorus once more. In double stops. In harmonics. With arpeggios thrown in. And once more, largo. Sure and full. Sobbing organ notes, whimpering grace notes. Superb, baron! And done with a half smile at the darkened faces out front. The tired faces that blinked stolidly at Viotti. A smile at the orchestra leader who stands with his mouth open waiting as if the song were still in the air.

Applause. All of us this time. More applause. Say this guy can fiddle, he can. Come on, baron, another tune. The tired faces yammer for another ditty. "Träumerei." All right, let her go, Paganini. And after that the "Missouri Waltz."

I will stay for the next show. I will stay for the three shows. And each time this magnifico will come out and make music. But better than that. I will go back stage and talk with him. I will ask him: "How does it happen, sir, that a man who can fiddle like you, a man who could play a duet with Kreisler—how does it happen you're fiddling in a neighborhood movie and vaudeville house?"

And he will unfold a story. Yes, there's a story there. Something happened to this nobleman of the soiled white vest and the marvelous fingers. There was an occurrence in this man's life which would make a good climax for a second act.

No, that would spoil the picture. To find out, to learn the clumsy mechanism behind this charming spectacle would take away. Better like this. The lady at the piano. Ah, indeed, the lady at the piano, a very elderly lady with a thin nose and hair that was once extremely beautiful, perhaps she had something to do with it? The orchestra pounds and scrapes away. And the movie jumps around and the heroine weeps, but somebody saves her. "Where there is no faith there cannot be true love," confesses the hero, folding her in his well-pressed arms. And that's that.

Now our friend, the baron, again. No, better to leave. He has left his smile in the wings this time. He is very serious or perhaps very tired. Two times tonight to play. Too much —too much.

My hat, and I will walk out on his nobs. And, anyway, Huneker wrote the story long ago. About a piano player in Coney Island that he called—what was it? Oh, yes, "A Chopin of the Gutter."

TEN-CENT WEDDING RINGS

A gloomy day and the loop streets grimace behind a mist. The electric signs are lighted. The buildings open like great fans in the half dark.

The streets invite a mood of melodrama. Windows glint evilly. Doorways grin with rows of electric teeth. This, *donnerwetter!* is the Great City of the old-time ten-twenty-thirty thrillers. The devourer of innocence, the strumpet of stone.

I walk along humming a bar of villainous music, the "skeeter scale" that the orchestra used to tum tum tum taaaa-tum in the old Alhambra as the two dockwallopers and the leering Chinaman were climbing in through little Mabel's hall bedroom window to abduct her.

Those were happy days for the drama, when a scoundrel was a scoundrel and wore a silk hat to prove it, and a hero was a two-fisted man, as anybody could tell by a glance at his marcelled hair and his open-at-the-throat shirt.

Tum tum tum tum taaaa-tum. Pizzicato pianissimo, says the direction on the score. So we are all set for a melodrama. Here is the Great City back-drop. Here are the grim-faced crowds shuffling by under the jaundice glare of electric signs. And Christmas is coming. A vague gray snow trickles out of the gloom.

A proper time for melodrama. All we need is a plot. Come, come now—a plot alive with villains and weeping maidens. Halto! The window of the 5- and 10-cent store! a tumble of gewgaws and candies and kitchen utensils. Christmas tree tinsel and salted peanuts, jazz music and mittens.

The curtain is up. Egad, what a masterly scene. A kitchen Coney Island. A puzzle picture of isles, signs, smells, noises. Cinderella wandering wistfully in the glass-bead section looking for a fairy godmother.

A clinking obbligato by the cash registers. The poor are buying gifts. This garish froth of merchandise is the back-

ground of their luxuries. This noisy puzzle-picture store is their horn of plenty. A sad thought and we'll dismiss it. What we want is plot.

Perhaps the jazz-song booster singing out of the side of his mouth with tired eyes leering at the crowd of girls: "Won't You Let Me Love You If I Promise to Be Good?" And "Love Me, Turtle Dove." And "Lovin' Looie." And "The Lovin' Blues."

All lovin'. Jazz songs, ballads, sad, silly, boobish nut songs—all about love me—love me. All about stars and kisses, moonlight and "she took my man away." There are telephones all over the walls and the song booster's voice pops out over the salted-peanut section, over the safety-pin and brassware section. A tinny, nasal voice with a whine and a hoarseness almost hiding the words.

The cash registers clink, clink. "Are you waited on, madam? Five cents a package, madam." The crowds, tired eyed, shabbily dressed, bundle-laden, young, old—the crowds shuffle up and down, staring at gewgaws, and the love-me love songs follow them around. Follow them to the loose-bead counter where Madge with her Japanese puffs of hair, her wad of gum and her black shirtwaist that she keeps straightening out continually by drawing up her bosom and pressing down on her hips with her hands—where Madge holds forth.

Tum tum tum tum taaaa-tum—halto! Here is our plot. Outside the pizzicato of the crowds, the Great City, shining, dragon-eyed, through the mist—the City That Has No Heart. And here under our nose, twinkling up at our eyes, a huge tray full of 10-cent wedding rings. End of Act One.

Act Two, now—Madge, the sharp-tongued, weary-eyed young woman behind the counter. Love-me love songs in her ear and people unraveling, faces unraveling before her. Who buys these wedding rings, Madge? And did you ever notice anything odd about your customers? And why do you suppose they buy ten-cent wedding rings, Madge?

"Just a moment," says Madge. "What is it, miss? A ring? What kind? Oh, yes. Ten cents. Gold or platinum just the same. Yes."

Two giggling girls move off. And Madge, chewing gently on her wad of gum and smoothing her huge hair puffs out with the coyly stiffened palms of her hands, talks.

"Sure, I get you. About the wedding rings. Sure, that's easy. We sell about twenty or thirty of them every day. Oh, mostly to kids—girls and boys. Sometimes an old Johnny comes in with a moth-eaten fur collar and blows a dime for a wedding ring. But mostly girls.

"I sometimes take a second look at them. They usually giggle when they ask for the ring. And they usually pretend it's for somebody as a joke they're buying it. Or sometimes they walk around the counter for a half hour and get me nervous as a cat. 'Cause I know what they want and they can't get their gall up to come and ask for it. But finally they make the break and come up and pick out a ring without saying a word and hand over ten cents.

"There was one girl no more than sixteen just this morning. She come here all full of pep and kidded about things and said wasn't them platinum wedding rings just too grand for words, and so on. Then she said she wanted a half-dozen of them, and was there a discount when bought in such quantity? I started wrapping them up when I looked at her and she was crying. And she dropped her sixty cents on the counter and said: 'Never mind, never mind. I don't want them. I can't wear them. They'll only make it worse.'"

A middle-aged-looking man interrupts. "What is it, sir?" asks Madge. "Anything in rings? What kind?" Oh, just plain rings," says the man with a great show of indifference, while his eyes ferret among the trinkets on the counter. And then, very calmly: "Oh, these will do, I guess." Two wedding rings, and he spent twenty cents. Madge follows him with her eyes. "That's it," she whispers, "usually the men buy two. One for themselves and one for the girl. Or if it's the girl that's buying them it's one for herself and one for her girl chum who's going with her and the two fellas on the party. Say, take it from me, these rings don't ever hear no wedding marches."

Back into the gloomy street again. A plot in our head, but who's the villain and who's the heroine and the hero? An easy answer to that. The crowd here—sad faced, tired-walking, bundle-laden. The crowd continually dissolving amid street cars and autos is the villain.

A crowd of shoppers buying slippers for uncle and shawls for mother and mufflers for brother and some bars of soap for the bathroom. Buying everything and anything that fill the fan-shaped buildings with their glinting windows. Buying carpet sweepers and window curtains and linoleum.

Pizzicato, pianissimo, professor—little-girl gigglers and hard-faced dock wallopers and slick-haired lounge lizards and broken-hearted ones—twenty a day they sidle up to Madge's counter, where the love me, love me songs razz the heavy air, and shoot a dime for a wedding ring.

WHERE THE "BLUES" SOUND

"That St. Louis woman
  Wid her diahmond rings,
Pulls mah man 'round
  By her apron strings—"

A voice screeches above the boom and hurrah of the black and white 35th Street cabaret. The round tables rock. Waiters careen. Balanced trays float at crazy angles through the tobacco smoke. Hats flash. Firecracker voices explode. A guffaw dances across a smear of faces. Congo gleams, college boy pallors, the smiles of black and white men and women interlace. A spotlight shoots its long hypotenuse upon the floor. In its drifting oval the entertainer, her shoulders back, her elbows out, her fists clenched and her body twisting into slow patterns, bawls in a terrifying soprano—

"If it waren't foh her powdah
  And her stohe bought hair,
The man Ah love
  Would not have gone nowhere—"

Listen for the tom-tom behind the hurrah. Watch for the torches of Kypris and Corinth behind the glare of the tungstens. This is the immemorial bacchanal lurching through the kaleidoscope of the centuries. Pan with a bootlegger's grin and a checked suit. Dionysius with a saxophone to his lips. And the dance of Paphos called now the shimmie.

Listen and watch and through the tumult, rising like a strange incense from the smear of bodies, tables and waiters, will come the curious thing that is never contained in the vice reports. The gleam of the devil himself—the echo of some mystic cymbal note.

Later the music will let out a tinny blaze of sound. Men and women will press together and a pack of bodies will sway on the dance floor. The tungstens will go out and the spotlight will throw colors—green, purple, lavender, blue, violet—

119

and as the scene grows darker and the colors revolve a howl will fill the place. But on the dance floor a silence will fasten itself over the swaying bodies and there will be only the sound of feet pushing. The silence of a ritual—faces stiffened, eyes rolling—a rigid embrace of men and women creeping cunningly among the revolving colors and the whiplike rhythms of the jazz band.

"Lost souls," says the vice reports, and the vice reports speak with a calm and knowing voice. Women whose bodies and faces are like shells of evil; vicious seeming men with a rasp in their laughter. These are among those present. Aphrodite is a blousy wench in the 35th and State streets neighborhood. And her votaries, although they offer an impressive ensemble, are a sorry lot taken face by face.

Izzy, who is an old timer, sits at a table and takes it in. Izzy's eyes and ears have learned to pick details in a bedlam. He can talk softly and listen easily through the height of the cabaret racket. The scene hits Izzy as water hits a duck's back.

"Well," he says, "it's a good night tonight. The slummers are out in full force rubberin' at each other. Well, this is a funny world, take it from me. Me? Huh, I come here every night or so to have a little drink and look 'em over for a while. Ain't nothing to see but a lot o' molls and a lot of sucker guys. Them? Say, they never learn no better. Tough guys ain't no different from soft guys, see? They all fall for the dames just as hard and just as worse. There's many a good guy in this place that's been gave a tumble by them, see?

"There, I got an idee he'd blow in tonight. He ain't missed a Saturday night for months. And he usu'lly makes it four or five times a week. That guy over there wit' the mop o' gray hair. Yeah, that's him. Well, he's the professor. I spotted him in the district a year or so ago. He had a dame wit' him who I know, see? A terrible broad. Say, maybe you've heard of him. His name is Weintraub. I picked it up from the dame he's goin' wit', see? He ought to be in your line. He was a reg'lar music professor before he come down. The leader of a swell orchestra somewhere in the east or in Europe, I guess. The dame don't know for sure, but she told me he was some baby on music.

"Well, that's him there, see? He comes in like this and sits down near the band. Look at him. Do you make him? The way he's movin' his hands? See, he's leadin' the band. Sure" — Izzy laughed mirthlessly — "that's what the guy's doin'. Nuts, see? Daffy. He comes in here like that and I always watch him. He sits still and when the music starts up he begins wit' his hands. Ain't he the berries?

"Now keep your eye on him. You'll see somethin' pretty quick. He's alone tonight. I guess the dame has shook him for the evenin'. Look, he's still conductin'. Ain't he rich? But he's got a good face, you might say. Class, eh? You'd know he was a musician.

"I tell you I begin to watch him the first time I saw him. And from the beginnin' he's always conductin' when the band starts in. The dame is usu'lly wit' him and she don't like it. She tries to stop him, but he don't see her for sour apples. He keeps right on like now, beatin' time wit' his hands. Look, the poor nut's growin' excited. Daffy. Can you beat it? There he goes. See? That's on account of Jerry. Jerry's the black one on the end wit' the saxophone. Ha, Jerry always does it.

"I told Jerry about this guy and Jerry tried it on him the first night. He pulled a sour one, you know, blew a mean one through the horn and his nobs nearly fell out of his seat. Like now. See, he's through. He won't conduct the band any more tonight. He's sore. No sir, he won't conduct such a lot of no-good boilermakers like Jerry. Can you beat it?"

Izzy's eyes follow a stoop-shouldered gray-haired man from one of the tables. A thin-faced man with bloodshot eyes.

He walks as if he were half asleep. The crowd swallows him and Izzy laughs again without mirth.

"He's done for the night. That's low down of Jerry. But Jerry says it gets his goat to see this daffy guy comin' in here night after night and leadin' the band from the table. So the smoke blows that sour note every time his nobs gets started on his conductin' and it always knocks his nobs for a gool. He never stays another minute, but lights out right away.

"Look, there's his dame. The one wit' the green hat, sittin' wit' the guy with the cheaters over there. Yeah, that's her. I don't know why she ain't wit' him tonight. Prob'ly a lovers' quarrel." And Izzy grinned. "She's a tough one, take it from me. I don't know how she hooked the professor, but she did. She used to be swelled up about him. And once she got him a job in Buxbaum's old place, she told me, to work in the orchestra. But his nobs kicked. Said he'd cut his throat before playin' in a roughneck orchestra and who did she think he was to do such a thing? He says to her: 'I'm Weintraub—Weintraub, d'ye understand?' And he hauls off and wallops her one and she guve up tryin' to get him a job. It makes her sore to watch him sittin' around like tonight and conductin' the orchestra. She says it ain't because he's daffy, but on account of his bein' stuck up."

The woman with the green hat had left her table. Izzy's shrewd eyes picked her out again—this time standing against a far wall talking to the professor, and the professor was rubbing his forehead and saying "No, no," with his hands.

And now the entertainer was singing again:

"Got de St. Louis Blues, jes' as blue as Ah can be,
Dat man has a heart like a rock ca-ast in de sea,
Or else he would not have gone so far away from me."

VAGABONDIA

Here they come. Five merry travelers in a snorting, dust-caked automobile. Wanderers, egad! Bowling rakishly across the country. Dusters and goggles and sunburn. Prairie nights have sung to them. Little towns have grinned at them. Mountains, valleys, forests and stars have danced across their windshield.

The newspaper man stood watching them haul up to the Adams Street curb. His heart was tired of tall buildings and the endless grimace of windows. Here was a chariot out of another world. Motor vagabonds. Scooting into a city with a swagger to their dust-caked wheels. And scooting out again.

The newspaper man thought, "The world isn't buried yet. There's still a restlessness left. Things change from triremes to motor boats, from Rosinante to automobiles. But adventure merely mounts a new seat and goes on. Dick Hovey sang it once:

> I am fevered with the sunset,
> I am fretful with the bay,
> For the wander thirst is on me
> And my soul is in Cathay.

The five merry travelers crawled out and stretched themselves. They doffed their goggles and slipped off their linen dusters and changed forthwith from a group of flying gnomes into five tired-looking citizens of California. Two middle aged women. Two middle-aged men and a son.

One of the men said, "Well, we'll lay up here for awhile, I got a blister on my hand from the wheel."

One of the women answered, "I must buy some hairpins, Martin."

The newspaper man said to himself, "What ho! I'll give them a ring. Why not? A story of the modern wanderlust.

123

Anyway, they're not averse to publicity seeing they've got two 'coast to coast' pennants on the back of their machine. What they've seen. Why they've journeyed. A tirade against the monotony of business. And I'll stick in one of Hovey's stanzas, the one that goes:

> There's a schooner in the offing
> With her topsails shot with fire,
> And my heart has gone aboard her
> For the Islands of Desire.

"You can say," said the spokesman of the wanderers, "that this is Martin S. Stevers and party. I am Mr. Stevers of the Stevers Linseed Oil Company in San Francisco. Here's my card."

"Thanks," said the newspaper man, taking the card.

"And now," spake on the spokesman of the wanderers, "what can I do for you?"

Newspaper men are perhaps the only creatures who as a type never learn how to ask questions. An embarrassment caused by the stupidity of the gabby great whom they interrogate daily puts a crimp into their tongues. Their questions wince in anticipation of the banalities they are doomed to elicit. Their curiosity collapses under the shadow of the inevitable, impending bromide.

Thus the newspaper man, wearily certain that regardless of what he asks or how he asks it, he will hear for answers only the clumsy asininities behind which the personalities, leaders and sacred white cows pompously attitudinize, gets so that he mumbles a bit incoherently.

But here was a different case. Here were merry travelers with memories of wind-swept valleys and star-capped mountains to chatter on. So the newspaper man unearthed his vocabulary, tilted his hat a trifle and smiled invitingly.

"Well," said he to the spokesman of the wanderers, "The kind of story I'd like to get would be a story about five

124

people wandering across the country. You know. Hills, sunsets, trees and how those things drive away the monotony that fills up the hearts of city folk. What you enjoyed on the trip and the advantages of a rover over a swivel-chair statistician."

An eloquence was beginning to skip around on the newspaper man's tongue. His heart, weary of tall buildings and the endless grimace of city windows, began to warm under the visions his phrases aroused.

Then he paused. One of the women had interrupted. "Go on Martin, you can tell him all that. And don't forget about the lovely hotel breakfast room in Des Moines."

Martin, however, hesitated. He was a heavy-set, large-faced man with expansive features almost devoid of expression. Suddenly his face lighted up. His hands jumped together and he rubbed their palms enthusiastically.

"I see," he said with profundity. "I see."

"Yes," breathed the newspaper man.

"Well," said Mr. Stevers, "the first thing I'd like to tell you, young man, is about the car. You won't believe this, but we've been making twenty miles on a gallon, that is, averaging twenty miles on each and every gallon, sir, since we left San Francisco. Pretty good, eh?"

On a piece of scratch paper the newspaper man obediently wrote, "twenty miles, gallon."

"And then," went on the spokesman for the wanderers, "Our speed, eh? You'd like to know that? Well, without stretching the thing at all, and you can verify it from any of my party, we've averaged twenty-six miles an hour all the time out. I tell you the old boat had to travel some to do that."

"Twenty-six miles," scribbled the newspaper man, adding after it, "The man's an idiot."

Mr. Stevers, unmindful, loosened up. The price of gasoline. The price of breakfasts. The condition of the roads. How long a stretch they had been able to do without a halt. How many hours a day he himself had stuck at the wheel. When he had finished the newspaper man bowed and walked abruptly away.

The newspaper man's thoughts form a conclusion.

"It's true, then," he thought, "the world's becoming as stupid as it looks. People are drying up inside with facts, figures, dollar signs. This man and his party would have got as much out of their cross-country trip if they'd all been blind-folded and shot through a tunnel two thousand feet under the ground. Man is like an audience and he has walked out on mystery and adventure. The show kind of tired him. And got his goat. It would have been a good yarn otherwise, the motor vagabonds. I'd have ended with Hovey's verse:

> I must forth again tomorrow,
> With the sunset I must be
> Hull down on the trail of rapture
> In the wonder of the sea.

Mumbling the lines to himself, the newspaper man strode on through the crowded loop with a sudden swagger in his eyes.

NIRVANA

The newspaper man felt a bit pensive. He sat in his bedroom frowning at his typewriter. About eight years ago he had decided to write a novel. Not that he had anything particular in his mind to write about. But the city was such a razzle-dazzle of dreams, tragedies, fantasies; such a crazy monotone of streets and windows that it filled the newspaper man's thought from day to day with an irritating blur.

And for eight years or so the newspaper man had been fumbling around trying to get it down on paper. But no novel had grown out of the blur in his head.

The newspaper man put on his last year's straw hat and went into the street, taking his pensiveness with him. Warm. Rows of arc lights. A shifting crowd. There are some streets that draw aimless feet. The blazing store fronts, clothes shops, candy shops, drug-stores, Victrola shops, movie theatres invite with the promise of a saturnalia in suspense.

At Wilson Avenue and Sheridan Road the newspaper man paused. Here the loneliness he had felt in his bedroom seemed to grow more acute. Not only his own aimlessness, but the aimlessness of the staring, smiling crowd afflicted him.

Then out of the babble of faces he heard his name called. A rouged young flapper, high heeled, short skirted and a jaunty green hat. One of the impudent little swaggering boulevard promenaders who talk like simpletons and dance like Salomes, who laugh like parrots and ogle like Pierettes. The birdlike strut of her silkened legs, the brazen lure of her stenciled child face, the lithe grimace of her adolescent body under the stiff coloring of her clothes were a part of the blur in the newspaper man's mind.

She was one of the things he fumbled for on the type-writer——one of the city products born of the tinpan bacchanal of the cabarets. A sort of frontispiece for an Irving Berlin ballad. The caricature of savagery that danced to the cari-

127

cature of music from the jazz bands. The newspaper man smiled. Looking at her he understood her. But she would not fit into the typewritten phrases.

"Wilson Avenue," he thought, as he walked beside her chatter. "The wise, brazen little virgins who shimmy and toddle, but never pay the fiddler. She's it. Selling her ankles for a glass of pop and her eyes for a fox trot. Unhuman little piece. A cross between a macaw and a marionette."

Thus, the newspaper man thinking and the flapper flapping, they came together to a cabaret in the neighborhood. The orchestra filled the place with confetti of sound. Laughter, shouts, a leap of voices, blazing lights, perspiring waiters, faces and hats thrusting vivid stencils through the uncoiling tinsel of tobacco smoke.

On the dance floor bodies hugging, toddling, shimmying; faces fastened together; eyes glassy with incongruous ecstasies.

The newspaper man ordered two drinks of moonshine and let the scene blur before him like a colored picture puzzle out of focus. Above the music he heard the childishly strident voice of the flapper:

"Where you been hiding yourself? I thought you and I were cookies. Well, that's the way with you Johns. But there's enough to go around, you can bet. Say boy! I met the classiest John the other evening in front of the Hopper. Did he have class, boy! You know there are some of these fancy Johns who look like they were the class. But are they? Ask me. Nix. And don't I give them the berries, quick? Say, I don't let any John get moldy on me. Soon as I see they're heading for a dumb time I say 'razzberry.' And off your little sugar toddles."

"How old are you?" inquired the newspaper man abstractedly.

"Eighteen, nosey. Why the insult? I got a new job yesterday with the telephone company. That makes my sixth job this year. Tell me that ain't going good? One of the

Johns I met in front of the Edgewater steered me to it. He turned out kind of moldy, and say! he was dumb. But I played along and got the job.

"Say, I bet you never noticed my swell kicks." The flapper thrust forth her legs and twirled her feet. "Classy, eh? They go with the lid pretty nice. Say, you're kind of dumb yourself. You've got moldy since I saw you last."

"How'd you remember my name?" inquired the newspaper man.

"Oh, there are some Johns who tip over the oil can right from the start. And you never forget them. Nobody could forget you, handsome. Never no more, never. What do you say to another shot of hootch? The stuff's getting rottener and rottener, don't you think? Come on, swallow. Here's how. Oh, ain't we got fun!"

The orchestra paused. It resumed. The crowd thickened. Shouts, laughter, swaying bodies. A tinkle of glassware, snort of trombones, whang of banjos. The newspaper man looked on and listened through a film.

The brazen patter of his young friend rippled on. A growing gamin coarseness in her talk with a nervous, restless twitter underneath. Her dark child eyes, perverse under their touch of black paint, swung eagerly through the crowd. Her talk of Johns, of dumb times and moldy times, of classy times and classy memories varied only slightly. She liked dancing and amusement parks. Automobile riding not so good. And besides you had to be careful. There were some Johns who thought it cute to play caveman. Yes, she'd had a lot of close times, but they wouldn't get her. Never, no, never no more. Anyway, not while there was music and dancing and a whoop-de-da-da in the amusement parks.

The newspaper man, listening, thought, "An infant gone mad with her dolls. Or no, vice has lost its humanness.

She's the symbol of new sin——the unhuman, passionless whirligig of baby girls and baby boys through the cabarets."

They came back from a dance and continued to sit. The din was still mounting. Entertainers fighting against the racket. Music fighting against the racket. Bored men and women finally achieving a bedlam and forgetting themselves in the artifice of confusion.

The newspaper man looking at his young friend saw her taking it in. There was something he had been trying to fathom about her during her breathless chattering. She talked, danced, whirled, laughed, let loose giggling cries. And yet her eyes, the part that the rouge pot or the bead stick couldn't reach, seemed to grow deader and deader.

The jazz band let out the crash of a new melody. The voices of the crowd rose in an "ah-ah-ah." Waiters were shoving fresh tables into the place, squeezing fresh arrivals around them.

The flapper had paused in her breathless rigmarole of Johns and memories. Leaning forward suddenly she cried into the newspaper man's ear above the racket:

"Say this is a dumb place."

The newspaper man smiled.

"Ain't it, though?" she went on. There was a pause and then the breathless voice sighed. She spoke.

"Gee!"——with a laugh that still seemed breathless——"gee, but it's lonely here!"

THE INDESTRUCTIBLE MASTERPIECE

"You come with me to the Art Institute today," said Max Kramm. "My friend Broun has an exhibition. You know Broun? Ah, I think he is today the greatest living artist. No, we will walk. It is only four or five blocks. And I tell you a story."

A story from Max Kramm is worth attention even though it is hot and though the Boul Mich pavement feels like a stove griddle through the leather of one's shoes. For the Dante-faced Max, in addition to being one of the leading piano professors of the country, the billiard champion of the Chicago Athletic Club and the most erudite porcelain connoisseur in Harper Avenue, is one of the survivors of the race of raconteurs that flourished in the time of nickel cigars and the free lunch.

"I have eight more lessons to administer today," sighed Max with a parting glower at the premises of the Chicago Musical College, "But when my old friend Broun has an exhibition I go."

"It was when we lived together in a studio in North Avenue," said Max. "Jo Davidson, Walter Goldbeck and the bunch, we all roomed together in the same neighborhood and we were poor, I can tell you. But young. And that makes up for a lot of things.

"Broun and I, we room together in a little attic where I have a piano and he paints. Even in those days we all knew Frank Broun would be a great painter if he didn't starve to death first. And the chances looked even.

"Well, there was Schneider, of course. You never heard of him, I'll bet you. No, he don't paint. And he don't sing and he don't play the piano. He was somebody much more important than such things. Schneider was the proprietor of a beer saloon in North Avenue. Where is he now, I wonder? Well, in those days he saved our life twice a day regularly.

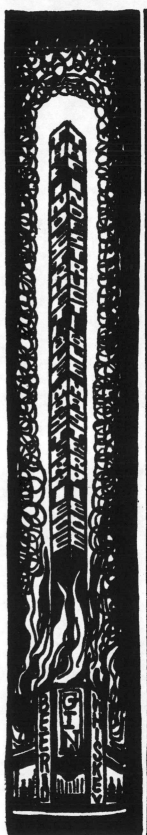

"Broun and I we keep alive for one whole year on Schneider's free lunch. Herring, pickles, rye bread, pepper beef, boiled ham, onions, pretzels, roast beef and a big jar full of fine cheese. And, I forgot, a jar full of olives and a dish of crackers. Oh, there was food fit for a king in Schneider's. You buy one glass beer, for five cents, and then you eat till you bust—for nothing.

"You can't imagine what that meant to us in those days. Broun and I, we sometimes have so much as ten cents a day between us and on this we must live. So at noon we both go into Schneider's. Broun says, 'You want a drink, Max? I say, 'No, Frank.' Then I engage Schneider in talk while Broun makes away with a meal. Then Broun does the talking and it is my turn.

"Well, it got so that the good Schneider finally points out to us one day. 'Max,' he says, 'and Frank, I tell you something. You boys owe me three dollars and you come in here and eat all your meals and you don't even pay for the one glass beer you buy any more. I am sorry, but your credit is exhausted.'

"So you can imagine what Broun and I feel when we get home. No more Schneider's, no more food, and eventually we see ourselves both starving to death.

" 'Max' says Broun, 'I have an idea.' And he did.

"Like all great ideas, it was simple. Broun figures that what we need to do is to convince Schneider we have wonderful prospects and so Schneider will give us back our credit. So Broun sits down that day and all day and most of the night he paints. I think it was the last canvas he had in the studio, too. And a big one. You know all of Broun's landscapes are big.

"Well, he paints and paints, and when he is finished we take the picture to Schneider, the two of us carrying it. I tell Schneider that it is one of the old masters which we just received from Berlin from my father's studio. Then Broun

132

says that Schneider must keep it in his place. It is too valuable to hang in our attic. Schneider looks at the picture and, it being so big, he half believes it.

"Then Broun and I go to the bank and draw out our $10 which we have saved up for a rainy day. And we go down town and get the picture insured for $2,000. You can imagine Schneider. We bring the insurance gink out there and when he gives us the policy and we show it to Schneider—well, our credit is re-established. Herring, rye bread, roast beef, pickles and cheese once more. We eat.

"Schneider is more proud of that picture than a peacock. And every day we drop in to see if it is all right and Broun always goes behind the bar and dusts it off a little and draws himself another drink. There is never any question any more of our credit. Don't we own a picture insured for $2,000? The good Schneider is glad to have such affluent customers, you can believe me.

"Well, things go on like this for some months. Then I am coming home one night with Broun and the fire engines pass us. So Frank and I we go to the fire.

"It is Schneider's beer saloon. We see it a block off. Frank turns pale and he holds my arm and he whispers, 'Max the picture! It is burning up!'

"I look at Broun and I suppose I tremble a little myself. Who wouldn't? Two thousand dollars! 'Max,' says Broun, 'We go around the world together. And I saw a suit today and a cane I must have.'

"But we couldn't talk. We walk slowly to the beer saloon. We walk already like plutocrats, arm in arm, and our faces with a faraway look. We are spending the two thousand, you can imagine.

"The saloon is burning fine. Everything is going up in smoke. Broun and I, we hold on to each other. We see Jo Davidson running to the fire and we nod at him politely. Money makes a big difference, you know.

133

"And then we hear a cry. I recognize Schneider and I see him break loose from the crowd. He runs back into the burning saloon, a fireman after him. Broun and I, we stand and watch. He is probably gone after one of his kids. But I count the kids who are all in the street and they are all there.

"Then Schneider comes out and the fireman, too. And they are carrying something. Broun falls against the delicatessen store window and groans. And I close my eyes. Yes, it is the picture.

"Schneider sees us and comes rushing. He is half burned up. But the picture is not touched. He and the fireman hand us the picture. As for me, I turn away and I lose command of the English language.

" 'You boys trusted me,' says Schneider, 'and I remembered just in time. I remembered your picture. I may not be an artist, but I don't let a masterpiece burn up. Not in my saloon. So I save it. It is the only thing I save out of the whole saloon.' And he wrings Broun's hand, and I say, 'thanks.' That night, all night long, I played Beethoven. The Ninth Symphony is good for feelings such as mine and Broun's."

It is cooler in the Art Institute and Max, smiling in memory of other days, looks at the Broun exhibition.

"I could finish the story by telling you excitedly that this landscape here is the picture Schneider saved," he went on, pointing to one of the large canvases. "But no. It wouldn't be the truth. I have the picture home. It is not yet worth $2,000, but in a few years more, who knows? Maybe I have cause to thank Schneider yet."

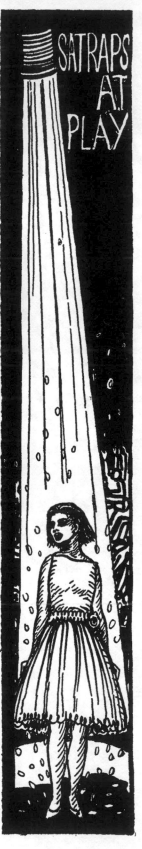

SATRAPS AT PLAY

The elfin-faced danseuse puts it over. Her voice sounds like a run-down fifteen-cent harmonica. But that doesn't matter. Not at two a. m. in an all-night cabaret. You don't need a voice to knock us out of our seats. You need something else—pep.

"I wanna be—in Tennuhsee," the elfin-faced one squeaks. And the ladies of the chorus grin vacuously and kick their pink tights. One, two, kick! One, two, kick! I wanna be—in Tennuhsee. One, two, kick! The third one on the other side looks all right. No, too fat. There's one. The one at the end. Pretty, ain't she? Who? You mean the one with the long nose? No, whatsamatter with you? The one with the eyes. See. She's bending over now. Some kid.

Two a. m. outside. Dark streets. Sleepy chauffeurs dreaming of $10 tips. All-night Greek restaurants. Twenty-second Street has gone to bed. But we sit in the warm cabaret, devilishly proud of ourselves. We're a part of the gang that stays awake when the stars are out.

And the elfin-faced one cuts loose. Attaboy, girlie! Legs shooting through the tobacco smoke. Eyes like drunken birds. A banjo body playing jazz capers on the air. It ain't art. But who the devil wants art? What we want are con-niption fits. This is the way the soul of Franz Liszt looked when he was writing music. Mumba Jumba had a dream that looked like this one night when the jungle moon arched its back and spat at his black linen face.

All right. Three a. m. Bring out the lions and the Christians now. The master of ceremonies is a fat man with little, ineffectual hands and a voice that bows and genuflects and throws itself politely worshipful at our feet.

Amateur night, says the voice, and some ladies and gen-tlemen will seek to entertain us with a few specialties for our amusement. And will the ladies and gentlemen of the audi-ence applaud according to the merit of each performer? For the one who gets the most applause, he or she will win the grand first prize of fifty bones.

Attaboy! Will we applaud? Say, bring 'em out! Bring 'em out! Ah, here she is. A pale, trembling little morsel with frightened eyes and a worn blue serge skirt. The floor is slippery. "Miss Waghwoughblngsz," says the voice, "will sing for your entertainment."

A terrified little squeak. A Mae Marsh grimace of courage. Good! Say, she's great! Look at her try to swing her body. And her arms have lost their joints. And she's forgotten the words. Poor little tyke. Throw her something. Pennies. While she's singing. See who can hit her.

So we throw her pennies and nickels and dimes. They land on her head and one takes her on the nose. And her voice dies away like a baby bird falling out of a nest. And she stands still—jerking her mouth and the pennies falling all around her. And a cynical-looking youth bounces out and picks them up. Bravo! She tried to bow and slipped. Another round of applause for that. All right, take her away. What did she sing? What was the song that mumbled itself through the laughter and the rain of pennies?

Ladies and gentlemen, Mr. Sghsgbrszsg will endeavor to entertain you with a ballad for your amusement. That's fine. After three a. m. outside. Cold and dark. But nothing cold or dark about us. We're just getting started. Bring 'em out. Bring out the ballad singer.

Ah, there's a lad for you. His shoes all shined and a clean collar on and his face carefully shaved at home. But his hands wouldn't wash clean. The shop grime lingers on his hands and in his broken nails. But his eyes are blue and he's going to sing. The boys at the shop know his songs. The noon hour knows them.

But his voice sounds different here under the beating tungstens. It quavers. Something about Ireland. A little

137

bit of heaven. He can't sing. If he was in his shirt sleeves and the collar was off and his face didn't hurt from the dull safety razor blade—it would sound better. But—pennies for him. Hit the singing boy in the eye and win the hand-painted cazaza.

"A little bit of heaven called Ireland," is what he's singing. And the noises start. The pennies and nickels rain. Finis! Not so good. He sang it all the way through and his voice grew better and better. Take him away. We didn't like the way his eyes blazed back at us when the pennies fell. Not so good. Not so good.

Here she is. Little Bertha, the Sewing Machine Girl. In the flesh. And walking across the slippery dance floor with her French heeled patent leathers wiggling under her. Bertha's the doodles. This is the way she stood at the piano at Sadie's party. This is the way she smiled at the errand boys and counter jumpers at Sadie's party. This is the way she bowed and this is the song she sang to them that they applauded so much.

And this is too good to be true. Bravo six times. Dimes and quarters and a majestic half dollar that takes Bertha on the ear. Bravo eleven times. Bertha stands smirking and moving her shoulders and singing in a piping little shop-girl voice. Encore, *cherie!* Encore! And it goes to Bertha's head. The applause and laughter, the lights and the pounding of the pennies falling out of heaven around her feet—these are too much for Bertha. She ends. Her arms make a gesture, a weak little gesture as if she were embracing one of the errand boys in a vestibule, saying good-night. A vague radiance comes over Bertha's face. Bravo twenty-nine times. The grand prize of fifty bones is hers. Wait and see if it ain't.

More lions and more Christians. Bring 'em out. The sad-looking boy with the harmonica. He forgets the tune all the time and we laugh and hit him with pennies. The clerk with the shock of black hair who does an Apache dance, and does it well. Too well. And the female impersonator who does a can-can female dance very well. Much too well.

Nobody wants them. We want Bertha, the Sewing Machine Girl. There was a thrill to her. The way she looked when the applause grew loud. The way her girl arms reached out toward something. As if we at the tables rolling around in our seats and laughing our heads off and all dressed up and guzzling sandwiches and ginger ale, as if we were something at a rainbow end.

Bring her on again. Line 'em up. Now we'll applaud the one we liked the best. For his nobs who gargled the Irish ballad, two bravos. If he hadn't got mad at us. Or if he'd got madder and spat a little more behind the music that came from him. But he didn't. The first gal who died on the floor. Whose heart collapsed. Whose eyes went blank with terror. Nine bravos for her. There was a thrill to her. Bravos for the rest of them, too. But Bertha wins the hand-painted cazaza. Fifty bucks for Bertha. Here you are, Bertha. You win.

Look, she's crying. That's all right, li'l' girl. That's all right. Don't cry. We just gave you the prize because you gave us a thrill. That's fair enough. Because of all the geniuses who performed for our amusement and whom we bombarded with pennies you were the only one who threw out your arms and your eyes to us as if we were rainbow's end.

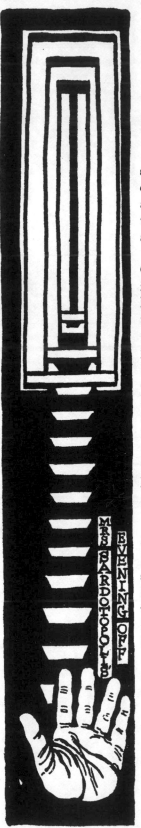

MRS. SARDOTOPOLIS' EVENING OFF

Mrs. Sardotopolis hurried along without looking into the store window. She was carrying her baby home from the doctor's office. The doctor said, "Hurry on. Get him home and don't buy him any ice cream on the way." Mrs. Sardotopolis lived in a place above a candy, book and notion store at 608 South Halsted street.

It was late afternoon. Greeks, Jews, Russians, Italians, Czechs, were busy in the street. They sat outside their stores in old chairs, hovered protectingly over the outdoor knick-knack counters, walked lazily in search of iced drinks or stood with their noses close together arguing.

The store windows glittered with crude colors and careless peasants' clothes. It was at such times as this, hurrying home from a doctor's office or a grocery store, that Mrs. Sardotopolis enjoyed herself. Her little eyes would take in the gleaming arrays of tin pans, calico remnants, picture books, hair combs and things like that with which the merchants of Halsted Street fill their windows.

But this time Mrs. Sardotopolis had seven blocks to go to her home and there was no time for looking at things. Despite the heat she had carefully wrapped the baby in her arms in a shawl.

When Mrs. Sardotopolis got home there would be eight other children to take care of. But that was a simple matter. None of them was sick. When the eight children weren't sick they tumbled, shrieked and squealed in the dark hallway or in the street. Anywhere. Mrs. Sardotopolis only listened with half an ear. As long as they made noise they were healthy. So from day to day she listened not for their noise but to hear if any of them grew quiet.

Joe had grown quiet. Joe was the baby, a year and a half, and quite a citizen. After several days Mrs. Sardotopolis couldn't stand Joe's quiet any more. His skin, too,

140

made her feel sad. His skin was hot and dry. So she had hurried off to the doctor.

There was hardly time in her day for such an errand. Now she must get home quickly. Mr. Sardotopolis and his three brothers would be home before it got dark. In the kitchen in the big pot she had left three chickens cooking.

A gypsy leaned out of a doorway. She was dressed in many red, blue and yellow petticoats and waists. Beads hung from her neck and her withered arms were alive with copper bracelets.

"Tell your fortune, missus," she called.

Mrs. Sardotopolis hurried by with no more than a look. Some day she would let the gypsy tell her fortune. It cost only twenty-five cents. But now there was no time. Too much to do. Her arms—heavy, tireless arms that knew how to work for fifteen hours each day—clung to the bundle Joe made in his shawl.

But the doctor was a fool. What harm could ice cream do? When anybody was sick ice cream could make them well. So Mrs. Sardotopolis lifted Joe up and turned her eyes toward an ice cream stand. She stopped. If Joe said, "Wanna," she would buy him some. But Joe didn't seem to know what she was offering, although usually he was quite a citizen. So she said aloud, "Wanna ice cream, Joe?"

To this Joe made no answer except to let his head fall back. Mrs. Sardotopolis grew frightened and walked fast.

As she came near her home Mrs. Sardotopolis was leaning over the bundle in her arms, crying, "Joe! Joe! Do you hear, Joe?"

The streets swarmed with the early evening crowds of men and women going home. In the cars the people stood packed as if they were sardines.

A few feet from her door beside the candy and notion store Mrs. Sardotopolis stopped. Her heavy face had grown white. She raised the bundle closer to her eyes and looked at it.

"Joe!" she repeated. "What's a matter, Joe?"

The bundle was silent. So Mrs. Sardotopolis pinched it. Then she stared at the closed eyes. Then she seized the bundle and crushed it desperately in her heavy arms, against her heavy bosom.

"Joe!" she repeated. "What's a matter, Joe?"

The glazier sitting in front of his glassware store stood up and blinked.

"Whatsamatter?" he asked.

Mrs. Sardotopolis didn't answer, but stood in front of her house, holding the bundle in her arms and repeating its name. A small crowd gathered. She addressed herself to several women of her race.

"I knew, before it come," she said. "He didn't want no ice cream."

Mrs. Sardotopolis walked upstairs and laid the bundle down on the table. It lay without moving and Mrs. Sardotopolis stood over it without moving. Then she sat down in a chair beside it and began to cry.

When Mr. Sardotopolis and his three brothers came home from driving the wagon they found her still crying.

"Joe is dead," she said.

The other children were all properly noisy. Mr. Sardotopolis said, "I will call my sisters and mother." He went over, looked at the child that lay dead on the table and stroked its head.

The sisters and mothers arrived. They took charge of the big pot with the three chickens in it, of the eight squalling little ones and of the silent bundle on the table. There were four sisters. As it grew dark Mrs. Sardotopolis found that she was sitting alone in a corner of the room. She felt tired. There was no use hugging the baby any more. Joe was dead. In a few days he would be buried. Tears. Yes, particularly since in a few months he would have had a smaller brother. Now Mrs. Sardotopolis was frightened. Joe was the first to die.

She walked out of the house, down the dark hallway into the street. "It will do her good," said her mother-in-law, who watched her.

In the street there was nothing to do. There were no errands to make. She could just walk. People were just walking. Young people arm in arm. It was a summer night in Halsted Street. Mrs. Sardotopolis walked until her eyes grew clearer. She took a deep breath and looked about her nervously. There was a gypsy leaning out of the doorway. Mrs. Sardotopolis stared at her.

"Tell your fortune, missus," called the gypsy.

Mrs. Sardotopolis nodded and entered the hallway. Her head felt dizzy. But there was nothing to do until tomorrow, when they buried Joe. With a curious thrill under her heavy bosom, Mrs. Sardotopolis held out her work-coarsened palm to the gypsy.

THE GREAT TRAVELER

Alexander Ginkel has been around the world. A week ago he came to Chicago and, after looking around for a few days, located in one of the less expensive hotels and started to work as a porter in a well-known department store downtown.

A friend said, "There's a man living in my hotel who should make a good story. He's been around the world. Worked in England, Bulgaria, Russia, Siberia, China and everywhere. Was cook on a tramp steamer in the south seas. A remarkable fellow, really."

In this way I came to call on Ginkel. I found him after work in his room. He was a short man, over 30, and looked uninteresting. I told him that we should be able to get some sort of story out of his travels and experiences. He nodded.

"Yes," he said, "I've been all around the world."

Then he became silent and looked at me hopefully.

I explained, "People like to read about travelers. They sit at home themselves and wonder what it would be like to travel. You probably had a lot of experiences that would give people a vicarious thrill. I understand you were a cook on a tramp steamer in the south seas."

"Oh, yes," said Ginkel, "I've been all over. I've been around the world."

We lighted pipes and Ginkel removed a book from a drawer in the dresser. He opened it and I saw it was a book of photographs—mostly pictures taken with a small camera.

"Here are some things you could use," he said. "You wanna look at them."

We went through the pictures together.

"This one here," said Ginkel, "is me in Vladivostok. It was taken on the corner there."

The photograph showed Ginkel dressed just as he was in the hotel room, standing near a lamp post on a street corner. There was visible a part of a store window.

"This one is interesting," said Ginkel, warming up. "It was taken in the archipelago. You know where. I forget the name of the town. But it was in the south seas."

We both studied it for a space. It showed Ginkel standing underneath something that looked like a palm tree. But the tree was slightly out of focus. So were Ginkel's feet.

"It is interesting," said Ginkel, "But it ain't such a good picture. The lower part is kind of blurred, you notice."

We looked through the album in silence for a while. Then Ginkel suddenly remembered something.

"Oh, I almost forgot," he said. "There's one I think you'll like. It was taken in Calcutta. You know where. Here it is."

He pointed proudly toward the end of the book. We studied it through the tobacco smoke. It was a photograph of Ginkel dressed in the same clothes as before and standing under a store awning.

"There was a good light on this," said Ginkel, "and you see how plain it comes out."

Then we continued without comment to study other photographs. There were at least several hundred. They were all of Ginkel. Most of them were blurred and showed odds and ends of backgrounds out of focus, such as trees, street cars, buildings, telephone poles. There was one that finally aroused Ginkel to comment:

"This would have been a good one, but it got light struck," he said. "It was taken in Bagdad."

When we had exhausted the album Ginkel felt more at ease. He offered me some tobacco from his pouch. I resumed the original line of questioning.

"Did you have any unusual adventures during your travels or did you get any ideas that we could fix up for a story," I asked.

"Well," said Ginkel, "I was always a camera bug, you know. I guess that's what gave me the bug for traveling. To take pictures, you know. I got a lot more than these, but I ain't mounted them yet."

"Are they like the ones in the book."

"Not quite so good, most of them," Ginkel answered. "They were taken when I hadn't had much experience."

"You must have been in Russia while the revolution was going on, weren't you?"

"Oh, yes. I got one there." He opened the book again. "Here," he said. "This was in Moscow. I was in Moscow when this was taken."

It was another picture of Ginkel slightly out of focus and standing against a store front. I asked him suddenly who had taken all the pictures.

"Oh, that was easy," he said. "I can always find somebody to do that. I take a picture of them first and then they take one of me. I always give them the one I take of them and keep the one they take of me."

"Did you see any of the revolution, Ginkel?"

"A lot of monkey business," said Ginkel. "I seen some of it. Not much."

The last thing I said was, "You must have come in for a lot of sights. We might fix up a story about that if you could give me a line on them." And the last thing Ginkel said was:

"Oh, yes, I've been around the world."

THUMBS UP AND DOWN

Later the art jury will sit on them. The art jury will discuss tone and modeling, rhythm and chiaroscuro and perspective. And in the light of these discussions and decisions the art jury will sort out the masterpieces that are to be hung in the Chicago artists' exhibition and the masterpieces that are not to be hung.

Right now, however, Louis and Mike are unwrapping them. Every day between nine and five Louis and Mike assemble in the basement of the Art Institute. The masterpieces arrive by the bushel, the truckload, the basketful. Louis unwraps them. Mike stacks them up. Louis then calls off their names and the names of geniuses responsible for them. Mike writes this vital information down in a book.

Art is a contagious business. Perfectly normal and marvelously wholesome-minded people are as likely to succumb to it as anybody else. It is significant that the Purity League meeting in the city a few weeks ago discussed the dangers which lay in exposing even decent, law-abiding people to art, any kind of art.

The insidious influence of art cannot, as a matter of fact, be exaggerated. I personally know of a number of very fine and highly respected citizens who have been lured away from their very business by art.

However, this is no place to sound the alarm. I will some day talk on the subject before the Rotary Club. To return to Louis and Mike. After Mike writes the vital information down in a book Louis carts the canvas over to a truck and it is ready for the jury room.

When they started on the job Louis and Mike were frankly indifferent. They might just as well have been unwrapping herring cases. And they were exceedingly efficient. They unwrapped them and catalogued them as fast as they came.

149

In three days, however, the workmanlike morale with which Louis and Mike started on the job has been undermined. They have grown more leisurely. They no longer bundle the pictures around like herring cases. Instead they look at them, try them this way and that way until they find out which way is right side up. Then they pass judgment.

Louis unwraps them. I was standing by in the basement with Bert Elliott, who has submitted a modernistic picture of Michigan Avenue, the Wrigley Building and the sky, called "Up, Straight and Across."

" 'The Home of the Muskrat,' " Louis called. Mike wrote it down. "Wanna look at it, Mike?"

"Yeah, let's see." Time out for critical inspection. "Say, this guy never saw a muskrat house. That ain't the way."

" 'Isle of Dreams,' " called Louis. "Hm! You can't tell which is right side up. I guess it goes like this."

"No. The other," said Mike. "Try it on its side. There, I told you so. 'Isle of Dreams.' I don't see no isle."

"Here's a cuckoo," called Louis, suddenly. " 'Mist.' "
"What?"

" 'Mist,' it says, only 'Mist,' Mike. I'll say he missed. It ain't no picture at all. That's a swell idee. Draw a picture in a fog and have the fog so heavy you can't see nothing, then you don't have to put any picture in. Can you beat it?"

"Go on. Try another."

"All right. Here's one. 'The Faithful Friend.' Now there's what I call a picture. I knowed a guy who owned a dog that looked just like this. A setter or something."

"Go on. That ain't a setter. It's a spaniel."

"You're cuckoo, Mike. Tell me it's a spaniel! Let's put it up ahead. It's probably one of the prize winners. Here's a daffy one. 'At Play.' What's at play? I don't see nothin' at play. Take a look, Mike."

"It's a sea picture. There's the sea, the gray part."

150

"You're nuts. Hennessey has a sea picture over the bar with some gals on the rocks. You know the one I mean. And if this is a sea picture I'm a orang-outang."

"Well, Louis, it's probably a different sea. Can you imagine anybody sending a thing like that in? It ain't hardly worth the work of unwrapping it. Hurry up, Louis, we're 'way behind."

"Well, take this, then. 'Children of the Ice.' Hm, I don't see no kids. I suppose this stuff here is the ice. But where's the kids?"

"He probably means the birds over there, Louis."

"If he means the birds why don't he say birds instead of children? Why don't he say 'birds of the ice'? What's the sense of saying 'children of the ice' when he means birds?"

"Go on, Louis. Don't argue with me. Hurry up."

"Here's some photographs."

"Them ain't photographs, you nut. They're portraits."

"Well, they look almost as good as photographs. 'My Favorite Pupil.' It's pretty good, Mike. See, there's the violin. He's a violin pupil. You can tell. Got it?"

"Yeah. Bring on the next."

A silence came over Louis. He stood for several minutes staring at something.

"Hurry up," calle Mike. "It's getting late."

"This is a mistake," called Louis. "Here's one that's a mistake."

"How come, Louis?"

"Well, look at it. You can see for yourself. The guy made a mistake."

"What does it read on the back? Hurry, we can't waste no more time."

"It reads 'Up, Down and Across' or something. It's a mistake though." Louis remained eyeing the canvas raptly. "It ain't finished, Mike. We ought to send it back."

"Let's see, Louis." Time out for critical inspection. "You're right. It is a mistake. 'Up, Down and Across,' you said. Well, we'll let it ride. It's not our fault. What's the name of the guy?"

"Bert Elliott," called Louis. A laugh followed. Louis turned to me and my friend.

"You see this?" he said. "I get it now. That's the Wrigley Building over there. What do you know about that?"

Louis seized his sides and doubled up. Mr. Elliott, beside me, cleared his throat and glanced apprehensively at his canvas.

"I'll say it's the first one he laughed at," said Mr. Elliott, pensively. "He didn't laugh at any of the others. Look, he's still looking at it. That's longer than he looked at any of the others."

"All right, Louis," from Mike. "Come on."

"Ho, ho," Louis went on, "I'd like to see this guy Elliott. Anybody who would draw a picture like that. Hold your horses, Mike, here's another. 'The Faun.' What's a faun, Mike? I guess he means fern. It looks like a fern."

"It does that, Louis. But we'll have to let it go as a faun. It's probably a foreign word. Most of these artists are foreigners, anyway."

Mr. Elliott and I left, Mr. Elliott remarking on the way down the Institute steps, "Ho, hum."

ORNAMENTS

Ornaments change, and perhaps not for the best. The scherzo architecture of Villon's Paris, the gabled caprice of Shakespeare's London, the Rip Van Winkle jauntiness of a vanished New York, these are ghosts that wander among the skyscrapers and dynamo beltings of modernity.

One by one the charming blunders of the past have been set to rights. Highways are no longer the casual folderols of adventure, but the reposeful and efficient arteries of traffic. The roofs of the town are no longer a rumble of idiotic hats cocked at a devil-may-care angle. Windows no longer wink lopsidedly at one another. Doorways and chimneys, railings and lanterns have changed. Cobblestones and dirt have vanished, at least officially.

Towns once were like improvised little melodramas. Men once wore their backgrounds as they wore their clothes—to fit their moods. A cap and feather, a gable and a latticed window for romance. A glove and rapier, a turret and a postern gate for adventure. And for our immemorial friend Routine a humpty-dumpty jumble of alleys, feather pens, cobblestones, echoing stairways and bouncing milk carts.

These things have all been properly corrected. Today the city frowns from one end to the other like a highly efficient and insanely practical platitude. Mood has given way to mode. An essential evolution, alas! D'Artagnan wore his Paris as a cloak. And perhaps Mr. Insull wears his Chicago as a shirt front. But most of us have parted company with the town. It is a background designed and marvelously executed for our conveniences. The great metronomes of the loop with their million windows, the deft crisscross of streets, the utilitarian miracles of plumbing, doorways, heating systems and passenger carriers—these are monuments to our collective sanity.

But if one is insane, if one has inherited one's grand-

153

father's characteristics as idler, loafer, lounger, dreamer, lover or picaroon, what then? Eh, one stays at home and tells it to the typewriter or, more likely, one gets run down, chewed up and bespattered while darting across State Street in quest of an invigorating vanilla phosphate.

Nevertheless—there's a word that speaks innate optimism, nevertheless, there are things which do not change as logically as do ornaments. Men and women, for instance. And although the town wears its mask of deplorable sanity and though Sunnyside Avenue seems suavely reminiscent of Von Bissing's troops goose-stepping through Belgium—there are men and women.

One naturally inquires, where? Quite so, where are there men and women in the city? One sees crowds. But men and women are lost. One observes crowds answering the advertisements. The advertisements say, come here, go there. And one sees men and women devotedly bent upon rewarding the advertisers.

Again, nevertheless, there are other observations to make. There are the taxicabs. Here in the taxicabs one may still observe men and women. Villon's Paris, Shakespeare's London and vanished New York, these are crowded into the taxicabs. In the taxicabs men and women still wear the furtive, illogical, questing, mysterious devil-may-care, wasterel adventure masks of their grandfathers' yesterdays.

What ho! A devilishly involved argument, that, when the taxicab owners plume themselves upon being the last word in the matter of deplorable efficiency, the ultimate gasp in the business of convenience! Nevertheless, although Mr. Hertz points with proper scorn to the sedan chair, the palanquin, the ox cart and the Ringling Brothers' racing chariots, we sweep a three-dollar fedora across the ground, raise our eyebrows and smile mysteriously to ourselves.

For on the days when our insanities grow somewhat persistent there is a solace in the spectacle of taxicabs that none of the advertisements of Mr. Hertz or his contemporaries can take away. For odds bodkins! gaze you through the little windows of these taxicabs. Pretty gals leaning forward eager-eyed, lips parted, with an air of piquing rendezvous to the parasols clutched in their dainty hands. Plump, heavy-jowled dandies reclining like tailored paladins in the leather cushions. Keen-eyed youths surrounded with heaps of bags and cases on a carefully linened quest. Nervous old women, mysteriously ragged creatures, rakish silk hats, bundles of children with staring fingers, strangely mustachioed and ribald-necked gentry.

A goodly company. A teasing procession for the eye and the thought. The cabs shoot by, caracoling through the orderly lines of traffic; zigzags of yellow, green, blue, lavender, black and white snorting along with a fine disdain. They speak of destinations reminiscent of the postern gate and the latticed window; of the waiting barque and the glowing tavern.

Of the crowds on the pavements; of the crowds in the passenger cars, elevators, lobbies, one wonders little where they are going. Answering advertisements, forsooth. Vertebrate brothers of the codfish. But these others! Ah, one stands on the curb with the vanilla phosphate playing havoc with one's blood and wonders a hatful.

These sybarites of the taxis are going somewhere. Make no doubt of that. These insanely assorted creatures bouncing on the leather cushions are launched upon mysterious and important enterprises. And these bold-looking jehus, black eyed, hard mouthed—a fetching tribe! A cross between Acroceraunian bandits and Samaritans. One may stare at a taxi scooting by and think with no incongruity of Carlyle's "Night of Spurs" —with Louis and his harried Antoinette flying the guillotine. And of other things which our inefficient memory prevents us from jotting down at this moment. But of other things.

Journalism is incomplete without its moral or at least its

overtones of morals. And we come to that now as an honest reporter should. Our moral is very simple. Any good platitudinarian will already have forestalled it. It is that the goodly company riding about in these taxicabs upon which we have been speculating are none other than these codfish of the pavements. The same, messieurs. A fact which gives us hope; briefly, hope for the fact that the world is not as sane as it looks and that, despite all the fine strivings of construction engineers, plumbers, advertisers and the like, men and women still preserve the quaint spirit of disorder and melodrama which once lived in the ornaments of the town.

THE WATCH FIXER

The wooden counter in front of Gustave is littered with tiny pieces of spring, tiny keys, almost invisible screws and odd-looking tools. Gustave himself is a large man with ponderous eyebrows and a thick nose. He stands behind his counter in the North Wells Street repair shop looking much too large for the store itself and grotesquely out of proportion with the springs, keys, screws and miniature tools before him.

Attached to Gustave's right eye is a microscope. It is fastened on by aid of straps round his large head. When he works he moves the instrument over his eye and when he rests he raises it so that it sticks out of his eyebrow.

Gustave is a watchmaker. When he was young he made watches of curious design. But for years he has had to content himself with repairing watches. Incased in his old-fashioned leather apron that hangs from his shoulders, the venerable and somewhat Gargantuan Gustave stands most of the day peering into the tiny mechanisms of watches brought into the old furniture shop. Gustave's partner is responsible for the furniture end of the business. As Gustave grows older he seems to lose interest in things that do not pertain to the delicate intricacies of watches.

I had a watch that was being fixed. Gustave said it would be ready in a half-hour. He slipped the microscope over his eye and, bending in his heavy round-shouldered way above the small watch, began to pry with his thick fingers. A pair of tiny pincers, a fragile-looking screwdriver and a set of things that looked like dolls' tools occupied him.

We talked, Gustave answering and evading questions and offering comments as he worked.

"Not zo hard ven you ged used to it," he said. "Und I am used to it. Vatches are my friends. I like to look into

157

dem und make dem go. Yes, I have been vorking on vatches for a long time. Years und years.

"No, I vas vunce in the manufagturing business. Long ago. It vas ven I vas married und had children. I come over from the old country den und I start in. Preddy soon ve had money to spare. Ve came oud here to Chicago und got a house. A very nice house.

"My vife was a danzer in the old country. Maybe you have heard of her. But never mind. I had dis vatch factory over here by the river. Dat vas thirty years ago. Und ve had a barn und horses.

"But you know how it is! Vat you have today you don't have tomorrow. Not so? My vife first. The nice house und the children vasn't enough for her. She must danze also. I vas younger und my head vas harder den. Und I said, 'No.' Alzo she vent avay. Yes, she vent avay. Und der vas two kids. My youngest a girl und my oldest a boy."

The microscope fastened itself closely to the inanimate springs and keys and screws. Gustave's thick fingers reached for a pair of baby pincers. And he continued now without the aid of questions in a low, gutteral voice:

"Vell, business got bad und I gave up the factory. Und I starded in someding else. Den my youngest she died. Yes, dat's how it goes. First vun ding und den anoder ding. Und preddy soon you have nodings.

"I tried to find my vife, but she vas hiding from me. Perhaps I vas hard headed in dem days. Ven you are young you are like dat. Now id is diff'rend. She iss dead und I am alive. Und if she had been my vife righd along she vould still be dead now. Alzo vat matter does it make?

"Dat vas maybe tventy years ago or maybe more. Maybe tventy-five years ago. Dings got all mixed up and my businesses got vorse und vorse. Und den my son ran avay und wrides me he become a sailor. So I vas alone."

"Dis vatch," sighed Gustave, "is very hard to figx. It iss an old vatch und not much good to begin vit. But I figx

158

him. Vat vas ve talking aboud? Oh, my business. Yes, yes. It goes like dat. I don't hear from my vife und I don't hear from my son. Und my liddle vun iss dead. Und so I lose my fine house und the horses und everyding.

"Preddy soon I got no job even und preddy soon I am almost a bum. I hang around saloons und drink beer und do noding but spend a little money I pick up now un den by doing liddle jobs. Ah, now I have it. It vas de liddle spring. See? Zo. Most of dese vatches iss no good vatsoever. Dey make vatches diff'rend now as dey used to. Chust vun minute or two more und I have him figxed so he don'd break no more for a vile. Und vat vas ve talking aboud?

"Ah, yes. Aboud how I drink beer und vas a bum. Dat's how it goes. Ven you are young you have less sense den ven you are old. Und I used to go around thinking I vould commit suicide. Yes, at night ven I vas all alone I used to think like dat. Everyding vas so oopside down und so inside oud. Vat's de use of living und vy go on drinking beer und becoming a vorse und bigger bum?

"Yes, it goes like dat. Ven I vas rich und happy und had my factory und my vife und children und horses und fine house I used to think vat a fine place the vorld vas und how simple it vas to be happy. Und den ven everyding vent avay I vas chust as big a fool und I used to think how terrible the vorld vas und how unhappiness vas all you could get.

"Yes, ten years ago, it vas. I started in again. I started in on vatches again. I got a job figxing vatches und a friend says he vould give me a chance. Und here I am. Still figxing vatches. Dey are my friends. Inside dey are all broken. Dey have liddle tings wrong vid dem und are inside oud und oopside down und I figx dem.

"I don' know vy, but figxing vatches made a new man from me. I don' think no more aboud my troubles und how oopside down and impozzible everyding is. But I look all de time into vatches und make dem go again. Yes, it iss like you say, a delicate business, und my fingers iss getting old for it, maybe. But I like dese liddle tools und all dese liddle things aboud a vatch I like to look at und hold und figx up.

"Because it iss so simple. Ezpecially ven you get acquainted vid how dey run und vy dey stop. Und der are zo many busted vatches. Zo nice outside und zo busted inside. I can'd explain maybe how it iss. But it iss like dat. Ven I hold de busted vatches under the micgrozcope, I feel happy I don' know. Some time maybe somebody pick me up like I vas a busted vatch und hold me under a micgrozcope und figx me up until I go tick tick again. Maybe dat's vy. Here. All done."

Gustave shifted the microscope up over his eyebrow and smiled ponderously across the counter.

"Put it on," he said, "but be careful. Dat's how vatches iss busted alvays. By bumping und paying no attention to dem."

SCHOPENHAUER'S SON

Life, alas, is an intricate illusion. God is a pack of lies under which man staggers to his grave. And man—ah, here we have Nature's only mountebank; here we have Nature's humorous and ingenuous experiment in tragedy. And thought —ah, the tissue-paper chimera that seeks forever to devour life.

It is the cult of the pessimist, the gentle malice of disillusion. And, like all other cults, it sustains its advocates. Thus, the city has no more debonairly-mannered, smiling-souled citizen to offer than Clarence Darrow. For years and years Mr. Darrow has been gently disproving the intelligence of man, the importance of life, and the necessity of thought. For years and years Mr. Darrow has been whimsically deflating the illusions in which man hides from the purposelessness of the cosmos. God, heaven, politics, philosophies, ambition, love—Mr. Darrow has deflated them time and again—charging from $1 to $2 a seat for the spectacle.

This is nothing against Mr. Darrow—that he charges money sometimes. For years and years Mr. Darrow has been enlivening the intellectual purlieus of the city with his debates. And Mr. Darrow's debates have been always worth $1, $2 and even $5—for various reasons. It is worth at least $5 to observe at first hand what a cheering and invigorating effect Mr. Darrow's pessimism has had upon Mr. Darrow after these innumerable years.

The story concerns itself with a funeral Mr. Darrow attended a few years ago. It is at funerals that Mr. Darrow's gentle malice finds itself crowned by circumstances. For to this son of Schopenhauer death is a weary smile that is proof of all his arguments.

This time, however, Mr Darrow was curiously stirred. For there lay dead in the coffin a man for whom he had held a deep affection. It was Prof. George B. Foster, the brilliant theologian of the University of Chicago.

During his life Prof. Foster had been a man worthy the steel of Mr. Darrow. Not that Prof. Foster was an unscrupulous optimist. He was merely an intellectual whose congenital tendencies were idealistic, just as Mr. Darrow's psychic and subconscious tendencies were anti-idealistic. And apart from this divergence of congenital tendencies Mr. Darrow and Prof. Foster had a great deal in common. They both loved argument. They both doted upon seizing an idea and energizing it with their egoism. They were, in short, ideal debaters.

Whenever Mr. Darrow and Prof. Foster debated on one of the major issues of reason a flutter made itself felt in the city—even among citizens indifferent to debate. Indifferent or not, one felt that a debate between Prof. Foster and Mr. Darrow was a matter of considerable importance. Things might be disproved or proved on such an occasion.

They were to have debated on "Is There Immortality?" when Prof. Foster's death canceled the engagement. This was one of the favorite differences of opinion between the two friends. Mr. Darrow, of course, bent all his efforts on disproving immortality. Prof. Foster bent all his on proving it. Considerable excitement had been stirred by the coming debate. The death of the brilliant theologian put an end to it.

Instead of the debate there was a funeral. Thousands of people who had admired the intellect, kindness and humanitarianism of Prof. Foster came to the memorial services held in one of the large theaters of the loop. Mr. Darrow came, his head bowed and grief in his heart. Friends like George Foster never replace themselves. Death becomes not a triumphant argument—an aloof clincher for pessimism, but a robber.

There were speakers who talked of the dead man's virtues, his love for people, scholarship and the arts, his keen brain and his genius. Mr. Darrow sat listening to the eulogy of his dead friend and tears filled his eyes. Poor George Foster— gone, in a coffin; to be buried out of sight in a few hours.

Then some one whispered to Mr. Darrow that a few words were expected of him.

It was Mr. Darrow's good-bye to his dear friend. He stood up and his loose figure and slyly malicious face wore an unaccustomed seriousness. The audience waited, but the facile Mr. Darrow was having difficulty locating his voice, his words. His eyes, blurred with tears, were still staring at the coffin. Finally Mr. Darrow began. His dear friend. Dead. So charming a man. So brilliant a mind. Dead now. He had been so amazingly alive it seemed incredible that he should be dead. It was as if part of himself—Mr. Darrow—lay in the coffin.

The eulogy continued, quiet, sincere, stirring tears in the audience and filling their hearts with a realization of the grief that lay in Mr. Darrow's heart. Then slowly the phrases grew clearer.

"We were old friends and we fought many battles of the mind," said Mr. Darrow. "And we were to have debated once more next week—on 'Is There Immortality?' It was his contention," whispered Mr. Darrow, "that there is immortality. He is gone now, but he speaks more eloquently on the subject than if he were still with us. There lies all that remains of my friend George Burman Foster—in a coffin. And had he lived he would have argued with me on the subject. But he is dead and he knows now, in the negation and darkness of death, that he was wrong—that there is no immortality—"

Mr. Darrow paused. He had after many years won his argument with Prof. Foster. But the victory brought no elation. Mr. Darrow's eyes filled again and he turned to walk from the stage. But before he left the mourners sitting around him heard him murmur:

"I wish poor George Foster had been right. There would be nobody happier than I to realize that his soul had survived —that there was still a George Foster. But—if he could come back now after the proof of death he would admit——yes, admit that——that there is no immortality."

And Mr. Darrow with his head bowed yielded the platform to his inarticulate and vanquished friend and debater.

WORLD CONQUERORS

The hall is upstairs. A non-committal sign has been tacked over the street entrance. It discloses that there is to be a discussion this night on the subject of the world revolution. The disclosure is made in English, Yiddish and Russian.

A thousand people have arrived. They are mostly west siders, with a sprinkling of north and south side residents. There seem to be two types. Shop workers and a type that classifies as the intelligentsia. The workers sit calmly and smoke. The intelligentsia are nervous. Dark-eyed women, bearded men, vivacious, exchanging greetings, cracking jokes.

The first speaker is a very bad orator. He is a workingman. An intensity of manner holds the audience in lieu of phrases. He says nothing. Yet every one listens. He says that workingmen have been slaves long enough. That there is injustice in the world. That the light of freedom has appeared on the horizon.

This, to the audience, is old stuff. Yet they watch the talker. He has something they one and all treasured in their own hearts. A faith in something. The workingmen in the audience have stopped smoking. They listen with a faint skepticism in their eyes. The intelligentsia, however, are warming up. For the moment old emotions are stirring in them. Sincerity in others—the martyr spirit in others—is something which thrills the insincerity of all intelligentsia.

Suddenly there is a change in the hall. Our stuttering orator with the forceful manner has made a few startling remarks. He has said, "And what we must do, comrades, is to use force. We can get nowhere without force. We must uproot, overthrow and seize the government."

Scandal! A murmur races around the hall. The residents from the north and south sides who have favored this discussion of world revolution with their uplifting presence are uneasy. Somebody should stop the man. It's one thing

to be sincere, and another thing to be too sincere and tell them that they should use force.

Now, what's the matter? The orator has grown violent. It is somebody in the back of the hall. Heads turn. A policeman! The orator swings his arms, and in his foreign tongue, goes on. "They are stopping us. The bourgeoisie! They have sent the *polizei!* But we stand firm. The police are powerless against us. Even though they drive us from this hall."

The orator is all alone in his excitement. The audience has, despite his valorous pronouncements, grown nervous. And the policeman walking down the aisle seems embarrassed. He arrives at the platform finally. He hands a card to the orator. The orator glances at the card and then waves it in the air. Then he reads it slowly, his lips moving as he spells the words out. The audience is shifting around, acting as if it wanted to rise and bolt for the door.

"Ah," exclaims the orator, "the policeman says that an enemy of the revolution has smashed an automobile belonging to one of the audience that was standing in front of the hall. The number of the automobile is as follows." He recites the number slowly. And then: "If anybody has an automobile by that number standing downstairs he better go and look after it."

A substantial looking north sider arises and walks hurriedly through the hall. The orator decides to subside. There is a wait for the chief speaker, who has not yet arrived. During the wait an incident develops. There are two lights burning at the rear of the stage. A young woman calls one of the officials of the meeting.

"Look," she says, "those lights make it impossible for us to see the speaker who stands in front of them. They shine in our eyes."

The official wears a red sash across the front of his coat. He is one of the minor leaders among the west side soviet radicals. He blinks. "What do you want of me?" he inquires

166

with indignation. "I should go and turn the lights out? You think I'm the janitor?"

"But can't you just turn the lights off?" persists the young woman.

"The janitor," announces our official with dignity, "turns the lights on and he will turn them off." Wherewith the Tarquin of the proletaire marches off. Two minutes later a man in his short sleeves appears, following him. This man is the janitor. The audience which has observed this little comedy begins to laugh as the janitor turns off the offending lights.

The chief speaker of the evening has arrived. He is a good orator. He is also cynical of his audience. A short wiry man with a pugnacious face and a cocksure mustache. He begins by asking what they are all afraid of. He accuses them of being more social than revolutionary. As long as revolution was the thing of the hour they were revolutionists. But now that it is no longer the thing of the hour, they have taken up other hobbies.

This appears to be rather the truth from the way the intelligentsia take it. They nod approval. Self-indictment is one thing which distinguishes the intelligentsia. They are able to recognize their faults, their shortcomings.

Now the speaker is on his real subject. Revolution. What we want, he cries, is for the same terrible misfortune to happen in this country that happened in Russia. Yes, the same marvelous misfortune. And he is ready. He is working toward that end. And he wishes in all sincerity that the audience would work with him. Start a reign of terror. Put the spirit of the masses into the day. The unconquerable will to overthrow the tyrant and govern themselves. He continues—an apostle of force. Of fighting. Of shooting, stabbing and barricades that fly the red flag. He is sardonic and sarcastic and everything else. And the audience is disturbed.

There are whispers of scandal. And half the faces of the intelligentsia frown in disapproval. They came to hear economic argument, not a call to arms. The other half is stirred.

It is almost eleven. The hall empties. The streets are alive. People hurry, saunter, stand laughing. Street cars, store fronts, mean houses, shadows and a friendly moon. These are part of the system. Three hours ago they seemed a powerful, impregnable symbol. Now they can be overthrown. The security that pervades the street is an illusion. Force can knock it out. A strange force that lies in the masses who live in this street.

The audience moves away. The intelligentsia will discuss the possibility of a sudden uprising of the proletaire and gradually they will grow cynical about it and say, "Well, he was a good talker."

The orator finally emerges from the building. He is surrounded by friends, questioners. For two blocks he has company. Then he is alone. He stands waiting for a street car. Some of the audience pass by without recognizing him.

The street car comes and the orator gets on. He finds a seat. His head drops against the window and his eyes close. And the car sweeps away, taking with it its load of sleepy men and women who have stayed up too late—including a messiah of the proletaire who dreams of leading the masses out of bondage.

THE MAN FROM YESTERDAY

"You'll not use my name," he said, "because my family would be exceedingly grieved over the notoriety the thing would bring them."

Fifty or sixty or seventy—it was hard to tell how old he was. He looked like a panhandler and talked like a scholar. Life had knocked him out and walked over him. There was no money in his pocket, no food in his stomach, no hope in his heart. He was asking for a job—some kind of writing job. His hands were trembling and his face twitched. Despair underlay his words, but he kept it under. Hunger made his body jerked and his eyes shine with an unmannerly eagerness. But his words remained suave. He removed a pair of cracked nose-glasses and held them between his thumb and forefinger and gestured politely with them. Hungry, dirty, hopeless, his linen gone, his shoes torn, something inside his beaten frame remained still intact. There was no future. But he had a past to live up to.

He was asking for a job. What kind of job he didn't know. But he could write. He had been around the world. He was a cosmopolite and a rhymester and a press agent and a journalist. He pulled himself together and his eyes struggled hard to forget the hunger of his stomach.

"In the old days," he said, enunciating in the oracular manner of a day gone by—"ah, I was talking with Jack London about it before he died. Dear Jack! A great soul. A marvelous spirit. We were in the south seas together. Yes, the old days were different. Erudition counted for something. I was Buffalo Bill's first press agent. Also I worked for dear P. T. Barnum. I was his publicity man.

"Doesn't the world seem to have changed, to you?" he asked. "I was talking to George Ade about this very thing. Strange, isn't it? George and I are old friends. Who? Dickie Davis of the *Sun?* Certainly—a charming fellow. Stephen Crane? Genius, my friend, genius was his. That was

169

the day when O. Henry was in New York. There was quite a crowd of us. We used to foregather in some comfortable grog shop and discuss. Ah, life and letters were talked about a great deal in those days."

His voice had the sound of a man casually relating incidents of his past. But his eyes continued to shine eagerly. And between sentences there were curious pauses. The pauses asked something.

"A most curious thing occurred the other evening," he smiled. "I had to pay for my oysters by writing a rhyme for the waiter. An anecdote by a dilettante, a gracefully turned plea worthy of M'sieur Brummell. "You know, it grows more and more difficult to obtain employment. My wardrobe is practically gone." He glanced with apparent amusement at his weary-willie makeup. His hand moved tremblingly to his neck. "My collar is soiled," he murmured, apologizing with eyes that managed to smile, "and the other evening I lost my stick."

Then the hunger and the hopelessness of the man broke through the shell of his manner. He needed a job, a job, a job! Something to do to get him food and shelter. His fingers tried to place the cracked nose-glasses back in position.

"I would—pardon me for mentioning this—I would much rather sit with a man like you and discuss the phases of life and literature of interest to both of us. But I would write almost anything. I have written a great deal. And I have managed money. There was a time—" A look of pain came into his eyes. This was being vulgar and not in line with the tradition that his enunciation boasted.

"I have known a great many people. I don't desire to bore you with talk of celebrities and all that. But I assure you, I have been somebody. Oh, nothing important or perhaps very worth while. I dislike this sort of thing, you know." Another smile twisted his lips. "But, when one is down to the last—er—to the last farthing, so to speak, one swallows a bit of his pride. That's more than an aphorism with me. To go on, I have handled great sums of money. I have traveled all over the world, I have eaten and spoken with men of genius all my life. My youth was a very interesting one and—and perhaps we could go somewhere for dinner and—and I could tell you things of writing men of the past that—that might appeal to you. Marvelous fellows. There was O. Henry and London and Davis and Phillips and Stevie Crane. I dislike imposing myself on you this way, but—if I didn't think you would be interested in a discussion with a man who—who admires the beautiful things of life and who has lived a rather varied existence I would not—"

The cracked nose-glasses were back in place and he had stopped short. Despair and hunger now were talking out of his eyes. They had come too close to his words. They must never come into his words. That would be the one defeat that would drive too deeply into him. Of the past, of the easy-going, charmingly garrulous past, all that was left to this nomad of letters was its manner. He could still sit in his rags as if he were lounging in the salon of an ocean liner, still gesture with his nose-glasses as if he were fixing the attention of a Richard Harding Davis across a bottle of Chateau Yquem.

So he remained silent. Let his eyes and the twitching of his face betray him. His words never would. His words would always be the well-groomed, carefully modulated, nicely considerate words of a gentleman. He resumed:

"So you have nothing. Ah, that's rather—rather disturbing. Just a moment—please. I don't mean to impose on you. Won't you sit down—so I will feel more at ease? Thank you, sir. Perhaps there is something in the way of a—of another kind of job. Anything about a theater, a newspaper office, a magazine, a circus, an hotel. I know them all. And if you could only keep an eye open for me. Thank you, sir. I am glad to see that men of letters are still considerate of their fellow craftsmen. Ah, you would have liked Jack London.

171

Did you know him? You know, we live in an age of jazz. Yes, sir, the tempo is fast. Life has lost its andante. Materialism has triumphed. There is no longer room for the spirit to expand. Machines are in the way. Noises invade the sanctity of meditative hours."

It was cold outside the cigar store. The man from yesterday stepped into the street. He stood smiling for a moment and for the moment in the courteous friendliness of his rheumy eyes, in the mannerly tilt of his head there was the picture of a sophisticated gentleman of the world nodding an adieu outside his favorite chophouse. Then he turned. The mannerly tilt vanished. There was to be seen a man—fifty, sixty or seventy, it was hard to tell how old—shuffling tiredly down the street, his body huddled together and his shoulders shivering.

THUMBNAIL LOTHARIOS

Here's the low down, gentlemen. The Miserere of the manicurist. Peewee, the Titian-haired Aphrodite of the Thousand Nails has been inveigled into submitting her lip-stick memoirs to the public eye.

Peewee is the melting little lady with the vermilion mouth and the cooing eyes who manicures in a Rialto hotel barber shop. She is the one whose touch is like the cool caress of a snowflake, whose face is as void of guile as the face of the Blessed Damosel.

There are others, scissor-Salomés and nail-file Dryads. Mr. Flo Ziegfeld has nothing on George, the head barber, when it comes to an eye for color and a sense for curve. But they are busy at the moment. The hair-tonic Dons and the mud-pack Romeos are giving the girls a heavy play. Peewee alone is at leisure. Therefore let us gallop quickly to the memoirs.

"H'm," says Peewee, "I'll tell you about men. Of course what I say doesn't include all men. There may be exceptions to the rule. I say may be. I hope there are. I'd hate to think there weren't. I'd get sad."

Steady, gentlemen. Peewee's doll face has lost guile-lessness. Peewee's face has taken on a derisive and ominous air.

"I'll give you the low down," says she with a sniff. "Men? They're all alike. I don't care who they are or what their wives and pastors think of them or what their mothers think of them. I got them pegged regardless. Young and old, and some of them so old they've gone back to the milk diet, they all make the same play when they come in here.

"And they're all cheap. Yes, sir, some are cheaper than others, of course. There's the patent-leather hair lounge-lizard. I hand him the fur-lined medal for cheapness. But I got a lot of other medals and I give them all away, too.

173

"Well, sir, they come in here and you take hold of their hand and start in doing honest work and, blooey! they're off. They're strangers in town. And lonesome! My God, how lonesome they are! And they don't know no place to go. That's the way they begin. And they give your hand a squeeze and roll a soft-boiled eye at you.

"Say, it gets kind of tiring, you can imagine. Particularly after you've been through what I have and know their middle names, which are all alike, they all answering to the name of cheap sport. Sometimes I give them the baby stare and pretend I don't know what's on their so-called minds. And sometimes when my nerves are a little ragged I freeze them. Then sometimes I take them up. I let them put it over.

"You'd be surprised. Liars! They're all rich. The young ones are all bond salesmen with wealthy fathers and going to inherit soon. The middle-aged ones are great manufacturers. The old ones are retired financiers. You should ought to hear the lads when they're hitting on all six."

Peewee wagged a wise old head and her vermilion mouth registered scorn at 105 degrees Fahrenheit. A very cold light, however, kindled in her beautiful eyes.

"Yes, yes, I've taken them up," she went on. "I've let them stake me to the swell time. Say, ten dollars to one that these manicured millionaires don't mean any more than the Governor's pardon does to Carl Wanderer. Not a bit. I don't want to get personal, but, take it from me, they're all after one thing. And they're a pack of selfish, mushy-headed tin horns with fishhook pockets, the kind you can't pull anything out of.

"Well, to get back. About the first minute you get the big, come-on squeeze. Then next the big talk about being strangers in your town. Then next they open with the big, hearty invitations. Will you be their little guide? And ain't you the most beautiful thing they ever set eyes on! And say, if they'd only met you before they wouldn't be living around

hotels now, lonesome bachelors without a friend. I forgot
to tell you, they're all single. No, never married. Even some
of the most humpbacked married men you ever saw, who come
in here dragging leg irons and looking a picture of the Common
People, they're single, too. I've seen them slip wedding rings
off their fingers to make their racket stand up.

"Then after they've got along and think they've got you
biting they begin to get fresh. They tell you you shouldn't
ought to work in a barber shop, a girl as beautiful as you. The
surroundings ain't what they should be. And they'd like to
fix you up. Yes, they begin handing out their castles in Rome
or Spain or whatever it is. Cheap! Say, they are so cheap they
wouldn't go on the 5- and 10-cent store counter.

"Sometimes you can shame them into making good in
a small way. But it's too much work. Oh, yes, they give
tips. Fifty cents is the usual tip. Sometimes they make it
$2.00. They think they're buying you, though, for that.

"As I was saying, the patent-leather hair boys are the
worst. They're the ones who call themselves loop hounds.
They know everybody by their first name and sometimes
they've got all of $6.50 in their pocket at one time. And if
you're out some evening with a friend—a regular fella, they
pop in the next day and say, 'Hello, Peewee, who was that
street sweeper I see you palling with last night? Oh, he
wasn't! Well, I had him pegged either as a street sweeper or
a plumber!'"

"That's their speed. And they come again and again.
They never give up. They've got visions of making a conquest
some day—on $1.50. And when a new girl comes into the
shop—boy, don't the buzzards buzz! I came here six months
ago and they started it on me. But I wasn't born yesterday.
I'd been a manicure in Indianapolis. And they're just the same
in Indianapolis as they are in Chicago. And they're just the
same in Podunk.

"Now, I'm not going to mention any names. But take

175

your city directory and begin with Ab Abner and go right on through to Zeke Zimbo and don't skip any. And you'll get a clear idea about the particular gentlemen I'm talking about."

Peewee sighed and shook her head.

"Are you busy?" inquired the head manicurist.

"Not at all," said Peewee, "not at all."

Peewee's biographer asked a final question. To which she responded as follows:

"Well, I'll get married. Maybe. When I find the exception I was telling you about—the gentleman who isn't a stranger in town and in need of a little guide. There must be one of them somewhere. Unless they was all killed in the war."

THE SOUL OF SING LEE

The years have made a cartoon out of Sing Lee. A withered yellow face with motionless black eyes. Thin fingers that move with lifeless precision. Slippered feet that shuffle as if Sing Lee were yawning.

A smell of starch, wet linen and steam mingles with an aromatic mustiness. The day's work is done. Sing Lee sits in his chair behind the counter. Three walls look down upon him. Laundry packages—yellow paper, white string—crowd the wall shelves. Chinese letterings dance gayly on the yellow packages.

Sing Lee, from behind the counter, stares out of the window. The Hyde Park police station is across the way. People pass and glance up:

> Sing Lee, Hand Laundry,
> 5222 Lake Park Avenue.

Come in. There is something immaculate about Sing Lee. Sing Lee has been ironing out collars and shirts for thirty-five years. And thirty-five years have been ironing Sing Lee out. He is like one of the yellow packages on the shelves. And there is a certain lettering across his face as indecipherable and strange as the dance of the black hieroglyphs on the yellow laundry paper.

Something enthralls Sing Lee. It can be seen plainly now as he sits behind the counter. It can be seen, too, as he works during the day. Sing Lee works like a man in an empty dream. It is the same to Sing Lee whether he works or sits still.

The world of collars, cuffs and shirt fronts does not contain Sing Lee. It contains merely an automaton. The laundry is owned by an automaton named Sing Lee, by nobody else. Now that the day's work is done he will sit like this for an hour, two hours, five hours. Time is not a matter of hours to Sing Lee. Or of days. Or even of years.

The many wilted collars that come under the lifeless hands of Sing Lee tell him an old story. The story has not varied for thirty-five years. A solution of water, soap and starch makes the collars clean again and stiff. They go back and they return, always wilted and soiled. Sing Lee needs no further corroboration of the fact that the crowds are at work. Doing what? Soiling their linen. That is as final as anything the crowds do. Sing Lee's curiosity does not venture beyond finalities.

Sing Lee is a resident of America. But this is a formal statistic and refers only to the automaton that owns the hand laundry in Lake Park Avenue. Observe a few more formal facts of Sing Lee's life. He has never been to a movie or a theater play. He has never ridden in an automobile. He has never looked at the lake.

Thus it becomes obvious that Sing Lee lives somewhere else. For a man must go somewhere in thirty-five years. Or do something. There is a story then, in Sing Lee. Not a particularly long story. Life stories are sometimes no longer than a single line—a sentence, even a phrase. So if one could find out where Sing Lee lives one would have a story perhaps a whole sentence long.

"Mukee kai, Sing Lee."

A nod of the thin head.

"Business good?"

Another nod.

"Pretty tired, washing, ironing all day, eh?"

A nod.

"When are you going to put in a laundry machine?"

A shake of the thin head.

"When are you going to quit, Sing Lee?"

Another shake of the thin head.

"You're not very gabby tonight, Sing."

A dignified answer to this: "I thinking."

"What about, Sing Lee?"

A faint smile. The smile seems to set Sing Lee in motion.
It comes from behind the automaton. It is perhaps Sing Lee's
first gesture of life in weeks.

"You don't mind my sitting here and smoking a pipe,
eh?"

The minutes pass. Sing Lee stands up. He turns on a
small electric light. This is a concession. This done, he opens
a drawer behind the counter and removes a little bronze
casket. The casket is placed on the counter. Slowly as if in
a deep dream Sing Lee lights a match and holds it inside the
casket. A thin spiral of lavender smoke unwinds from its
mouth.

Sing Lee watches the spiral of smoke. It wavers and
unwinds. A finger writing; an idiot flower. Then it opens
up into a large smoke eye. Smoke eyes drift casually away.
An odor crawls into the air. Sing Lee's eyes close gently
and his thin body moves as he takes a deep breath.

His eyes still closed, Sing Lee speaks.

"You writer?" he murmurs.

"Yes."

"I too," says Sing Lee. "I write poem."

"Yes? When did you do that?"

"Oh, long ago. Mebbe year. Mebbe five years."

Sing Lee reaches into the open drawer and takes out
a large sheet of rice paper. It is partly covered with Chinese
letters up and down.

"I read you in English," says Sing Lee. His eyes remain
almost shut. He reads:

> The sky is young blue.
> Many fields wait.
> Many people look at young blue sky.
> Old people look at young blue sky.
> Many birds fly.
> At night moon comes and young blue sky is old.
> Many young people look at old sky.

"Did you write that about Chicago, Sing Lee?"

"No, no," says Sing Lee. His eyes open. The smoke eyes from the incense pot drift like miniature ghost clouds behind him and creep along the rows of yellow laundry packages.

"No, no," says Sing Lee. "I write that about Canton. I born in Canton many years ago. Many, many years ago."

MRS. RODJEZKE'S LAST JOB

Mrs. Rodjezke scrubbed the corridors of the Otis building after the lawyers, stenographers and financiers had gone home. During the day Mrs. Rodjezke found other means of occupying her time. Keeping the two Rodjezke children in order, keeping the three-room flat, near the corner of Twenty-ninth and Wallace streets, in order and hiring herself for half-day cleaning, washing or minding-the-baby jobs filled this part of her day. As for the rest of the day, no fault could be found with the manner in which Mrs. Rodjezke used that part of her time.

At five-thirty she reported for work in the janitor's quarters of the office building. She was given her pail, her scrub brush, mop and bar of soap and with eight other women who looked curiously like herself started to work in the corridors. The feet of the lawyers, stenographers and financiers had left stains. Crawling inch by inch down the tiled flooring, Mrs. Rodjezke removed the stains one at a time. Eight years at this work had taken away the necessity of her wearing knee pads. Mrs. Rodjezke's knees did not bother her very much as she scrubbed.

In the evening Mrs. Rodjezke usually rode home in the street car. There were several odd items about Mrs. Rodjezke that one could observe as she sat motionless and staring in her seat waiting for the 2900 block to appear. First, there were her clothes. Mrs. Rodjezke was not of the light-minded type of woman that changes styles with the season. Winter and summer she wore the same.

Then there were her hands. Mrs. Rodjezke's fingernails were a contrast to the rest of her. The rest of her was somewhat vigorous and buxom looking. The fingernails, however, were pale—a colorless light blue. And the tips of her fingers looked a trifle swollen. Also the tips of her fingers were different in shade from the rest of her hands.

Another item of note was her coiffure. Mrs. Rodjezke was always indifferently dressed, her clothes looking as if they had been thrown on and pinned together. Yet her coiffure was almost a proud and careful-looking thing. It proclaimed, alas, that the scrubwoman, despite the sensible employment of her time, was not entirely free from the vanities of her sex. The deliberate coiling and arranging of her stringy black hair must have taken a good fifteen minutes regularly out of Mrs. Rodjezke's otherwise industrious day.

These items are given in order that Mrs. Rodjezke may be visualized for a moment as she rode home on a recent evening. It was very hot and the papers carried news on the front page: "Hot Spell to Continue."

Mrs. Rodjezke got off the car at 29th and Halsted streets and walked to her flat. Here the two Rodjezke children, who were 8 and 10 years old respectively, were demanding their supper. After the food was eaten Mrs. Rodjezke said, in Bohemian:

"We are going down to the beach to-night and go in swimming."

Shouts from the younger Rodjezkes.

When the family appeared on the 51st Street beach it was alive with people from everywhere. They stood around cooling off in their bathing suits and trying to forget how hot it was by covering themselves in the chill sand.

Mrs. Rodjezke's bathing suit was of the kind that attracts attention these days. It was voluminous and hand made and it looked as if it might have functioned as a "wrapper" in its palmier days. For a long time nobody noticed Mrs. Rodjezke. She sat on the sand. Her head felt dizzy. Her eyes burned. And there was a burn in the small of her back. Her knees also burned and the tips of her fingers throbbed.

These symptoms failed to startle Mrs. Rodjezke. Their absence would have been more of a surprise. She sat staring at the lake and trying to keep track of her children. But their dark heads lost themselves in the noisy crowds in front of her and she gave that up. They would return in due time. Mrs. Rodjezke must not be criticized for a maternal indifference. The children of scrubwomen always return in due time.

Mrs. Rodjezke had come to the lake to cool off. The idea of going for a swim had been in her head for at least three years. She had always been able to overcome it, but this time somehow it had got the better of her and she had moved almost blindly toward the water front.

"I will get a rest in the water," she thought.

But now on the beach Mrs. Rodjezke found it difficult to rest. The dishes weren't washed in the kitchen home. The clothes needed changing on the beds. And other things. Lots of other things.

Mrs. Rodjezke sighed as the shouts of the bathers floated by her ears. The sun had almost gone down and the lake looked dull. Faintly colored clouds were beginning to hide the water. It was no use. Mrs. Rodjezke couldn't rest. She sat and stared harder at the lake. Yes, there was something to do. Before it got too dark. Something very important to do. And it wasn't right not to do it. The scrubwoman sighed again and put her hand against her side. The burn had dropped to there. It had also gone into her head. But that was a thing which must be forgotten. Mrs. Rodjezke had learned how to forget it during the eight years.

A girl saw it first. She was laughing in a group of young men from the hotel. Then she exclaimed, suddenly:

"Heavens! Look at that woman!"

The group looked. They saw a middle-aged woman in a humorous bathing costume crawling patiently down the beach on her hands and knees. Soon other people were looking. Nobody interfered at first. Perhaps this was a curious exercise. Some of them laughed.

But the woman's actions grew stranger. She would stop as she crawled and lift up handfuls of water from the edge of the lake. Then she would start scratching in the sand. A crowd collected and the beach policeman arrived. The beach policeman looked down at the woman on her hands and knees.

She had stopped and her face had grown sad.

"What's the matter here?" the policeman asked of her.

The woman began to cry. Her tears flooded her round worn face.

"I can't finish it to-night," she sobbed, "not now anyway. I'm too tired. I can't finish it to-night. And the soap has floated away. The soap is gone."

Mrs. Rodjezke was taken up by the policeman with the two Rodjezke children, who had, of course, returned in due time. They cried and cried and the group went to the police station.

"I don't know what's wrong with the poor woman," said the beach policeman to the Hyde Park police sergeant. "But she was moving up and down like she was trying to scrub the beach."

"I guess," said the sergeant, "we'll have to turn her over to the psychopathic hospital."

There's a lot more to the story, but it has nothing to do with Mrs. Rodjezke's last job.

QUEEN BESS' FEAST

Elizabeth Winslow, who was a short, fat woman with an amazing gift of profanity and "known to the police" as "Queen Bess," is dead. According to the coroner's report Queen Bess died suddenly in a Wabash Avenue rooming house at the age of seventy.

Twenty-five years ago Queen Bess rented rooms and sold drinks according to the easy-going ideas of that day. But there was something untouched by the sordidness of her calling about this ample Rabelaisian woman. There was a noise about Queen Bess lacking in her harpy contemporaries.

"Big-hearted Bess," the coppers used to call her, and "Queenie" was the name her employees had for her. But to customers she was always Queen Bess. In the district where Queen Bess functioned the gossip of the day always prophesied dismally concerning her. She didn't save her money, Queen Bess didn't. And the time would come when she'd realize what that meant. And the idea of Queen Bess blowing in $5,000 for a tally-ho layout to ride to the races in! Six horses and two drivers in yellow and blue livery and girls all dressed like sore thumbs and the beribboned and painted coach bouncing down the boulevard to Washington Park—a lot of good that would do her in her old age!

But Queen Bess went her way, throwing her tainted money back to the town as fast as the town threw it into her purse, roaring, swearing, laughing—a thumping sentimentalist, a clownish samaritan, a Madam Aphrodite by Rube Goldberg. There are many stories that used to go the rounds. But when I read the coroner's report there was one tale in particular that started up in my head again. A mawkish tale, perhaps, and if I write it with too maudlin a slant I know who will wince the worst—Queen Bess, of course, who will sit up in her grave and, fastening a blazing eye on me, curse me out for every variety of fat-head and imbecile known to her exhaustive calendar of epithets.

185

Nevertheless, in memory of the set of Oscar Wilde's works presented to my roommate twelve years ago one Christmas morning by Queen Bess, and in memory of the six world-famous oaths this great lady invented—here goes. Let Bess roar in her grave. There's one thing she can't do and that's call me a liar.

It was Thanksgiving day and years ago and my roommate Ned and I were staring glumly over the roofs of the town.

"I've got an invitation for Thanksgiving dinner for both of us," said Ned. "But I feel kind of doubtful about going."

I inquired what kind of invitation.

"An engraved invitation," grinned Ned. "Here it is. I'll read it to you." He read from a white card: "You are cordially invited to attend a Thanksgiving dinner at the home of Queen Bess, —— Street and Wabash Avenue, at 3 o'clock. You may bring one gentleman friend."

"Why not go?" I asked.

"I'm a New Englander at heart," smiled Ned, "and Thanksgiving is a sort of meaningful holiday. Particularly when you're alone in the great and wicked city. I've inquired of some of the fellows about Queen Bess's dinner. It seems that she gives one every Thanksgiving and that they're quite a tradition or institution. I can't find out what sort they are, though. I suspect some sort of an orgy on the order of the Black Mass."

At 2 o'clock we left our room and headed for the house of Queen Bess.

A huge and ornamental chamber known as the ballroom, or the parlor, had been converted into a dining-room. Ned and I were early. Six or seven men had arrived. They stood around ill at ease, looking at the flamboyant paintings on the wall as if they were inspecting the Titian room of some museum. Ned, who knew the town, pointed out two of the six

186

as men of means. One was manager of a store. One was a billiard champion in a Michigan Avenue club.

Gradually the room filled up. A dozen more men arrived. Each was admitted by invitation as we had been. Sally, the colored mammy of the house, took charge and bade us be seated. Some twenty men took their places about the long rectangular table. And then a pianist entered. I think it was Prof. Schultz. He played the piano in the ballrooms of the district. He came in in a brand-new frock coat and patent leather shoes and sat down at the ivories. There was a pause and then the professor struck up, doloroso pianissimo, the tune of "Home, Sweet Home."

As the first notes carrying the almost audible words, "Mid pleasures and palaces" arose from the piano the folding doors at the end of the ballroom parted and there appeared Queen Bess, followed by fifteen of the girls who sold drinks for her. Queen Bess was dressed in black, her white hair coiffured like a hospital superintendent's. Her girls were dressed in simple afternoon frocks. Neither rouge nor beads were to be seen on them. And as the professor played "Home, Sweet Home" Queen Bess marched her companions solemnly down the length of the ballroom and seated them at the table.

I remember that before the numerous servitors started functioning Queen Bess made a speech. She stood up at the head of the table, her red face beaming under her white hair and her black eyes commanding the attention of the men and women before her.

"All of you know who I am, blankety blank," said Queen Bess, "and, blankety blank, what a reputation I got. All of you know. But I've invited you to this blankety blank dinner, hoping you will humor me for the afternoon and pretend you forget. I would like to see you enjoy yourselves at the banquet board, eat and drink what wine there is and laugh and be thankful, but without pulling any blankety blank rough stuff. I would like to see you enjoy yourselves as if you were

187

in—in your own homes. Which I take it none of you gentlemen have got, seeing you are sitting here at the board of Queen Bess.

"Now, gentlemen," she concluded, "if it's asking too much of you to forget, the fault is mine and not yours. And nobody will be penalized or bawled out, blankety blank him, for being unable to forget. But if you can forget, and if you can let us enjoy ourselves for an afternoon in a blankety blank decent and God-fearing way—God love you."

And Queen Bess sat down. We ate and drank and laughed till seven o'clock that evening. And I remember that not one of the twenty men present used a profane word during this time; not one of them did or said anything that wouldn't have passed muster in his own home, if he had one. And that no one got drunk except Queen Bess. Yes, Queen Bess in her black dress got very drunk and swore like a trooper and laughed like a crazy child. And when the party was over Queen Bess stood at the door and we passed out, shaking hands with her and giving her our thanks. She stood, steadying herself against the door beam, and saying to each of us as she shook our hands:

"God love you. God love you for bringing happiness to a blankety blank blank like old Queen Bess."

THE DAGGER VENUS

The great Gabriel Salvini, whose genius has electrified the populace of a thousand vaudeville centers, sat in his suite at the Astor Hotel and listened glumly to the strains from a phonograph.

"What is the use?" growled the great Salvini. "It is no use. You listen to her."

"New music for your act, signor?"

"No, no, no. My wife. You hear her? She lie on the floor. The phonograph music play. The man call from the phonograph, 'one, two; one, two; one, higher; one, two.' And my wife, she lie on the floor and she kick up. She kick down. She roll over. She bend back. She bend forward. But it is no use."

"Madam is reducing, then, signor?"

"Bah! She kick. She roll. She jump. I say 'Lucia, what good for you to kick and jump when tonight you sit down and you eat; name of God, how you eat! Potatoes and more potatoes. Bread with butter on it. Meat, pie, cream, candy—ten thousand devils! She eat and eat until the eyes stick out. There is no more place to put. And I say, 'Lucia, you eat enough for six weeks every time you set down to the table.' I say, 'Lucia, look how the MacSwiney of Ireland go for thirty weeks without eating one bite.' Bah!"

"It is difficult to make a woman stop eating, signor."

"Difficult! Aha, but she must stop, or what become of me, the great Salvini, who have 200 medals? Look! I will show you from my book what they say of me. They say, 'Salvini is the greatest in his line.' They say, 'Here is genius; here is a man whose skill transcends the imagination.' So what I do if madam keep on growing fatter? Ah, you hear that music? It drive me crazy. I sit every day and listen. You hear her kick. Bang, bang! That's how she kick up when she lie on the back. Ah, it is tragedy, tragedy!"

I nodded in silence as the great Salvini arose and moved across the room, a dapper figure in a scarlet dressing gown and green silk slippers. He returned with a fresh load of cigarettes. I noticed his hands—thin, gentle-looking fingers, like a woman's. They quivered perceptibly as he lighted his smoke, and I marveled at this—that the wizard fingers of the great Gabriel Salvini should shake!

"I tell you my story," he resumed. "I tell no one else. But you shall hear it. It is a story of—of this." And he clapped his hand despairingly over his heart. "I suffer. Name of God, I suffer every day, every night. And why? because! You listen to her. She still kick and kick and kick. And I sit here and think 'Where will it all end?' Another five pounds and I am ruined.

"It is ten years ago I meet her. Ah, so beautiful, so sweet, so light—like this." And the great Salvini traced the wavering elfin proportions of the Lucia of his youth in the air with his hands.

"And I say to her, 'My beloved, my queen, you and I will be married and we will work together and grow famous and rich.' And she say, 'Yes.' So we marry and begin work at once. I am in Milan, in Italy. And all through the honeymoon I study my Lucia. For my work is hard. All through the honeymoon I use only little stickers I throw at her. I begin that way. Five, six, seven hours a day we practice. Ah, so sweet and beautiful she is as she stand against the board and I throw the little stickers at her. She smile at me, 'Have courage, Salvini.' And I see the love in her eyes and am happy and my arm and wrist are sure.

"Then I buy the knives to throw at her. I buy the best. Beautiful knives. I have them made for her special. For not a hair of my beloved's head must be touched. And we practice with the knives. I am then already famous. Everybody in Italy knows Salvini, the great knife thrower. They say, 'Never has there been a young man of such genius with the knives.' But I am only begin.

"Our début is a success. What do I say, 'Success!' Bah! It is like wildfire. They stand up and cheer. 'Salvini, Salvini!' they cry. And she, my beloved, stand against the board framed by the beautiful knives that fit exactly around her—to an inch, to a quarter inch, to a hair from her ears and neck. And she stand, and as they cheer for Salvini, the great Salvini, I see her smile at me. Ah, how sweet she is! How happy I am!

"And so we go on. I train all the time. Soon I know the outline of my Lucia so well I can close my eyes and throw knives at her, and always they come with the point only a hair away from her body. I pin her dress against the board. Her arms she stretch out and I give her two sleeves of knives. And for five years, no for eight years, everything go well. Never once I touch her. Always I watch her eyes when I throw and her eyes give me courage.

"But then what happen? Ah, ten thousand devils, she begin. She grow fat. One night I send a knife through the skin of her arm. I cannot go on with the act. I must stop. I break down and weep. For I love her so much the blood that comes from her arm drive me crazy. But I say, 'How did the great Salvini make such a mistake? It is incredible.' Then I look at her and I see something. She is getting fat. Name of God, I shudder. I say, 'Lucia, we are ruined. You get fat. I can only throw knives at you like you were, like we have studied together. You get fat. I must change my throw. I cannot!'"

The great Salvini raised his shoulders in a despairing shrug.

"Two years ago that was," he whispered. "She weigh one hundred fifty pounds when we marry. So pretty, so light she is. But now she weigh already two hundred pounds, and she is going up. She will not listen to me.

"It is the eat, the eat, the terrible eat which do this. And every night when we perform I shiver, I grow cold. I stand looking at her as she take her place on the board. And I see she have grow bigger. Perhaps it is nothing to you, a woman grown bigger. But to Salvini it is ruin.

"I throw the knife. Zip it goes and I close my eyes each time. I no longer dare give her the beautiful frame as before. But I must throw away. Because for eight years I have thrown at a target of 150 pounds. And my art cannot change.

"Some day she will be sorry. Yes, some day she will understand what she is doing to me. She will eat, eat until she grow so fat that it is all my target that I mastered on the honeymoon. And I will throw the knife over. She will no longer be Lucia, and it will hit. Name of God, it will hit her and sink in."

"Well, she will have learned a lesson then, signor."

"She will have learned. But me, I will be ruined. They will laugh. They will say, 'Salvini, the great Salvini, is done. He cannot throw the knives any more. Look, last night he hit his wife. Twice, three, times he threw the knives into her.' *Sapristi!* It is the stubbornness of womankind.

"I will tell you. Why does she eat, eat, eat? Why does she grow fat? Because she no longer loves me. No, she do it on purpose to ruin me."

And the great Salvini covered his ears with his hands as the phonograph continued relentlessly, "one, two, one, two, higher, two."

LETTERS

One of the drawers in my desk is full of letters that people have sent in. Some of them are knocks or boosts, but most of them are tips. There are several hundred tips on stories in the drawer.

Today, while looking them over I thought that these tips were a story in themselves. To begin with, the different kinds of stationery and the different kinds of handwriting. You would think that stationery and handwriting so varied would contain varied suggestions and varied points of view.

But from the top of the pile to the bottom—through 360 letters written on 360 different kinds of paper—there runs only one tip. And in the 360 different kinds of handwriting there runs only one story.

"There is a man I see almost every day on my way home from work," writes one, "and I think he would make a good story. There is something queer about him. He keeps mumbling to himself all the time." This tip is on plain stationery.

"—and I see the old woman frequently," writes another. "Nobody knows who she is or what she does. She is sure a woman of mystery. You ought to be able to get a good story out of her." This tip is on pink stationery.

"I think you can find him around midnight walking through the city hall. He walks through the hall every midnight and whistles queer tunes. Nobody has ever talked to him and they don't know what he does there. There is certainly a queer story in that man." This tip is written on a business letterhead.

"She lives in a back room and so far as anybody knows has no occupation. There's something awfully queer about her and I've often wondered what the mystery about her really was. Won't you look her up and write it out? Her address is—" This tip is on monogrammed paper.

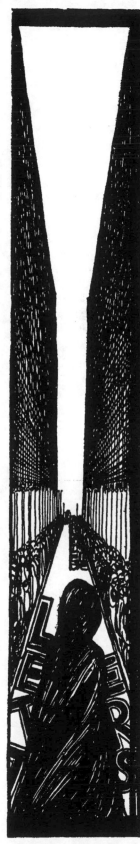

"I've been waiting for you to write about the queer old man who hangs out on the Dearborn Street bridge. I've passed him frequently and he's always at the same place. I've wondered time and again what his history was and why he always stood in the same place." This tip is on a broker's stationery.

"He sells hot beans in the loop and he's an old-timer. He's always laughing and whenever I see him I think, 'There's a story in that old man. There's sure something odd about him.' " This tip is on scratch paper.

"I saw her first several years ago. She was dressed all in black and was running. As it was past midnight I thought it strange. But I've seen her since and always late at night and she's always running. She must be about forty years old and from what I could see of her face a very curious kind of woman. In fact, we call her the woman of mystery in our neighborhood. Come out to Oakley Avenue some night and see for yourself. There's a wonderful story in that running woman, I'm certain." This tip is signed "A Stenographer."

They continue—tips on strange, weird, curious, odd, old, chuckling, mysterious men and women. Solitaries. Enigmatic figures moving silently through the streets. Nameless ones; exiles from the free and easy conformity of the town.

If you should read these letters all through at one sitting you would get a very strange impression of the city. You would see a procession of mysterious figures flitting through the streets, an unending swarm of dim ones, queer ones. And then as you kept on reading this procession would gradually focus into a single figure. This is because all the letters are so nearly alike and because the mysterious ones offered as tips are described in almost identical terms.

So the dim ones, the queer ones, would become a composite, and you would have in your thought the image of a single one. A huge, nebulous caricature—hooded, its head lowered, its eyes peering furtively from under shaggy brows, its thin fingers fumbling under a great black cloak, its feet moving in a soundless shuffle over the pavement.

Sometimes I have gone out and found the "woman of mystery" given in a letter. Usually an embittered creature living in the memory of wrongs that life has done her. Or a psychopathic case suffering from hallucinations or at war with its own impulses. And each of them has said, "I hate people. I don't like this neighborhood. And I keep to myself."

The letters all ask, "Who is this one?"

But that doesn't begin to answer the question the letters ask, "Who is it?"

The story of the odd ones is perhaps no more interesting than the story that might be written of the letters that "tip them off." A story here, of the harried, buried little figures that make up the swarm of the city and of the way they glimpse mystery out of the corners of their eyes. Of the way they pause for a moment on their treadmill to wonder about the silent, shuffling caricature with its hooded face and its thin fingers groping under its heavy black cloak.

In another drawer I have stored away letters of another kind. Letters that the caricature sends me. Queer, marvelous scrawls that remind one of spiders and bats swinging against white backgrounds. These letters are seldom signed. They are written almost invariably on cheap blue lined pad paper.

There are at least two hundred of them. And if you should read them all through at one sitting you would get a strange sense that this caricature of the hooded face was talking to you. That the Queer One who shuffles through the streets was sitting beside you and whispering marvelous things into your ear.

He writes of the stars, of inventions that will revolutionize man, of discoveries he has made, of new continents to be visited, of trips to the moon and of buried races that live beneath the rivers and mountains. He writes of amazing crimes he has committed, of weird longings that will not let him sleep. And, too, he writes of strange gods which man should worship. He pours out his soul in a fantastic scrawl. He says: "One is all. God looked down and saw ants. The wheel of life turns seven times and you can see between. You will sometime understand this. But now you have curtains on your eyes."

Now that you have read all the letters the city becomes a picture. An office in which sits a well-dressed business man dictating to a pretty stenographer. They are hard at work, but as they work their eyes glance furtively out of a tall, thin window. Some one is passing outside the window. A strange figure, hooded, head down, with his hands moving queerly under his great black cloak.

THE MOTHER

She sat on one of the benches in the Morals Court. The years had made a coarse mask of her face. There was nothing to see in her eyes. Her hands were red and leathery, like a man's. They had done a man's work.

A year-old child slept in her arms. It was bundled up, although the courtroom itself was suffocating. She was waiting for Blanche's case to come up. Blanche had been arrested by a policeman for—well, for what? Something about a man. So she would lose $2.00 by not being at work at the store today. Why did they arrest Blanche? She was in that room with the door closed. But the lawyer said not to worry. Yes, maybe it was a mistake. Blanche never did nothing. Blanche worked at the store all day.

At night Blanche went out. But she was a young girl. And she had lots of friends. Fine men. Sometimes they brought Blanche home late at night. Blanche was her daughter.

The woman with the sleeping child in her arms looked around. The room was nice. A big room with a good ceiling. But the people looked bad. Maybe they had done something and had been arrested. There was one man with a bad face. She watched him. He came quickly to where she was sitting. What was he saying? A lawyer.

"No, I don't want no lawyer," the woman with the child mumbled. "No, no."

The man went back. He kept pretty busy, talking to lots of people in the room. So he was a lawyer. Blanche had a lawyer. She had paid him $10. A lot of money.

"Shh, Paula!" the woman whispered. Paula was the name of the sleeping child. It had stirred in the bundle.

"Shh! Mus'n't. Da-ah-ah-ah——"

She rocked sideways with the bundle and crooned over it. Her heavy coarsened face seemed to grow surprised as she stared into the bundle. The child grew quiet.

197

The judge took his place. Business started. From where she sat the woman with the child couldn't hear anything. She watched little groups of men and women form in front of the judge. Then they went away and other groups came.

The lawyer had said not to worry. Just wait for Blanche's name and then come right up. Not to worry.

"Shh, Paula, shh! Da-ah-ah-ah——"

There was Blanche coming out of the door. She looked bad. Her face. Oh, yes, poor girl, she worked too hard. But what could she do? Only work. And now they arrested her. They arrested Blanche when the streets were full of bums and loafers, they arrested Blanche who worked hard.

Go up in front like the lawyer said. Sure. There was Blanche going now. And the lawyer, too. He had a better face than the other one who came and asked.

"And is this the woman?"

The lawyer laughed because the judge asked this.

"Oh, no," he said; "no, your honor, that's her mother. Step up, Blanche."

What did the policeman say?

"Shh! Paula, shh! Da-ah——" She couldn't hear on account of Paula moving so much and crying. Paula was hungry. She'd have to stay hungry a little while. What man? That one!

But the policeman was talking about the man, not about Blanche.

"He said, your honor, that she'd been following him down Madison Street for a block, talking to him and finally he stopped and she asked him——"

"Shh! Paula, don't! Bad girl! Shh!"

That man with the black mustache. Who was he?

"Yes, your honor, I never saw her before. I walk in the street and she come up and talk to me and say, 'You wanna come home with me?'"

"Blanche, how long has this been going on?"

Look, Blanche was crying. Shh, Paula, shh! The judge
was speaking. But Blanche didn't listen. The woman with
the child was going to say, "Blanche, the judge," but her tongue
grew frightened.

"Speak up, Blanche." The judge said this.

She could hardly hear Blanche. It was funny to see her
cry. Long ago she used to cry when she was a baby like Paula.
But since she went to work she never cried. Never cried.

"Oh, judge! Oh, judge! Please—"

Shh, Paula! Da-ah-ah-ah—" Why was this? What
would the judge do?

"Have you ever been arrested before, Blanche?"

No, no, no! She must tell the judge that. The woman
with the child raised her face.

"Please, judge," she said, "No! No! She never arrested
before. She's a good girl."

"I see," said the judge. "Does she bring her money
home?"

"Yes, yes, judge! Please, she brings all her money home.
She's a good girl."

"Ever seen her before, officer?"

"Well, your honor, I don't know. I've seen her in the
street once or twice, and from the way she was behavin', your
honor, I thought she needed watchin'."

"Never caught her, though, officer?"

No, your honor, this is the first time."

"Hm," said his honor.

Now the lawyer was talking. What was he saying? What
was the matter? Blanche was a good girl. Why they arrest
her?

"Shh, Paula, shh! Mus'n't." She held the child closer
to her heavy bosom. Hungry. But it must wait. Pretty
soon.

He was a nice judge. "All right," he said, you can go,
Blanche. But if they bring you in again it'll be the House of

the Good Shepherd. Remember that. I'll let you go on account of her."

A nice judge. "Thank you, thank you, judge. Shh, Paula! Goo-by."

Now she would find out. She would ask Blanche. They could talk aloud in the hallway.

"Blanche, come here." A note of authority came into the woman's voice. A girl of eighteen walking at her side turned a rouged, tear-stained face.

"Aw, don't bother me, ma. I got enough trouble."

"What was the matter with the policeman?"

"Aw, he's a boob. That's all."

"But what they arrest you for, Blanche? I knew it was a mistake. But what they arrest you for, Blanche? I gave him $10."

"Aw, shut up! Don't bother me."

The woman shrugged her shoulders and turned to the child in her arms.

"Da-ah-ah, Paula. Mamma feed you right away. Soon we find place to sit down. Shh, Paula! Mus'n't. Da-ah-ah—"

When she looked up Blanche had vanished. She stood still for a while and then, holding the year-old child closer to her, walked toward the elevator. There was nothing to see in her eyes.

CLOCKS AND OWL CARS

As they say in the melodramas, the city sleeps. Windows have said good-night to one another. Rooftops have tucked themselves away. The pavements are still. People have vanished. The darkness sweeping like a great broom through the streets has emptied them.

The clock in the window of a real estate office says "Two." A few windows down another clock says "Ten minutes after two."

The newspaper man waiting for a Sheffield Avenue owl car walks along to the next corner, listening for the sound of car wheels and looking at the clocks. The clocks all disagree. They all hang ticking with seemingly identical and indisputable precision. Their white faces and their black numbers speak in the dark of the empty stores. "Tick-tock, Time never sleeps. Time keeps moving the hands of the city's clocks around and around."

Alas, when clocks disagree what hope is there for less methodical mechanisms, particularly such humpty-dumpty mechanisms as tick away inside the owners of clocks? The newspaper man must sigh. These clocks in the windows of the empty stores along Sheffield Avenue seem to be arguing. They present their arguments calmly, like meticulous professors. They say: "Eight minutes of two. Three minutes of two. Two. Four minutes after two. Ten minutes after two."

Thus the confusions of the day persist even after the darkness has swept the streets clean of people. There being nobody else to dispute, the clocks take it up and dispute the hour among themselves.

The newspaper man pauses in front of one half-hidden clock. It says "Six." Obviously here is a clock not running. Its hands have stopped and it no longer ticks. But, thinks the newspaper man, it is not to be despised for that. At least it is the only clock in the neighborhood that achieves perfect

accuracy. Twice a day while all the other clocks in the street are disputing and arguing, this particular clock says "Six" and of all the clocks it alone is precisely accurate.

In the distance a yellow light swings like an idle lantern over the car tracks. So the newspaper man stops at the corner and waits. This is the owl car. It may not stop. Sometimes cars have a habit of roaring by with an insulting indifference to the people waiting for them to stop at the corner. At such moments one feels a fine rage, as if life itself had insulted one. There have been instances of men throwing bricks through the windows of cars that wouldn't stop and cheerfully going to jail for the crime.

But this car stops. It comes to a squealing halt that must contribute grotesquely to the dreams of the sleepers in Sheffield Avenue. The night is cool. As the car stands silent for a moment it becomes, with its lighted windows and its gay paint, like some modernized version of the barque in which Jason journeyed on his quest.

The seats are half filled. The newspaper man stands on the platform with the conductor and stares at the passengers. The conductor is an elderly man with an unusually mild face.

The people in the car try to sleep. Their heads try to make use of the window panes for pillows. Or they prop their chins up in their palms or they are content to nod. There are several young men whose eyes are reddened. A young woman in a cheap but fancy dress. And several middle-aged men. All of them look bored and tired. And all of them present a bit of mystery.

Who are these passengers through the night? And what has kept them up? And where are they going or coming from? The newspaper man has half a mind to inquire. Instead he picks on the conductor, and as the car bounces gayly through the dark, cavernous streets the mild-faced conductor lends himself to a conversation.

"I been on this line for six years. Always on the owl car," he says. "I like it better than the day shift. I was married, but my wife died and I don't find much to do with my evenings, anyway.

"No, I don't know any of these people, except there's a couple of workingmen who I take home on the next trip. Mostly they're always strangers. They've been out having a good time, I suppose. It's funny about them. I always feel sorry for 'em. Yes, sir, you can't help it.

"There's some that's been out drinking or hanging around with women and when they get on the car they sort of slide down in their seats and you feel like there was nothing much to what they'd been doing. Pessimistic? No, I ain't pessimistic. If you was ridin' this car like I you'd see what I mean.

"It's like watchin' people afterwards. I mean after they've done things. They always seem worse off then. I suppose it's because they're all sleepy. But standin' here of nights I feel that it's more than that. They're tired sure enough but they're also feeling that things ain't what they're cracked up to be.

"I seldom put anybody off. The drunks are pretty sad and I feel sorry for them. They just flop over and I wake them up when it comes their time. Sometimes there's girls and they look pretty sad. And sometimes something really interestin' comes off. Once there was a lady who was cryin' and holdin' a baby. On the third run it was. I could see she'd up and left her house all of a sudden on account of a quarrel with her husband, because she was only half buttoned together.

"And once there was a man whose pictures I see in the papers the next day as having committed suicide. I remembered him in a minute. Well, no, he didn't look like he was going to commit suicide. He looked just about like all the other passengers—tired and sleepy and sort of down."

The mild-faced conductor helped one of his passengers off.

"Don't you ever wonder what keeps these people out or where they're going at this time of night?" the newspaper man pursued as the car started up again.

"Well," said the conductor, "not exactly. I've got it figured out there's nothing much to that and that they're all kind of alike. They've been to parties or callin' on their girls or just got restless or somethin'. What's the difference? All I can say about 'em is that you get so after years you feel sorry for 'em all. And they're all alike—people as ride on the night run cars are just more tired than the people I remember used to ride on the day run cars I was on before my wife died."

The clock in a candy store window says "Three-twelve." A few windows down, another clock says "Three-five." The newspaper man walks to his home studying the clocks. They all disagree as before. And yet their faces are all identical— as identical as the faces of the owl car passengers seem to the conductor. And here is a clock that has stopped. It says "Twenty after four." And the newspaper man thinks of the picture the conductor identified in the papers the next morning. The picture said something like "Twenty after four" at the wrong time. It's all a bit mixed up.

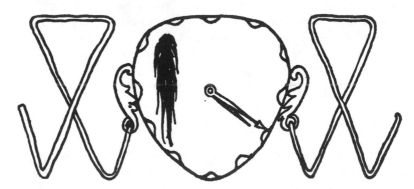

CONFESSIONS

The rain mutters in the night and the pavements like dark mirrors are alive with impressionistic cartoons of the city. The little, silent street with its darkened store windows and rain-veiled arc lamps is as lonely as a far-away train whistle.

Over the darkened stores are stone and wooden flat buildings. Here, too, the lights have gone out. People sleep. The rain falls. The gleaming pavements amuse themselves with reflections.

I have an hour to wait. From the musty smelling hallway where I stand the scene is like an old print—an old London print—that I have always meant to buy and put in a frame but have never found.

Writing about people when one is alone under an electric lamp, and thinking about people when one stands watching the rain in the dark streets, are two different diversions. When one writes under an electric lamp one pompously marshals ideas; one remembers the things people say and do and believe in, and slowly these things replace people in one's mind. One thinks (in the calm of one's study): "So-and-so is a Puritan . . . . he is viciously afraid of anything which will disturb the idealized version of himself in which he believes—and wants other people to believe. . . ." Yes, one thinks So-and-so is this and So-and-so is that. And it all seems very simple. People focus into clearly outlined ideas—definitions. And one can sit back and belabor them, hamstring them, pull their noses, expose their absurdities and derive a deal of satisfaction from the process. Iconoclasm is easy and warming under an electric light in one's study.

But in the rain at night, in the dark street staring at darkened windows, watching the curious reflections in the pavements—it is different in the rain. The night mutters and whispers.

"People," one thinks, "tired, silent people sleeping in the dark."

Ideas do not come so easily or so clearly. The ennobling angers which are the emotion of superiority in the iconoclast do not rise so spontaneously. And one does not say "People are this and people are that. . . ." No, one pauses and stares at the dark chatter of the rain and a curious silence saddens one's mind.

Life is apart from ideas. And the things that people say and believe in and for which they die and in behalf of which they invent laws and codes—these have nothing to do with the insides of people. Puritan, hypocrite, criminal, dolt—these are paper-thin masks. It is diverting to rip them in the calm of one's study.

Life that warms the trees into green in the summer, that sends birds circling through the air, that spreads a tender, passionate glow over even the most barren wastes—people are but one of its almost too many children. The dark, the rain, the lights, people asleep in bed, the wind, the snow that will fall tomorrow, the ice, flowers, sunlight, country roads, pavements and stars—all these are the same. Through all of them life sends its intimate and sacred breath.

One becomes aware of such curious facts in the rain at night and one's iconoclasm, like a broken umbrella, hangs useless from one's hand. Tomorrow these people who are now asleep will be stirring, giving vent to outrageous ideas, championing incredulous banalities, prostrating themselves before imbecile superstitions. Tomorrow they will rise and begin forthwith to lie, quibble, cheat, steal, fourflush and kill, each and all inspired by the solacing monomania that every one of their words and gestures is a credible variant of perfection. Yes, tomorrow they will be as they were yesterday.

But in this rain at night they rest from their perfections, they lay aside for a few hours their paper masks. And one can contemplate them with a curious absence of indignation

207

or criticism.   There is something warm and intimate about
the vision of many people sleeping in the beds above the darkened store fronts of this little street.   Their bodies have been in
the world so long—almost as long as the stones out of which
their houses are made.   So many things have happened to
them, so many debacles and monsters and horrors have swept
them off their feet. . . . and always they have kept on—
persisting through floods, volcanic eruptions, plagues and wars.

Heroic and incredible people.   Endlessly belaboring
themselves with ideas, gods, taboos, and philosophies.   Yet
here they are, still in this silent little street.   The world has
grown old.   Trees have decayed and races died out.   But here
above the darkened store fronts lies the perpetual miracle
. . . . People in whom life streams as naïve and intimate as
ever.

Yes, it is to life and not people one makes one's obei-
sance.   Toward life no iconoclasm is possible, for even that
which is in opposition to its beauty and horror must of necessity be a part of them.

It rains.   The arc lamps gleam through the monotonous
downpour.   One can only stand and dream. . . . how
charming people are since they are alive. . . . how charming the rain is and the night. . . . And how foolish arguments are. . . . how banal are these cerebral monsters who
pose as iconoclasts and devote themselves grandiloquently and
inanely to disturbing the paper masks. . . .

I walk away from the musty smelling hallway.   A dog
steps tranquilly out of the shadows nearby.   He surveys the
street and the rain with a proprietary calm.

It would be amusing to walk in the rain with a strange
dog.   I whistle softly and reassuringly to him. He pauses and
turns his head toward me, surveying me with an air of vague
discomfort.   What do I want of him? . . . . he thinks . . . .

who am I? .·. . . have I any authority? . . . . what will happen to him if he doesn't obey the whistle?

Thus he stands hestitating. Perhaps, too, I will give him shelter, a kindness never to be despised. A moment ago, before I whistled, this dog was tranquil and happy in the rain. Now he has changed. He turns fully around and approaches me, a slight cringe in his walk. The tranquillity has left him. At the sound of my whistle he has grown suddenly tired and lonely and the night and rain no longer lure him. He has found another companionship.

And so together we walk for a distance, this dog and I, wondering about each other. . . .

AN IOWA HUMORESQUE

In a room at the Auditorium Hotel a group of men and women connected with the opera were having tea. As they drank out of the fragile cups and nibbled at the little cakes they boasted to each other of their love affairs.

"And I had the devil of a time getting rid of her," was the motif of the men's conversation. The women said, "And I just couldn't shake him. It was awful."

There was one—an American prima donna—who grew pensive as the amorous boasting increased. An opulent woman past 35, dark-haired, great-eyed; a robust enchantress with a sweep to her manner. Her beauty was an exaggeration. Exaggerated contours, colors, features that needed perspective to set them off. Diluted by distance and bathed by the footlights she focused prettily into a Manon, a Thaïs, an Isolde. But in the room drinking tea she had the effect of a too startling close-up—a rococo siren cramped for space.

The barytone leaned unctuously across the small table and said to her with a preposterous archness of manner:

"And how does it happen, my dear, that you have nothing to tell us?"

"Because she has too much," said one of the orchestra men, laughingly.

The prima donna smiled.

"Oh, I can tell a story as well as anybody," she said. "In fact, I was just thinking of one. You know I was in Iowa last month. And I visited the town where I was born and lived as a girl—until I was nineteen. It's funny."

Again the pensive stare out of the window at the chill-looking autumn sky and the sharp outlines of the city roofs.

"Go on," her hostess cried. To her guests she added, in the social curtain-raiser manner peculiar to rambunctious hostesses, "if Mugs tells anything about herself you can be sure it'll be something immense. Go on, Mugs." Mugs is one of the nicknames the prima donna is known by among her friends.

"We went to school together," the prima donna smiled, "John and I. And I don't think I've ever loved anybody as I loved him. He used to frighten me to death. You see, I was ambitious. I wanted to be somebody. And John wanted me to marry him. Somehow marriage wasn't what I wanted then. There were other things. I had started singing and at night I used to lie awake, not wanting to sleep. I was so taken up with my dreams and plans that I hated to lose consciousness. That's a fact.

"Well, John grew more and more insistent. And one evening he came to call on me. I was alone on the porch. John was about twenty-three then. That was about twenty years ago. He was a tall, good-looking, sharp-faced young man with lively eyes. I thought him marvelous at the time. And he stood on the steps of the porch and talked to me. I never forgot a word he said. I have never heard anything so wonderful since."

The barytone shrugged his shoulders politely and said "Hm!"

"Oh, I know," smiled the prima donna, "you're the Great Lover and all that. But you never could talk as John did that evening on the porch—in Iowa. He stood there and said, 'Mugs, you're going to regret this moment for the rest of your life. There'll be nights when you'll wake up shivering and crying and you'll want to kill yourself. Why? Because you didn't marry me. Because you had your chance to marry me and turned it down. Remember. Remember how I'm standing here talking to you—unknown—a country boy. Remember that when you hear of me again.'

" 'What are you going to do?' I asked.

"'I'm going to be president of the United States,' he said. And he said it so that there was truth in it. As I looked at him standing on the steps I felt frightened to death. There he was, going to be president of the United States, and there was I, throwing the greatest chance in the world away. He knew I believed him and that made it worse. He went on talking in a sort of oracular singsong that drove me mad.

" 'I'm not asking you again. You've had your chance, Mugs. And you've thrown it away. All right. It'll not be said afterward that John Marcey made a fool of himself. Good-bye.' "

The prima donna sighed. "Yes," she went on, looking into her empty teacup; "it was good-bye. He walked away, erect, his shoulders high, his body swinging. And I sat there shivering. I had turned down a president of the United States! Me, a gawky little Iowa girl. And, what was worse, I was in love with him, too. Well, I remember sitting on the porch till the folks came home from prayer meeting and I remember going to bed and lying awake all night, crying and shivering.

"I didn't see John Marcey again. I stayed only a week longer and then I came to Chicago to study music. My folks were able to finance me for a time. But I never forgot him. It was John who had started me for Chicago. And it was John who kept me practicing eight hours a day, studying and practicing until I thought I'd drop.

"I was going to make good. When he became president I was going to be somebody. I wasn't going to do what he said I would, wake up cursing myself and remembering my lost chance. So I went right on working my head off and finally it was Paris and finally it was a job in London. And I never stopped working.

"But the funny part was that I gradually forgot about John Marcey. When I had arrived as an opera singer he was entirely dead for me. But last month I visited my home town. I was passing through and couldn't resist getting off and looking up people I knew as a girl. My folks are dead, you know.

"And when I walked down the street—the same old funny little Main Street—I remembered John Marcey. And, would you believe it, that same feeling of fear came back to me as I'd had that night on the porch when he made his 'remember' speech. I got curious as the devil about John and felt afraid to inquire. But finally I was talking to an old, old man who runs the drug-store on the corner of Main and Sixth streets there. I'd recognized him through the window and gone inside and shaken hands; and I asked him:

" 'Do you remember John Marcey?'

" 'Marcey——Marcey?' he repeated. 'Oh, yes. Old Marse. Why, yes. Sure.' And he kept nodding his head. Then I asked with my heart in my mouth, 'What's become of him?' And the old druggist who was looking out of his store window adjusted his glasses and pointed with his finger. 'There he is. There he is. Wait a minute. I'll call him.'

"And there was John, my president of the United States, hunched over on the seat of a garbage wagon driving a woebegone nag down the street. I grabbed hold of the druggist and said, 'Don't, I'll see him later.'

"Well, I couldn't stay in that town another minute. I hurried to the station and waited for the next train and kept thinking of John driving his garbage wagon, and his battered felt hat and his hangdog face until I thought I'd go mad.

"That's all," laughed the prima donna, "That's my love story." And she stared pensively into the empty teacup as the barytone moved a bit closer and began:

"I'll tell you about a Spanish girl I met in Prague that'll interest you——"

THE EXILE

The newspaper man told the story apropos of nothing at all. There was a pause in the talk among the well-dressed dinner guests. A very satisfied-looking man said:

"Well, thank God, this radical excitement is over."

Every one agreed it was fortunate and the newspaper man, an insufferably garrulous person, interjected: "That reminds me of Bill Haywood."

"Oh, yes," said the hostess, "he was the leader of all that terrible thing, wasn't he?"

"He was," said the newspaper man. "I knew him fairly well. I covered the I. W. W. trial in Judge Landis' court, where he and a hundred or so others were sent to prison."

"What was the charge against them?" inquired the satisfied one.

"I forget," said the newspaper man, "but I remember Haywood. The trial, of course, had something to do with the war. The war was going on then, you remember."

"Oh, yes, indeed," exclaimed the hostess. "It will take a long time to forget the war." And her eyes brightened.

"You were going to tell us about the I. W. W. trial," pursued the hostess a few minutes later.

"Oh, there's nothing much about that," said the newspaper man. "I was principally interested in Bill Haywood for a moment. You know they sent him to jail for twenty years or so. Anyway, that was his sentence."

"The scoundrel ran away," said the very satisfied one. "Funny they should let a man as unprincipled and dangerous as Haywood slip through their hands after sending him to jail."

"Yes, they let him escape to Russia, of all places," declared the hostess with indignation. "Where he could do the most harm. Oh, the government is so stupid at times it simply drives one furious. Or makes you laugh. Doesn't it?"

"Yes, he skipped his bond or something," said the newspaper man, "and became an exile."

The satisfied one snorted.

"Exile!" he derided. "You don't call a man an exile who runs away from a country he has always despised and fought against?"

"The last time I saw him," went on the newspaper man, as if he were unruffled, "was about four or five days before he disappeared. I was surprised to see him. I thought he was serving his time in jail. I hadn't been following the ins and outs and I wasn't aware he had got appeals and things and was still at large."

"Yes," said the satisfied one, "that's the trouble with this country. Too lenient toward these scoundrels. As if they were entitled to—"

"Justice," murmured the newspaper man. "Quite so. Our enemies are not entitled to justice. It is one of my oldest notions."

"But tell us about what this Haywood said," pursued the hostess. "It must have been funny meeting him."

"It was," said the newspaper man. "It was at the Columbia theater between acts in the evening. I had gone to see a burlesque show there. And between acts I was on the mezzanine floor. I went out to get a glass of water.

"As I was coming back whom do I see leaning against the railing but old Bill Haywood. I hadn't seen him for about two years, I guess. But he hadn't changed an iota. The same crooked-lipped smile. And his one eye staring ahead of him with a mildly amused light in it. A rather striking person was Bill. I suppose it was because he always seemed so calm outside.

"He remembered me and when I said hello to him he called me by name and I walked to his side. I started talking and said: 'Well, what are you doing here? I thought you were serving time in six jails.'

215

" 'Not yet,' said Haywood, 'but in a few days. The sentence starts next week.'

" 'Twenty years?'

" 'Oh, something like that.'

"Well," said the newspaper man, "I suddenly remembered that he was in a theater and I got kind of curious. I asked what he was doing in the theater and he looked at me and grinned.

" 'I'm all in,' he said. 'Been going the pace for about a month now. Out every night. Taking in all the glad spots and high spots.'

"This was so curious coming from Big Bill that I looked surprised. And he went on talking. Yes, sir, this Big Bill Haywood, the terror of organized society, was saying good-bye to his native land as if he were a sentimental playboy. He wasn't going to jail because by that time he had all his plans matured for his escape to Russia.

"But he knew he was going to leave the country and perhaps never come back again. So he was making the rounds.

" 'I've been to almost every show in town,' he went on talking, 'all the musical comedies, all the dramas, all the west side melodramas. I've been to almost all the cafés, the swell ones with the monkey-suit waiters and the old ones I've known myself for years. I drew up a list of all these places in town about a month ago and I've been following a schedule ever since.'

"I asked him," said the newspaper man, "if he liked the plays he'd seen. Bill grinned at that.

" 'It ain't that,' said Bill. 'No, it ain't that. It's only seeing them. You know, there's nothing like these kind of things anywhere else in the world.'

"And then the theater got dark and we said good-bye casually and went to our different seats. I didn't see Haywood again. About a week or so later I read the headline that he had fled the country. Nobody knew where he was, but people suspected. And then two weeks after that there was the story that he had reached Russia and was in Moscow.

"Well, when I read that," said the newspaper man, "I remembered all of a sudden how he had stood leaning against the railing at the Columbia theater saying good-bye to something. Making the rounds for a month saying good-bye in his own way to all the places he would never see again. Kind of odd, I thought, for Bill Haywood to do that. That isn't the way Nietzsche would have written a radical. But Dickens might have written it that way, like Bill.

"That's why whenever I see his name in print now," pursued the newspaper man, "I always think of the burlesque chorus on the stage kicking their legs and yodeling jazzily and Big Bill Haywood staring with his one eye, saying good-bye with his one eye.

"Tell me he's not an exile!" laughed the newspaper man suddenly.

ON A DAY LIKE THIS

On a day like this, he says, on a day like this, when the wind plays cello music across the rooftops. . . . I think about things. The town is like a fireless, dimly lighted room. Yesterday the windows sparkled with sunlight. To-day they stare like little coffin tops.

On a day like this, he says, on this sort of a day I walk along smoking a pipe and wonder what I was excited about yesterday. Then I remember, he says, that once it rained yesterday and I waited under the awning till it ended. I remember, he says, that once I walked swiftly down this street toward a building on the corner. It was vastly important that I reach this building. I remember, he says, that there were days I hurried down Clark Street and days I ran down Monroe Street. Now it is windy again. There is long silence over the noises of the street. The sky looks empty and old.

There were people gathered around an automobile that had bumped into the curbing. I stopped to watch them, he says. There was a man next to me with a heavy gray face, with loose lips and with intent eyes. There was another man and another—dozens of men—all of them people who had been hurrying in the street to get somewhere. And here they were standing and looking intently at an automobile with a twisted wheel.

I became aware that we were all looking with a strange intensity at this automobile; that we all stood as if waiting for something. Dozens of men hurrying somewhere suddenly stop and stand for ten, twenty, thirty minutes staring at a broken automobile. There was a reason for this. Always where there is a machine at work, digging or hammering piles, where there is a horse fallen, an auto crashed, a flapjack turner, a fountain pen demonstrator; where there is a magic clock that runs, nobody knows how, or a window puzzle that turns in a

218

drug-store window or anything that moves behind plate glass —always where there is any one of these things there are people like us standing riveted, attentive, unwavering.

People on artificial errands, hurrying like obedient automations through the streets; stern-faced people with dignified eyes, important-stepping people with grave decision stamped upon them; careless, innocuous-looking people—all these people look as if they had something in their heads, as if there were things of import driving them through the streets. But this is an error. Nothing in their heads. They are like the fish that swim beneath the water—a piece of shining tin captures their eyes and they pause and stare at it.

The broken automobile holds their eyes, holds them all riveted because—because it is something unordinary to look at, to think about. And there is nothing unordinary to look at or think about in their heads.

And I too, he says, on this day when the wind played cello music across the rooftops, stood in the crowd. We were all children, I noticed, more than that—infants. Open-mouthed infantile wonder staring out of our tired, gray faces. Men, without thought, men making a curious little confession in the busy street that they were not busy, that there is nothing in life at the moment that preoccupies them—that a broken automobile is a godsend, a diversion, a drama, a great happiness.

I smoked my pipe, he says, and began to wonder again. Why did they stare like this? And at what? And who were these staring ones? And what was it in them that stared? I thought of this, he says. Dead dreams, and forgotten defeats stood staring from the curb at the broken automobile. Men who had survived themselves, who had become compliant and automatic little forces in the engine of the city—these were ourselves on the curb.

And this is a weary thing to remember about the city. When I am tired, he says, and the plot of which I am hero, villain and Greek chorus suddenly vanish from my mind, I pause and look at something behind plate glass. A bauble catches my eye. Long minutes, half hours pass. There is a marvelous plentitude of baubles to look at. Machines digging, excavations, scaffoldings, advertisements, never are lacking.

And at such times I begin to notice how many of us there are. The hurry of the streets is an illusion. The noises that rise in clouds, and the too-many suits of clothes and hats that sweep by—all these things are part of an illusion. The fact drifts through my tired senses that there is an amazing silence in the street—the silence inside of people's heads. Everywhere I look I find these busy ones, these energetic ones stopped and standing like myself before a bauble in a window, before a broken automobile.

Of people, authors always make great plots. Authors always write of adventures and intrigues, of emotions and troubles and ideas which occupy people. People fall in love, people suffer defeats, people experience tragedies, happinesses, and there is no end to the action of people in books.

But here is a curious plot, he says, on a day like this. Here is a crowd around a broken automobile. The broken automobile has trapped them, betrayed them. They realize the broken automobile as a "practical" excuse to stop walking, to stop moving, to stop going anywhere or being anybody. Their serious concentration on the broken wheel enables them to pretend that they are logically interested in practical matters. Without which pretense it would be impossible for them to exist. Without which pretense they would become consciously dead. They must always seem, to themselves as well as to others, logically interested in something. Yes, always something.

But the plot is—and do not misunderstand this, he cautions—that the pretense here around the broken automobile grows shallow enough to plumb. There is nothing here. Two dozen men standing dead on a curbing, tricked into confessional by a little accident.

So I will begin a book tomorrow, he says, and empties his pipe as he talks, which will have to do with the make-believe of people in streets—the make-believe of being alive and being somebody and going somewhere.

And saying this, this garrulous one walks off with a high whistle on his lips and a grave triumph sitting on his shoulders.

JAZZ BAND IMPRESSIONS

The trombone player has a straight part. He umpah umps with the conventional trombone fatalism. Whatever the tune, whatever the harmonies, trombone umpah umps regardless. Umpah ump is the soul of all things. Cadenzas, glissandos, arpeggios, chromatics, syncopations, blue melodies —these are the embroidery of sound. From year to year these change, these pass. Only the umpah ump remains. And tonight the trombone player plays what he will play a thousand nights from tonight—umpah ump.

The bassoon and the bull fiddle—they umpah ump along. Underneath the quaver and whine of the jazz they beat the time, they make the tuneless rhythm. The feet dancing on the crowded cabaret floor listen cautiously for the trombone, the bassoon and the bull fiddle. They have a liaison with the umpah umps—the feet. Long ago they danced only to the umpah umps. There were no cadenzas, glissandos, arpeggios then. There was only the thumping of cedar wood on cedar wood, on ebony or taut deerskin.

Civilizations have risen, fallen and risen again. Armies, gods, races have been chewed into mist by the years. But the thumping remains. The feet of the dancers on the cabaret floor keep a rendezvous with the ebony on the taut deerskin, with the cedar wood beating on cedar wood.

The clarinet screeches, wails, moans and whistles. The clarinet flings an obbligato high over the heads of the dancers on the cabaret floor. It makes shrill sounds. It raves like a fireless Ophelia. It plays the clown, the tragedian, the acrobat.

A whimsical insanity lurks in the music of the clarinet. It stutters ecstasies. It postures like Tristan and whimpers like a livery-stable nag. It grimaces like Peer Gynt and winks like a lounge lizard, a cake eater.

It is not for the feet of the dancers on the crowded cabaret floor. The feet follow the umpah umps. The thoughts of the dancers follow the clarinet. The thoughts of the boobilariat dance easily to the tangled lyric of the clarinet. The thoughts tie themselves into crazy knots. The music of the clarinet becomes like crazily uncoiling whips. The thoughts of the dancers shake themselves loose from words under the spur of the whips. They begin to dance, not as the feet dance. There is another rhythm here. The rhythm of little ecstasies whimpering. Thus the thoughts of the dancers dance—dead hopes, wearied ambitions, vanishing youth do an inarticulate can-can in the heads of the dancers on the cabaret floor.

The cornet wears a wooden gag in its mouth and a battered black derby hangs over its end. Umpah ump from the trombone, the bull fiddle and the bassoon. Tangled lyrics from the clarinet. And the cornet cakewalks like a hoyden vampire, the cornet whinnies like an odalisque expiring in the arms of the Wizard of Oz.

Lust giggles at a sly jest out of the cornet. Passion thumbs its nose at the stars out of the cornet. The melody of jazz, the tin pan ghosts of Chopin, Tchaikowsky, Old Black Joe, Liszt and Mumbo Magumbo, jungle troubadour of the Congo, come whinnying out from under the pendant derby.

The dancers on the cabaret floor close their eyes and grin to themselves. The cornet kids them along. When they grow sad it burlesques their sorrow. The cornet laughs at them. It leers like a satyr master of ceremonies at them. It is Pan in a clown suit, Silenus on a trick mule, Eros in a Pullman smoker.

Laugh, dance, jerk, wiggle and kid all you want—but the Lady of the Sea Foam whispers a secret. Aphrodite, become a female barytone, still takes herself very seriously. Aphrodite, alas, is always serious. She gurgles a sonorous plaint out of the saxophone. The cornet sneers at her. The clarinet sneaks up on her and tweaks her nose. The trombone, the bull fiddle and the bassoon ignore her altogether. And the dancers on the cabaret floor are too busy to dance to her simple wails.

Yet there is no mistake. Aphrodite, the queen, abandoned by her courtiers and surrounded by this galaxy of mountebanks, is still Aphrodite. Big-bosomed, sleepy-eyed and sad lipped she walks invisible among the dancers on the cabaret floor and they listen to her voice out of the saxophone.

The drums, the piano and the violin give her a fluttering drape. But there are things to be seen. This is not the Aphrodite of the Blue Danube waltz—but a duskier, more mystical lady. There are no roses on her cheeks, no lilies in her skin. She is colored like a panther flower and her limbs are heavy with taboo magic. But she is still imperial. In vain the mountebanks and burlesqueries of her court. Her lips place themselves against the hearts of the dancers on the cabaret floor. And she croons her ancient hymns.

The hearts of the dancers give themselves to the saxophone. Their feet keep a rendezvous with the umpah umps. Their thoughts dance on the slack wire of the clarinet. Their veins beat time to the whinny of the derby wreathed cornet. The fiddles and the drums are partners for their arms and their muscles. But their hearts embrace shyly the Mother Aphrodite. Their hearts listen sadly and proudly and they almost forget to dance.

Midnight approaches. Enameled faces, stenciled smiles, painted eyes and slants of colored hats—these are the women. Careless, polite, suave, grinning—these are the men. The jazz band plays. The cabaret floor, jammed, seems to be moving around like a groaning turnstile.

Bodies are hidden. The spotlight from the balcony begins to throw a series of colors. Melody is lost. The jazz band is hammering like a mad blacksmith. Whang! Bam!

Whang! Bam! Nobody hears the music of the band. Bodies together move on the turnstile floor. This is the part of the feast of Belshazzar that the authorities censored in a Griffith movie. This is the description of Tiberius's court that the authorities suppressed. Here are the poems that hide on the forbidden shelves of the public library.

The pulp of figures dissolves. The hammering band has finished. Men and women, grown suddenly polite and social, return to their tables. Citizens of a neighborhood, toilers, clerks, fourflushers, wives, husbands, gropers, nobodies, less-than-nobodies—watch and see where they go. Into the brick holes, into the apartment buildings. They pack themselves away like ants in an anthill.

The nobodies—the gropers, husbands, wage-earners, fourflushers—but they made a violent picture a moment ago. Under the revolving colors of the floodlight and the hammering, whinnying music of the jazz band they became again the mask of Dionysus—the ancient satanical mask which nature slips over her head when in quest of diversion.

NIGHT DIARY

Where is the moon? Gone. This inferior luminary cannot compete with the corset ad signs and the ice cream ad signs that blaze in the night sky. We stand on a bridge that connects State Street and look at the river.

There are night shapes. But first we see the dark water of the river and silver, gold and ruby reflections of the bridge lights. These hang like carnival ribbons in the water. The "L" trains crawl over the Wells Street bridge and the water below them becomes alive with a moving silver image. For a moment the reflection of the "L" trains in the river seems like a ghostly waterfall. Then it changes and becomes something else. What? The light reflections in the dark water are baffling. It is a game to stand on the bridge and make up similes about them. They look like this, like that, like something else. Like golden pillars, like Chinese writing, like monotonous exclamation points.

There are boat shapes. The river docks bulge with shadows. The boat shapes emerge slowly from the shadows. These shapes, unlike the river reflections, do not suggest similes. They bulge in the darkness and their vanished outlines remind one of something. What? Of boats, of ships, of men.

Men and ships. Little lanterns hang like elfin watchmen from the sterns of ships. The bulldog noses of tugboats sleep against the docks. High overhead the corset ad and the ice cream ad blaze, wink and go out and turn on so as to attract the preoccupied eyes of people far away. Then the bridges count themselves to the west. First bridge, second bridge, third bridge. Street cars, auto lights and vague noises jerk eerily over the bridges.

The sleeping tugboats, launches and lake craft remind one of nothing at all except that there are engines. But as one stares at them they become secret. There is something mysterious about abandoned engines. It is almost as if one saw the

227

bodies of men lying in shadows. Engines and men are insep-
arable. And these boats that sleep in the river shadows are
parts of men. Amputations.

The night shapes increase. There are buildings. They
drift along the river docks. Dark windows and faded brick
lines. Their rooftops are like the steps of a giant stairway
that has broken down. Where is the moon? Here are windows to mirror its distant silver. Instead, the windows sleep.
The nervous electric signs that wink and do tricks throw an
intermittent glare over the windows.

Do you know the dark windows of the city, you gentlemen
who write continually of temples and art? Come, forget
your love for things you never saw, cathedrals and parthenons
that exist in the yesterdays you never knew. Come, look at
the fire escapes that are stamped like letter Z's against the mysterious rectangles; at the rhythmic flight of windows whose
black and silver wings are tipped with the yellow winkings of
the corset and ice cream signs. The windows over the dark
river are like an alphabet, like the keyboard of a typewriter.
They are like anything you want them to be. You have only to
wish and the dark windows take new patterns.

Wall shapes arise. Warehouses that have no windows.
Huge lines loom in the shadows. A vast panel of brick without
windows rises, vanishes. Buildings that stand like playing
blocks. The half-hidden shapes, the tracks of windows, the
patterns of rooftops suggest things—fortresses, palaces, dun-
geons, wars, witches and cathedrals.

But after watching them they lose these false significances.
They suggest nothing. They are the amputations of men.
Things, playthings men have left behind for the corset and
the ice cream ads to wink at. And this is the real secret of their
beauty. The night devours their meaning and leaves behind
lines; angles, geometries, rhythms and lights. And these
things that have no meaning, that suggest nothing, that are
not the symbols of ideas or events—these become beautiful.

There are several people standing on this bridge—loiterers. Their elbows rest on the railing, their faces are hidden in their hands. They stare into the scene. A hoarse whistle toots at Wells Street. Bells clang far away. There is a scurry of dim noises in the dark. Something huge moves through the air. It is a bridge opening. Its arms make a massive gesture upward. A boat is coming through, a heavy shape drifting among the carnival ribbons that hang down in the black water.

Noises that have different tones. Boat whistles, bridge bells, electric alarm tinglings and the swish of water like the sound of wood tapping wood. Lights that have different colors. The yellow of electric signs. Around one of them that hoists its message in the air runs a green border. The electric lights quiver and run round the glaring frame like a mysterious green water. Red, gold and silver pillars in the water. Gray, blue and black shadows; elfin lanterns, "L" trains like illuminated caterpillars creeping over Wells Street, waterfalls of silver, Chinese writing in ruby; black, lead and silver windows and a thousand shades of darkness from bronze to strange greens. All these are things that the loitering ones leaning on the bridge rail know.

How nicely the hoods of automobiles hide the twisted lines of the gas engines under them. Smooth as chariots, curved and graceful as greyhounds, pigeons, rabbits—the

State Street begins after one passes odors. This is South Water Street. A swept, dusted and wonderfully silent street. White wings have scrubbed its worn body. But the odors deepen with the night. Farm odors, food odors—an aroma of decay surrounds them. By their smells one can almost detect the presence of chickens, eggs, oranges, cabbages, potatoes, plums and cantaloupes.

A group of movie theaters holds carnival at the entrance to the loop. People hurry under electric canopies, dig in their pockets for dollar bills and buy tickets. The buildings sleep along the river. The boats wait in the shadows. Movie signs, crossing cops, window tracks and different colored suits of clothes; odors, noises, lights and a mysteriously tender pattern of walls—these lie in the night like a reward.

We walk away with memories. When we are traveling some day, riding over strange places, these will be things we shall remember. Not words, but lines that mean nothing; and the scene from the bridge will bring a sad confusion into our heads. And we shall sit staring at famous monuments, battlefields, antiquities, and whisper to ourselves:

". . . . wish I was back. . . . wish I was back. . . ."

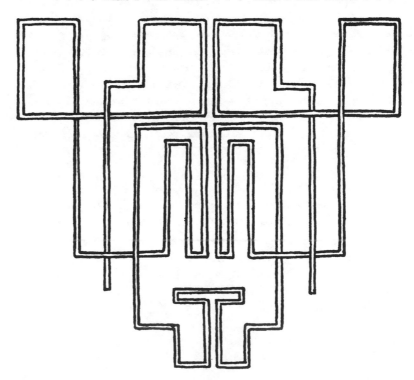

THE LAKE

The lake asks an old question as you ride to work or come home from work on the I. C. train. The train shoots along and out of the window the lake turns slowly like a great wheel. There is a curious optical illusion, as if the train were riding frantically on the rim of a great wheel and the wheel were turning in an opposite direction.

Perhaps this illusion makes it seem as if the lake were asking an old question as you ride along its edge—"Where you going?"

People looking out of the train window seem to grow sad as they stare at the lake. But this does not apply to train riders alone. In the summer time there are the revelers on the Municipal Pier and the beach loungers and all others who sit or take walks within sight of the water.

During the summer day the beaches are lively and the vari-colored bathing suits and parasols offer little carnival panels at the ends of the east running streets. As you pass them on the north side bus or on the south side I. C., the sun, the swarm of bathers smeared like bits of brightly colored paint across the yellow sand and the obliterating sweep of water remind you of the modernist artists whose pictures are usually lithographic blurs.

Yet winter and summer, even when the thousands upon thousands of bathers cover the sand like a shower of confetti and when there are shouts and circus excitements along the beach, people who look at the lake seem always to become sad. One wonders why.

Perhaps it is because the inanimate sweep of the water, its hugeness and silence, make one forget the petty things and the greedy trifles which form the routine of one's day. And when one forgets these things one remembers, alas, something they pleasantly obscured by their presence. A

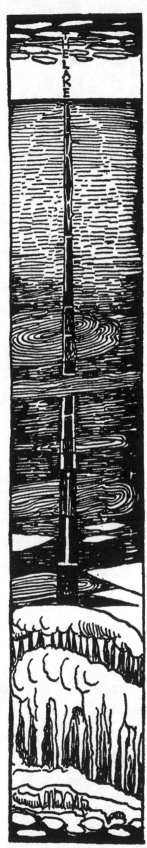

dream, perhaps, buried long ago. A hope, an emotion success-
fully interred under the amiable rubbish the days have piled
up.

Then, too, there is the question, "Where you going?"
And an answer to it that seems to come out of the long reaches
of water—"Come with me—somewhere—nowhere."

These thoughts play in people's minds without words.
They are almost more a part of the lake than of their thinking,
as if they were, in fact, lake thoughts.

Another reason why people grow sad when they look
at the water of the lake is perhaps that the lake offers them
an escape from the tawdry, nagging little responsibilities of
the day that go with being a citizen and a breadwinner. Not
that it invites to suicide. Quite the reverse; it invites to living.
To doing something that has a sweep to it; that has a swagger
to it. To setting sail for strange ports where strange adventures wait.

So, as the I. C. trains rush their thousands to work and
home again the citizens and breadwinners let their imagi-
nations gallop toward a faraway horizon. And these imagi-
nations come galloping back again and the breadwinners are
saddened—by a memory. Yes, they were for a moment
rovers, egad! swashbucklers, gentlemen and ladies of fortune
free of the rigamarole burdens that keep them on the I. C.
treadmill. And now they are again passengers. Going to
work. Going home to go to work again tomorrow.

It is easy to think that this is the secret of the sad little
grimace the lake brings to the eyes of the train riders.

This discourse is becoming a bit dolorous. But the subject rather requires an andante treatment. The city's press
agents will tell you quite another story about the lake—about
the "city's playground" and how conducive it is to healthful
sport and joyous recreation. But, on the other hand, there
is this other side, so to speak, of the lake. For the lake

belongs to those familiar things that surprise people into uncomfortable silences.

One could as easily write about the sky in this vein, since the lake, like the sky, challenges the monotony of people's lives with another monotony—the monotony of nature that seems to engulf, obliterate, reduce to puny proportions the routine by which people live and which, fortunately, they delude themselves into admiring.

There is also the question of beauty. This is a delicate issue to introduce into one's daily reading and the reader's pardon is solicited with proper humiliation. And yet, there is a question of beauty, of soul states and æsthetic nuances involved in the consideration of the lake.

Beauty by one definition is the sensatory excitement stirred in people by the rhythm of line, the vibration of color, the play of motion and the surprise of idea. It is usually a saddening effect that beauty produces and perhaps this is because beauty is something like an illumination that while admirable in itself throws into pathetic evidence all the ugly and unbeautiful things of one's life.

In this somewhat involved æsthetic principle there is probably another hint at the causes of the sadness people show when they look at the lake.

Today the lake wears its autumn aspect. Out of the train window one sees a wedge of geese flying south or occasionally a lone bird circling like an endless note over the water. The waves look cold and their symmetrical crisscross makes one think of the chill, lonely nights that beckon outside the coziness of one's home windows.

On summer days the lake is sometimes like a huge lavender leaf veined with gold. Sometimes it becomes festive and wears the awning stripes of cloud and sun. Or it grows serene and reminds one of a superb domesticity—as it lies pointed like a grate, arched like a saucer or the back of a sleeping kitten.

But today its autumn is a bit depressing. It no longer lures toward strange adventure. Instead its grayness seems to say to one, "Stay away—stay away. Hide away in warm houses and warm overcoats. Men are little things—puny things."

It is when one leaves the city and goes to visit or to live in another place where there is no lake that the lake grows alive in one's mind. One becomes thirsty for it and dreams of it. One remembers it then as something that was almost an essential part of life, like a third dimension. In some way one associates one's day dreams with the lake and falls into thinking that there is something unfinished, sterile about living with no lake at one's elbow.

In a short while, a month or so, the lake will become a stage for melodrama. The people riding on its edge will stare into mists. They will watch the huge mist shapes rolling back and forth over the hidden water. The blue of the sky, the cold sun, the fog and the freezing water will become actors in a great play and the train windows will be little prosceniums inclosing the melodrama of winter.

SERGT. KUZICK'S WATERLOO

"Offhand," said Sergt. Kuzick of the first precinct, "off-hand, I can't think of any stories for you. If you give me a little time, maybe I could think of one or two. What you want, I suppose, is some story as I know about from personal experience. Like the time, for instance, that the half-breed Indian busted out of the bridewell, where he was serving a six months' sentence, and snuck home and killed his wife and went back again to the bridewell, and they didn't find out who killed her until he got drunk a year later and told a bar-tender about it. That's the kind you want, ain't it?"

I said it was.

"Well," said Sergt. Kuzick, "I can't think of any off-hand, like I said. There was a building over on West Monroe Street once where we found three bodies in the basement. They was all dead, but that wouldn't make a story hardly, because nobody ever found out who killed them. Let me think awhile."

Sergt. Kuzick thought.

"Do you remember the Leggett mystery?" he inquired doubtfully. "I guess that was before your time. I was only a patrolman then. Old Leggett had a tobacco jar made out of a human skull, and that's how they found out he killed his wife. It was her skull. It come out one evening when he brought his bride home. You know, he got married again after killin' the first one. And they was having a party and the new bride said she didn't want that skull around in her house. Old Leggett got mad and said he wouldn't part with that skull for love or money. So when he was to work one day she threw the skull into the ash can, and when old Leggett come home and saw the skull missing he swore like the devil and come down to the station to swear out a warrant for his wife's arrest, chargin' her with disorderly conduct. He carried on

235

Sergt. Kuzick's Waterloo

so that one of the boys got suspicious and went out to the house with him and they found the skull in the ash can, and old Leggett began to weep over it. So one of the boys asked him, naturally, whose skull it was. He said it wasn't a skull no more, but a tobacco jar. And they asked him where he'd got it. And he begun to lie so hard that they tripped him up and finally he said it was his first wife's skull, and he was hung shortly afterward. You see, if you give me time I could remember something like that for a story.

"Offhand, though," sighed Sergt. Kuzick, "it's difficult. I ain't got it clear in my head what you want either. Of course I know it's got to be interestin' or the paper won't print it. But interestin' things is pretty hard to run into. I remember one night out to the old morgue. This was 'way back when I started on the force thirty years ago and more. And they was having trouble at the morgue owing to the stiffs vanishing and being mutilated. They thought maybe it was students carryin' them off to practice medicine on. But it wasn't, because they found old Pete—that was the colored janitor they had out there—he wasn't an African, but it turned out a Fiji Islander afterward. They found him dead in the morgue one day and it turned out he was a cannibal. Or, anyway, his folks had been cannibals in Fiji, and the old habit had come up in him so he couldn't help himself, and he was makin' a diet off the bodies in the morgue. But he struck one that was embalmed, and the poison in the body killed him. The papers didn't carry much on it on account of it not bein' very important, but I always thought it was kind of interestin' at that. That's about what you want, I suppose—some story or other like that. Well, let's see.

"It's hard," sighed Sergt. Kuzick, after a pause, "to put your finger on a yarn offhand. I remember a lot of things now, come to think of it, like the case I was on where a fella named Zianow killed his wife by pouring little pieces of hot lead into her ear, and he would have escaped, but he sold the body to the old county hospital for practicin' purposes, and while they was monkeying with the skull they heard something rattle and when they investigated it was several pieces of lead inside rattling around. So they arrested Zianow and got him to confess the whole thing, and he was sent up for life, because it turned out his wife had stabbed him four times the week before he poured the lead into her while she slept, and frightened him so that he did it in self-defense, in a way.

"I understand in a general way what you want," murmured Sergt. Kuzick, "but so help me if I can think of a thing that you might call interestin'. Most of the things we have to deal with is chiefly murders and suicides and highway robberies, like the time old Alderman McGuire, who is dead now, was held up by two bandits while going home from a night session of the council, and he hypnotized one bandit. Yes, sir, you may wonder at that, but you didn't know McGuire. He was a wonderful hypnotist, and he hypnotized the bandit, and just as the other one, who wasn't hypnotized, was searching his pockets McGuire said to the hypnotized bandit, 'You're a policeman, shoot this highwayman.' And the hypnotized one was the bandit who had the gun, and he turned around, as Alderman McGuire said, and shot the other, unhypnotized bandit and killed him. But when he reported the entire incident to the station—I was on duty that night—the captain wouldn't believe it, and tried to argue McGuire into saying it was a accident, and that the gun had gone off accidentally and killed the unhypnotized bandit. But the alderman stuck to his story, and it was true, because the hypnotized bandit told me privately all about it when I took him down to Joliet.

"I will try," said Sergt. Kuzick, "to think of something for you in about a week. I begin to get a pretty definite idea what you want, and I'll talk it over with old Jim, who used

237

to travel beat with me.   He's a great one for stories, old Jim
is.   A man can hardly think of them offhand like.   You give
me a week."   And the old sergeant sank into his wooden chair
and gazed out of the dusty station window with a perplexed
and baffled eye.

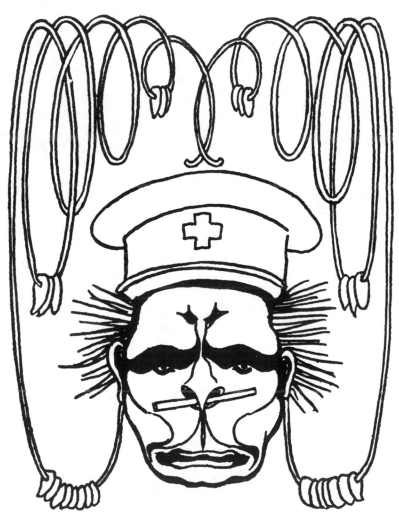

DEAD WARRIOR

Do you want to see the dead warriors come back, the fallen army come back, crawling out of its million coffins and walking back across the sea and across the prairie; the waxen face of youth come out of its million graves and its uniform hanging from its limp frame? Do you want to see the war dead, the young ones ripped to pieces in the trenches standing like tired beggars at your back door, dead hands and dead eyes and wailing softly: "I was so young. I died so soon. All of us from all the countries who died so soon, we grow lonely on the other side. Ah, my unlived days! My uneaten bread! My uncounted years! They lie in a little corner and nobody comes to them!"

It's a Jewish play called "The Dead Man" and every night in Glickman's Palace Theater on Blue Island Avenue a thousand men and women sit with staring eyes and watch this figure in its grave-clothes come dragging back like a tired beggar, come moaning back with the cry: "My unlived days! My uneaten bread! My uncounted years!"

He stands between Hamlet and Peer Gynt, this strangely motionless one who has thrown the west side into an uproar. There is no drama around him. He is a dead young man in uniform walking slowly, limply through three acts. This is all one remembers—that his eyes were open and unseeing, that his arms hung like a scarecrow's and that the fingers of his hands were curled in and motionless.

They talk to him in the play. The scene is a Jewish village in Poland. The war has ended. Famine, disease and poverty remain. Refugees, dying ones, starving ones, huddle together in the dismantled synagogue. No one knows what has happened. The armies have passed. Flame and blood brightened the sky for a time. Now the little village lies cut off from the world and its people clutch desperately to the hem

of life. No news has come. Wanderers stagger down the torn
roads with crazy tidings and the old men of the synagogue sit
shivering over their prayer books. A world has been blown
into fragments and this scene is one of the fragments.

Sholom Ash, who wrote this play, spent a time in villages
abroad as a Jewish relief worker and he brought back this
scene. A bedlam of despair, a merciless photograph that stares
across the footlights for a half-hour. The story begins. There
is a village leader in whose veins the will to live still throbs.
He exhorts the shivering ones. There will be a wedding. He
will give his daughter in marriage. There will be feasting.
The dead are dead. The duty of the living ones is to live. Let
the old women prepare food and the men will sing. Life will
begin over and a new village will be built up.

But the daughter hangs back. She talks of the young
man whom she married and who went away to war.

"He is dead, poor child," the father says.

"No, no, he isn't dead. I dreamed he was still alive," she
answers.

But the festival starts. The starving ones sing in the
broken synagogue. There will be a wedding. Life will begin.
But there is something in the ruined doorway. A uniform
stands in the doorway. A dark, waxen-faced young man who
seems asleep, whose arms hang limp, whose fingers curl in.
He comes forward and stands, a terribly idle figure. He is the
young man.

They greet him. His bride weeps with joy. His aged
mother presses his hands and weeps and murmurs in a whisper:
"Oh, how changed he is!" The synagogue shouts and cries its
welcome. But the young man's eyes stare and it would seem
almost that he is dead. Then he talks. His voice has a lifeless sound, his words are like a child reciting sleepily. There
is a gruesome oddity about him. But an old man explains.
"They come back like that," he says. "There is one who came

back who shrieks all night. And another who cannot remember anything."

Yet how strangely he talks! Of a country from which he has come—on the other side, it lies. Hysterical questions arise. Is there food there, are there houses there, is there milk for children and synagogues in which to pray? There is everything one desires, he says. So the questions rise and the answers come—curious child answers. But why is he so pale and worn if the country whence he comes is so remarkable? Ah, because he was lonely. All who are in this country are like him—lonely for the homes they left so soon. For their people. All who are in the country whence he came sit and remember only the things of the past. Yes, that is all one does in this marvelous country—remember the things of the past, over and over again.

They will go with him. The miser who has hidden away his gold, the widow and her two orphans, the hungry ones and despairing ones—they will all go back with him.

One comes out of the theater with a strange sense of understanding. The dead have spoken to one. It is never to be forgotten. The youth that was ripped to pieces in the trenches reached out his limp arms across a row of west side footlights and left a cry echoing in one's heart: "My unlived days! My uneaten bread! My uncounted years! They lie in a little corner waiting and no one comes to them."

Propaganda? Yes, a curious undertone of propaganda. The war propaganda of the dead, older than the fall of Liege by a hundred centuries. The primitive propaganda of the world mourning for its lost ones.

You will see the play, perhaps. Or you will wait until it is translated some day. But this month the west side is aglow with the genius of Sholom Ash and with the interpretative genius of Aaron Teitelbaum, who plays the dead man in uniform and who directed the production. I know of no performance today that rivals his.

241

THE TATTOOER

Here the city kind of runs over at the heel and flaunts a seven-year-old straw hat. Babylon mooches wearily along with a red nose dreaming in the sun, and Gomorrah leans against an ash can. It is South State Street below Van Buren. The ancient palaces of mirth and wonder blink with dusty lithographs.

"Long ago," says Dutch, "yeh, long ago it was different. Then people was people. Then life was something. Then the tattooing business was a business. When the old London Musee was next door and everybody knew how to have a good time."

The automatic piano in the penny arcade whangs dolorously into a forgotten tango. The two errand boys stand with their eyes glued on the interiors of the picture slot machines— "An Artist's Model" and "On the Beach at Atlantic City." A gun pops foolishly in the rear and the 3-inch bullseye clangs. In a corner behind the Postal Card Photo Taken in a Minute gallery sits Dutch, the world's leading tattooer. Sample tattoo designs cover the two walls. Dragons, scorpions, bulbous nymphs, crossed flags, wreathed anchors, cupids, butterflies, daggers and quaint decorations that seem the grotesque survivals of the mid-Victorian schools of fantasy. Photographs of famous men also cover the walls—Capt. Constantinus tattooed from head to foot, every inch of him; Barnum's favorites, ancient and forgotten kooch dancers, fire eaters, sword swallowers, magicians and museum freaks. And a two column article from the *Chicago Chronicle* of 1897, yellowed and framed and recounting in sonorous phrases ("pulchritudinous epidermis" is featured frequently) that the society folk of Chicago have taken up tattooing as a fad, following the lead of New York's Four Hundred, who followed the lead of London's most aristocratic circles; and that Prof. Al Herman, known from Madagascar to Sandy Hook as "Dutch," was the leading artist of the tattoo needle in the world.

Here in his corner, surrounded by the molding symbols and slogans of a dead world, Dutch is rounding out his career —a Silenus in exile, his eyes still bright with the memory of hurdy-gurdy midnights.

"Long ago," says Dutch, and his sigh evokes a procession of marvelous ghosts tattooed from head to toe and capering like a company of debonair totem poles over the cobblestones of another South State Street. But the macabre days are gone. The Barnum bacchanal of the nineties lies in its grave with a fading lithograph for a tombstone. Along with the fall of the Russian empire, the collapse of the fourteen points and the general dethronement of reason since the World's Fair, the honorable art of tattooing has come in for its share of vicissitudes.

"Oh, we still do business," says Dutch. "Human nature is slow to decline and there are people who still realize that if you got a handsome watch what do you want to do to it? Engrave it, ain't it? And if you got a handsome skin, what then? Tattoo, naturally. And we tattoo in seven colors now where it used to be three, and use electricity. Do you think it's crazy? Well, you should see who I used to tattoo in the old days. Read the article on the wall. As for being crazy, what do you say about the man who spends his last 50 cents to get into a baseball game, and gets excited and throws his only hat in the air and loses it, and the man who sits all day and all night with a fishpole on the pier and don't catch any fish? Yes, like I tell the judge who picked us up one day in Iowa, you know how they do sometimes when you follow the carnival. And he asks me why I shouldn't go to jail, and if tattooing ain't crazy, and I says give me three minutes and I prove my case. And I begin with the Romans, and how they was the brightest people we knew, and how they went in for tattooing, and how Columbus was tattooed, and all the sailors that was bright enough to discover America was tattooed, also. Then I say, what if Charlie Ross was tattooed?

243

Would he be lost to-day? And what if he had under his name the word Philadelphia? And in addition to that the date where he was born and his address and so on. Would he be lost then? 'You see,' I says, 'a man can't be tattooed enough for his own good,' and the judge says I win my case."

The automatic piano plays "Over There" and the shooting gallery rifles pop too insistently for a moment. Dutch contemplates a plug of fresh tobacco. Then he resumes. This time a more intimate tale—the story of his romance—a weird, grotesque amour with a gaudy can-can obbligato.

"Long ago," Dutch whispers; "yeh, I knew all the girls. I tattoned them all. And I live in this street for thirty years now. But nobody is interested any more in what used to be. How this street has become different! Ach, it is gone, all gone. Everything. Tattooing hangs on a little. Human nature demand it. But human nature is dying likewise. Yeh, I ask you what would old Barnum say if he should come back and see me sitting here? Me, who was as good any day as Capt. Constantinus? I hate to think what. In those days talent counted. If you could sing or dance or tattoo it meant something. Now what does it mean? Look at the dancers and singers they have, and who is there that tattooes any more? It's all gone to smash, the whole world."

Now amid the popping of the rifles and the tinny whanging of the piano Dutch draws forth a final package. He unwraps a yellowed newspaper. Photographs. One by one he shufflles them out and arranges them on the broken desk as if in some pensive game of solitaire. There is Dutch when he was a boy, when he was a sailor, when he grew up and became a world famous tattooer. There is Dutch surrounded by queens of the Midway, Dutch with his arms debonairly thrown round the shoulders of snake charmers and other bizarre and vanished contemporaries. The photographs are yellowed. They make a curious collection. They make the

244

soulless piano sound a bit softer. A "where are the snows of yesteryear" motif played on a can-can fife.

Finally a modern photo in a folder, unyellowed. A smiling, wholesome faced girl. Here Dutch pauses in his game of solitaire and looks in silence.

"My daughter," he says finally. "I sent her through college. Yeh, she's graduated now and has a fine job. I help her all I can. What? Is she tattooed?"

The world's greatest tattoo artist bristles and glowers at the designs on the walls, frowns at the cupids, nymphs, anchors, dragons and butterflies.

"I should say not," he mutters. "She don't belong in this street, not here. She's got a different life, and I help her all I can and she likes me. No, sir, in this street belongs only those who have a long memory. The new ones should start somewhere else. Not, mind you, that tattooing ain't good enough for anybody. But times have changed."

The piano obliges with "The Blue Danube." A customer saunters in. Dutch is all business. The electricity is switched on. A blue spark crackles. Dutch clears his throat and slaps the customer proudly on the back.

"Only a little more to go," he explains, "all over. Two more ships at sea and three dragons will do the job, Heinie. And then, h'm, you will get a job any day in any side show, I can guarantee you that."

Heinie grins hopefully.

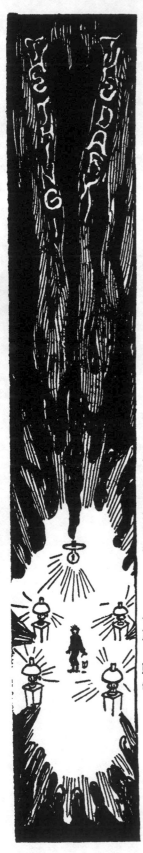

THE THING IN THE DARK

It has the usual Huron street ending. Emergency case. Psychopathic hospital. Dunning. But the landlady talked to the police sergeant. The landlady was curious. She wanted the police sergeant to tell her something. And the police sergeant, resting his chin on his elbow, leaned forward on his high stool and peered through the partition window at the landlady—and said nothing. Or rather, he said: " don't know. That's the way with people sometimes. They get afraid."

This man came to Mrs. Balmer's rooming-house in Huron Street when it was spring. He was a short, stocky man with a leathery face and little eyes. He identified himself as Joseph Crawford, offered to pay $5 a week for a 12 by 12 room on the third floor at the rear end of the long gloomy hallway and arrived the next day at Mrs. Balmer's faded tenement with an equally faded trunk. Nothing happened.

But when Mrs. Balmer entered the room the following morning to straighten it up she found several innovations. There were four kerosene lamps in the room. They stood on small rickety tables, one in each corner. And there was a new electric light bulb in the central fixture. Mrs. Balmer took note of these things with a professional eye but said nothing. Idiosyncrasies are to be expected of the amputated folk who seek out lonely tenement bedrooms for a home.

A week later, however, Mrs. Balmer spoke to the man.

"You burn your light all night," said Mrs. Balmer, "and while I have no objection to that, still it runs up the electric light bill."

The man agreed that this was true and answered that he would pay $1 extra each week for the privilege of continuing to burn the electric light all night.

Nothing happened. Yet Mrs. Balmer, when she had

time for such things as contemplation, grew curious about the man in the back room. In fact she transferred her curiosity from the Japanese female impersonator on the second floor and the beautiful and remarkably gowned middle-aged woman on the first floor to this man who kept four kerosene lamps and an electric bulb burning all night on the third floor.

For some time Mrs. Balmer was worried over the thought that this man was probably an experimenter. He probably fussed around with things as an old crank does sometimes, and he would end by burning down the house or blowing it up—accidentally.

But Mrs. Balmer's fears were removed one evening when she happened to look down the gloomy hallway and notice that this man's door was open. A gay, festive illumination streamed out of the opened doorway and Mrs. Balmer paid a social call. She found her roomer sitting in a chair, reading. Around him blazed four large kerosene lamps. But there was nothing elese to notice. His eyes were probably bad, and Mrs. Balmer, after exchanging a few words on the subject of towels, transportation and the weather, said good-night.

But always after that Mrs. Balmer noticed that the door remained open. Open doors are frequent in rooming-houses. People grow lonely and leave the doors of their cubby holes open. There is nothing odd about that. Yet one evening while Mrs. Balmer stood gossiping with this man in the doorway she noticed something about him that disturbed her. She had noticed it first when she looked in the room before saying hello. Mr. Crawford was sitting facing the portières that covered the folding doors that partitioned the room. The portières were a very clever ruse of Mrs. Balmer. Behind them were screwed hooks and these hooks functioned as a clothes-closet.

Mrs. Balmer noticed that Mr. Crawford, as she talked, kept staring at the portières and watching them and that he seemed very nervous. The next morning, when she was

247

straightening up the room, Mrs. Balmer looked behind the portières. An old straw hat, an old coat, a few worn shirts hung from the hooks. There was nothing else but the folding-door and this was not only locked but nailed up.

When two months had passed Mrs. Balmer had made a discovery. It had to do with the four kerosene lamps and the extra large electric bulb and the portières. But it was an irritating discovery, since it made everything more mysterious than ever in the landlady's mind.

She had caught many glimpses of this man in the back room when he wasn't looking. Of evenings he sat with his door opened and his eyes fastened on the portières. He would sit like that for hours and his leathery face would become gray. His little eyes would widen and his body would hunch up as if he were stiffening. But nothing happened.

Finally, however, Mrs. Balmer began to talk. She didn't like this man Crawford. It made her nervous to catch a glimpse of him in his too-brightly lighted room, sitting hour after hour staring at the portières—as if there was something behind them, when there was nothing behind them except an old hat and coat and shirt. She looked every morning.

But he paid his rent regularly. He left in the morning regularly and always returned at eight o'clock. He was an ideal roomer—except that there never is an ideal roomer—but Mrs. Balmer couldn't stand his lights and his watching the portières. It frightened her.

Screams sometimes sound in a rooming-house. One night—it was after midnight—Mrs. Balmer woke up. The darkened house seemed filled with noises. A man was screaming.

Mrs. Balmer got dressed and called the janitor. There was no doubt in her mind where the noises came from. Some of the roomers were awake and looking sleepily and frightenedly out of their doorways. Mrs. Balmer and the janitor

248

hurried to the back room on the third floor. It was Crawford screaming.

His door was closed, but it opened when the janitor turned the knob. Mr. Crawford was standing in front of the portières in the too-brightly lighted room and screaming. His arms, as if overcoming some awful resistance, shot out, and his hands seized the portieres. With the amazing screams still coming from his throat, Mr. Crawford tore crazily at the portières until they ripped from the rod above the folding-door. They came down and the man fell with them. Over him, hanging on the "clothes-closet" hooks, were revealed an old straw hat, an old coat and a worn shirt.

"You see," said Mrs. Balmer to the police sergeant, "he was afraid of something and he couldn't stand the dark. And the portières always frightened him. But the doctor wasn't able to do anything with him. The doctor says there was some secret about it and that Mr. Crawford went crazy because of this secret. The only thing they found out about him was that he used to be a sailor."

AN OLD AUDIENCE SPEAKS

Tired, madam? That is nothing remarkable. So are we, whose faces you see from across the footlights, faces like rows of wilted plants in the gloom of this decrepit theater. We are all very tired.

It is Saturday afternoon. For a little while yesterday there was spring in the streets. But now it has grown cold again. The wind blows. The buildings wear a bald, cheerless look.

What are we tired about? God knows. Perhaps because winter is so long in passing. Or, perhaps, because spring will be so long in passing. Tired of waiting for tomorrow.

So you dance for us. We have paid 50 cents each to see the show. This abominable orchestra is out of tune. The fiddles scrape, the piano makes clattering sounds. And you, madam, are tired. The gay purple tights, the gilded bodice, the sultana's toque, or whatever it is, do not deceive us. Your legs, madam, are not as shapely as they were once. And your body—ah, bodies grow old.

Yes, we are not deceived, madam. You have come to us —last. There were others before us, others reaching far back, to whom you gave your youth. Others for whom you danced when your legs were, perhaps, like two spring mornings, and when your body was, perhaps, like a pretty laugh.

Here are the tired ones. From the South Clark and South State streets bed-houses. The kinds of faces that the smart movie directors hire as "types" for the underworld scenes or the slum scenes.

It is Saturday afternoon and we walked up and down the street, looking at the lithographs outside the decrepit theater fronts. And when it got too cold to walk any farther we dropped in, forking out four bits for the privilege.

And we expect nothing, madam. There will be no great

music for us. And what scenery there is behind the footlights will be faded and patched. The jokes will be things that make no one laugh. And the dancers, madam, will be like you. Tired, heavy-faced dancers, whose legs flop, whose bodies bounce while the abominable orchestra plays.

But it is warm where we sit. We half shut our eyes and tired little dreams come to us. And you, madam, going wearily through your steps, are the Joy of Life. Your hoarse voice, singing indecipherable words about dearie and honey and my jazz baby, your sagging shoulders layered with powder and jerking to the music, the rigid, lifeless grin of your cruelly painted lips—these things and the torn, smeared papier-mâché ballroom interior—these are the Joy of Life.

Tired little dreams, worth almost the four bits. Do you remember other audiences, madam? As we remember other dancers? Do you recall the gay, dark glow of ornate auditoriums, and do you remember when you were young and there were many tomorrows? As we do? Oh, dearie, dearie, how mah heart grows weary, waitin' for mah baby for to come back home. Very good, madam. Although the voice is a bit cracked. Now dance. Lumber across the stage in your purple tights, wiggle around in your sultana's toque. That's the baby. And kick your legs at us as you exit. Ah, what a kick! But never mind. It is quite good enough for us. And —it reminds us.

We applaud. Does the noise sound ghastly? What is it we applaud? God knows. But applause is a habit. One applauds in a theater. How does it sound in the wings to you, madam, our applause? Rather meaningless, eh? And not interesting at all? Ah, we forgive you for that, for not feeling a great thrill at our applause. Nevertheless, it is a rather piquant thing, our applause. Considering how cold it is outside, how long winter is in passing. Considering how cheerless the buildings look.

Put on the red ball gown and come out and crack jokes with the hop-headed-looking juvenile lead. Greetings, madam. How marvelous you look in this ball gown! Ah, indeed! You were walking down the street the other day and chanced to meet. Hm, we've heard that joke, but we'll laugh again. Matrimony. I'll tell you what marriage is. A lottery. Yes, we've heard that one, too. Accept our laughter, nevertheless.

Your jokes, madam, are neither young nor refined. But —neither are we. And your wit is somewhat coarse and pointless. But so are we. And your voice is a trifle tired and cracked and loud. But so is our laughter. We are even, quite even, madam. If you were better once, so were we. If you remember sweeter laughter, why we remember more charming jests. Go on, Dolores, our lady of jokes, you're worth the four bits.

Now the street seems a bit colder because it was warmer in the theater. Where do we go from here? Up and down, up and down the old street. A very pleasant afternoon. Spent in laughter and applause. Once there was booze for a nickel and a dime. But it was found necessary to improve the morals of the nation. No booze today.

That is quite a brave photograph of you outside the theater, madam. The Dancing Venus. If we had tears we would shed them. The Dancing Venus, indeed! We smile as you smiled yourself when you saw it for the first time. But— good-by. Master Francois Villon sang it all long ago. Yesterdays, yesterdays, here is a street of yesterdays.

And we, the tired ones, the brutal-faced, bitter-eyed ones, the beaten ones—we walk up and down the cold street, peering at the cheerless buildings. Life takes a long time to pass. But without changing our bitter, brutal faces we bow this afternoon, madam, to the memory of you.

We paid four bits to see you. Our Lady of Jokes, and in this cold, sunless street we grin, we smirk, we leer a salutation to your photograph and the phrase beneath it that laughs mockingly back at us—Oh, Dancing Venus!

MISHKIN'S MINYON

We were discussing vacations and Sammy, who is eleven years old going on twelve, listened nervously to his father. Finally Sammy spoke up:

"I won't go," he bristled. "No, I won't if I gotta tell the conductor I'm under five. I ain't going."

Sammy's father coughed with some embarrassment.

"Sha!" said Feodor Mishkin, removing his attention from the bowl of fruit, "I see it takes more than naturalization papers to change a *landsmann* from Kremetchuk." And he fastened a humorous eye upon Sammy's father.

"It's like this," continued the Falstaffian one from Roosevelt Road: "In Russia where my friend here, Hershela comes from, that is in Russia of the good old days where there were pogroms and ghettos and *provocateurs*—ah, I grow homesick for that old Russia sometimes—the Jews were not always so honest as they might be. Don't interrupt me, Hershela. My friend here I want to tell a story to is a journalist and he will understand I am no 'antishemite' if I explain how it is that you want your son Sammy to tell the conductor he is under five."

Turning to me Mishkin grinned and proceeded.

"The Jews, as you know, are great travelers," he said. "They have traveled more than all the other peoples put together. And yet, they don't like to pay car fare, in Russia, particular. I can remember my father, who was a good rabbi and a holy man. Yes, but when it came time to ride on the train from one city to another he would fold up his long beard and crawl under the seat.

"It was only on such an occasion that my father would talk to a woman. He would actually rather cut off his right hand than talk to a woman in public that he didn't know. This was because Rabbi Mishkin, my father, was a holy man.

254

But he was not above asking a woman to spread out her skirts so that the inspector coming through the train couldn't see him under the seat.

"Of course, you had to pay the conductors. But a ruble was enough, not ten or twenty rubles like the fare called for. And the conductors were always glad to have Jews ride on their train because it meant a private revenue for them. I remember that the conductors on the line running through Kremetchuk had learned a few words of Yiddish. For instance, when the train would stop at a station the conductor would walk up and down the platform and cry out a few times—*mu kennt*. This meant that the inspector wasn't on the train and you could jump on and hide under the seats. Or if the inspector was on the train the conductor would walk up and down and yell a few times, *Malchamovis!* This is a Hebrew word that means Evil Angel and it was the signal for nothing doing.

"The story I remember is on a train going out of Kiev," said Mishkin. "Years ago it was. I was sitting in the train reading some Russian papers when I heard three old Jews talking. They had long white beards and there were marks on their foreheads from where they laid twillum. Yes, I saw that they were holy men and pretty soon I heard that they were upset about something. You know what? I'll tell you.

"For a religious Jew in the old country to pass an evening without a minyon is a sin. A minyon is a prayer that is said at evening. And to make a minyon there must be ten Jews. And they must stand up when they pray. Of course, if you are somewhere where there are no ten Jews, then maybe it's all right to say it with three or four Jews only.

"So these holy men on the train were arguing if they should have a minyon or not because there were only three of them. But finally they decided after a theological discussion that it would be all right to have the minyon. It was dark already and the train was going fast and the three Jews stood up in their place at the end of the car and began the prayer.

"And pretty soon I began to hear voices. Yes, from under nearly every seat. Voices praying. A mumble-bumble that filled the car. I didn't know what to make of it for a few minutes. But then I remembered. Of course, the car was full of rabbis or at least holy men and they were as usual riding with their beards folded up under the seats.

"So," smiled Mishkin, "the prayer continued and some of the passengers who were listening began to smile. You can imagine. But the three Jews paid no attention. They went on with the minyon. And now, listen, now comes the whole story. You will laugh. But it is true. I saw it with my own eyes.

"The prayer, like I told you, must be said standing up. At least it is a sin to say the last part of the prayer, particularly the 'amen,' without standing up. So as the prayer came towards its finish imagine what happened. From under a dozen seats began to appear old Jews with white beards. They crawled out and without brushing themselves off stood up and when the 'amen' finally came there were eleven Jews standing up in a group and praying. Under the seats it was completely vacant.

"And just at this moment, when the 'amen' filled the car, who should come through but the inspector in his uniform with his lantern. When he saw this whole car full of passengers he hadn't seen before he stopped in surprise. And the finish of it was that they all had to pay their fare—extra fare, too.

"It is a nice story, don't you think, Hershela," Mishkin laughed. "It shows a lot of things, but principally it shows that a holy man is a holy man first and that he will sacrifice himself to an inquisition in Madrid or a train inspector in Kiev for the simple sake of saying his 'amen' just as he believed it should be said and just as he wants to say it."

Sammy's father shrugged his shoulders.

"I don't see how what you say has anything to do with what my son said," he demurred. "Sammy looks user more than five and what harm is there in saving $15 if—"

Sammy interrupted with a wail.

"I won't go," he cried. "No, if I gotta tell the conductor I'm under five I better stay home. I don't wanna go. He'll know I'm 'leven going on twelve."

"All right, all right," sighed Sammy's father. "But you see," he added, turning to Mishkin, "it ain't on account of wanting to have a minyon that my son has such high ideas."

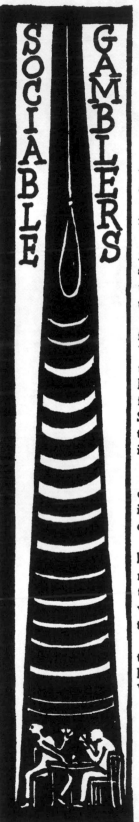

SOCIABLE GAMBLERS

"Yes, it do interfere with their game," said Bill Cochran, the deputy sheriff from Tom Freeman's office. He cut himself a slice of chewing tobacco and glanced meditatively out of the window of the Dearborn Street bastile. Whereat he repeated with gentle emphasis, "It do."

A long rain was leaning against the walls of the county jail. A dismal yellowish gloom drifted up and down the street. Deputy Cochran, with an effort, detached his eye from the lugubrious scene of the rain and the day-dark and spoke up brightly.

"But at that," said he, "I don't think their being doomed for to hang can be held entirely responsible for their losing. You see, I've made quite a study of the game o' rhummy, not to mention pinochle and other such games of chance, and if I do say so myself I doubt there's the man in Chicago, doomed for to hang or otherwise, who would find me an easy mark. Still, as I say, in the case of these gentlemen who you refer to— to wit, the doomed men as I have acted as death watch for— it do interfere with their game. There's no denying that."

Now the rain chattered darkly on the grated windows of the Dearborn Street bastile and Deputy Cochran tilted back in his chair and thought pensively and in silence of life and death and high, low, jack and the game.

"They pick me out for the death watch on account I have a way with doomed men," he remarked at last, his voice modestly self-conscious. "Some of the deputies is inclined to get a bit sad, you know. Or to let their nerves go away with them. But me, I feel as the best thing to do in the crisis to which I refer is to make the best of it.

"So when I sit in on the death watch I faces myself with the truth. I says to myself right away: 'Bill, this young feller here is to be hanged by the neck until dead, in a few hours. Which being the case, there's no use wasting any more time or thought on the matter.' So after this self-communication, I usually says to the young feller under observation by the death watch, 'Cheerio, m' lad. Is there anything in particular as you'd like to discuss.'

"I was a bit thick with the Abyssinian prince, Grover Redding, you recall. The man spent the whole time we were with him praying at the top of his voice and singing hymns. Not that I begrudged the fellow this privilege. But if you've ever heard a man who's going to be hanged in a few hours try to pass the time in continual prayers shouted at the top of his voice you'll understand our predicament.

"Then there was Antonio Lopez. I was death watch on him and a difficult task that was. The lad kept up his pretense that he fancied himself a rooster to the very end. He crouched on the chair on his feet and flapped his elbows like as they were wings and emitted rooster calls all night long. I tried to dissuade him and offered to play him any game he wished for any stake. But the only way he could reconcile himself to the approaching fatal dawn was to crow like a rooster. I thought to cheer him up toward the end by congratulating him on his excellent imitations, as I bore him no ill will despite he gave us all a terrible headache before the death march took him away."

Now the rain dropped in long, quick lines outside the window and the pavements below glowed like dark mirrors. Deputy Cochran, however, had become oblivious to the scene. His eyes withdrew themselves from the rain-dark and casually traced themselves over the memories his calling had left him.

"There was Blacky Weed some years ago," he went on. "And Viana, the choir boy. And to come down to more recent incidents, Harry Ward, the 'Lone Wolf.' I played cards with them all and can truthfully say I won most of the games played to which I refer, with the exception of those played with the 'Lone Wolf,' hanged recently, if you recall.

"I will say that the chief trouble with the doomed men as

I have engaged in games of chance with is their inability to concentrate. Now cards, to be properly played, requires above all a gift of the ability to concentrate. Recognizing this I have always refused to play for money with the doomed as I have been watch over, saying to them when they pressed the matter, 'No, m' lad. Let's make it just a sociable game for the fun there's in it rather than play for money.'

"There are others not so scrupulous," hinted Deputy Cochran. "Take for instance, the example of the newspaper man as was Eddie Brislane's friend and comforter. He was with him in the cell most of the time before the hanging, and two days before the aforesaid he paid Brislane $50 for a story to be printed exclusively in his paper. Then this newspaper man, which I consider unethical under the circumstances, played Brislane poker, and what with the doomed man's lack of concentration and his inability to take advantage of the turns of the game, therefore, this newspaper man won back his $50 and some few dollars besides.

"As for me, I doubt whether all my card playing with these doomed men, successful though it has been, has ever brought me as much as a half dollar. No, as I said, sociability is the object of these games and all I aim for is to put the doomed man at his ease for the time being."

Deputy Cochran suddenly smiled, although before an impersonal air had marked his discourse.

"There was the 'Lone Wolf,' as I mentioned," he continued. "A cold-blooded feller and a sinner to the end. But he was the best rhummy player as I have ever had the pleasure of matching skill with. Yes, sir, it was his ability for to concentrate. As I said, that is the prime ability necessary and the 'Lone Wolf' had more concentration than any one I have matched skill with in or out of the jail.

"That was an interesting evening we spent on the death watch for the 'Lone Wolf.' He regaled us for an hour or so telling us how he used to steal motor cars. Yes, sir, whenever the 'Lone Wolf' wanted a new car he just went out and took it. A cold-blooded feller, as I say.

"Then he asked if I would mind playing him a game of rhummy and I answered, 'No, Harry. As you are aware, I am here to oblige. So we got out the deck and Harry insisted upon gambling. 'Make it a dollar a hand,' he said. But I would listen to none of that. We played eight games in all and he beat me six of them. Perhaps I was not at my best that night. But I never played against such a cold-blooded feller. He took a positive joy in winning his games and on the whole acted like a bum winner, making the most of his unusual good luck. I hold no grudge for that, however. But I feel that if we could have continued the play some other time I'd easily have finished him off."

Now the sun was slowly recovering its place and the rain had become a light mist. Deputy Cochran seemed to regard this as a signal for a conclusion.

"Summing the matter all up, pro and con," he offered, "it do interfere with their game a lot. But I lay this to the fact that they all fancy they're going to be reprieved and they keep waiting and listening for an announcement which will save them from the gallows. I've known some of them to lead a deuce thinking it was an ace and vice versa. But at that I can fully recommend a good, sociable game of cards as the best way for a doomed man to pass the few hours before the arrival of the fatal moment."

RIPPLES

It rains. People carry umbrellas. A great financier has promised me an interview. The windows of his club look out on a thousand umbrellas. They bob along like drunken beetles.

Once in a blue moon one becomes aware of people. Usually the crowds and their endless faces are a background. They circle around one the way ripples circle around a stone that has fallen into the water. The torments, elation of others; the ambitions, defeats of others; the bedlam of others—who cares? They are no more than the ripples which one's ego creates in the plunge from youth to age.

Here, then, under the umbrellas outside the great financier's club, are people. One must marvel. They pass one another without so much as a glance. To each of them all the others—the bedlam of others—are ripples emanating from themselves. The great quests and struggles going on and the million agonies and tumults beating in the veins of the world —ripples. Yes, vague and vaguer ripples which surround the fact that one is going to buy a pair of suspenders; which circle the fact that one is invited out for dinner this evening.

Ah, the smug and oblivious ones under umbrellas! It rains, but the umbrellas keep off the rain. The world pours its distinctions and elations over their souls, but other umbrellas, invisible, keep off distractions and elations. And each of them, scurrying along outside the window of the great financier's club, is an omniscient world center to himself. The great play was written around him, a blur of disasters and ecstasies, a sort of vast and inarticulate Greek chorus mumbling an obbligato to the leitmotif which is at the moment the purchase of a pair of suspenders or a dinner invitation for the evening.

None so small under these umbrellas outside the window but fancies himself the center of the cosmos. None so stupid

but regards himself as the oracle of the times. And they scurry along without a glance at one another, each innately convinced that his ideas, his prejudices, his ambitions, his tastes are the Great Standard, the Normal Criterion. Puritan, paranoiac, sybarite, katatoniac, hardhead, dreamer, coward, desperado, beaten ones, striving ones, successful ones—all flaunt their umbrellas in the rain, all unfurl their invisible umbrellas to the world. Let it rain, let it rain—calamities and ecstasies tipped with fire and roaring with thunder—nothing can disturb the terrible preoccupation of the plunge from youth to age.

The pavements gleam like dark mirrors. The office window lights chatter in the gloom. An umbrella pauses. The great financier is giving directions to his chauffeur. The directions given, the great financier stands in the rain for a moment. His eyes look up and down the street. What does he see? Ripples, vague and vaguer ripples, that mark his passage from the limousine into the club.

He is wet. A servant helps him remove his coat. Then he comes to the window and sinks into a leather chair and stares at the rain and the umbrellas outside. The great financier has been abroad. His highly specialized mind has been poking among columns of figures, columns of reports. He desired to find out if possible what conditions abroad were. For six months the great financier closeted himself daily with other great financiers and talked and talked and discussed and talked.

But he says nothing. It is curious. The whole world and all its marvelous distractions seem to have resolved themselves into the curt sentence, "It rains." And somehow the great financier's faculty for the glib manipulation of platitudes which has earned him a reputation as a powerful economist seems for the moment to have abandoned him. His eyes

266

remind one of a boy standing on tiptoe and staring over a fence at a baseball game.

The conversation finally begins. It runs something like this. It is the great financier talking. "Europe. Oh, yes. Quite a mess. Things will pick up, however." A long pause. The umbrellas bob along. One, two, three, four, five—the financier counts up to thirty. Then he rubs his hands together as if he were taking charge of a situation freshly arisen at a board of directors' meeting and says in a jovial voice: "Where were we? Oh, yes. The European situation. Well, now, what do you want to know in particular?"

Ah, this great financier has columns of figures, columns of reports and columns of phrases in his head. Press a button and they will pop out. "Have a cigar?" the financier asks. Cigars are lighted. "A rotten day," he says. Doesn't look as if it will clear up, either, does it?" Then he says, "I guess this is an off day for me. No energy at all. I swear I can't think of a thing to tell you about the European situation."

He sits smoking, his eyes fastened on the scene outside the window. His eyes seem to be searching as if for meanings that withhold themselves. Yet obviously there is no thought in his head. A mood has wormed its way through the columns of figures, columns of reports, and taken possession of him. This is bad for a financier. It is obvious that the umbrellas outside are for the moment something other than ripples; that the great play of life outside is something other than an inarticulate Greek chorus mumbled as an obbligato for him alone.

The great financier is aware of something. Of what? He shakes his head, as if to question himself. Of nothing he can tell. Of the fact that a great financier is an atom like other atoms dancing in a chaos of atoms. Of the fact that each of the umbrellas crawling past under his window is as important as himself. The great financier's ego is taking a rest and dreams naked of words crowd in to distract him.

267

"We have in Europe a peculiar situation," he says. "England and France, although hitched to the same wagon, pull in different directions. England must build up her trade. France must build up her morale. These involve different efforts. To build up her trade England must re-establish Germany. To build up her morale France must see that Germany is not re-established and that it remains forever a beaten enemy."

The great financier looks at his watch suddenly. "By Jove!" he says. "By Jove!" He has to go. He is sorry the interview was a failure. But a rotten day for thinking. Back into his raincoat. A limousine has drawn up. A servant helps him to dress. In a moment another umbrella has joined the crawl of umbrellas over the pavement.

It rains. And a great financier is riding home to dinner.

PITZELA'S SON

"His name?" said Feodor Mishkin. "Hm! Always you want names. Is life a matter of names and addresses or is it something else?"

"But the story would be better, Feodor, with names in it."

The rotund and omniscient journalist from the west side muttered to himself in Russian.

"Better!" he repeated. "And why better? If I tell you his name is Yankel or Berella or Chaim Duvit do you know any more than if I tell you his name is Pitzela?"

"No. We will drop the matter. I will call him Chaim Yankel."

"You will call him Chaim Yankel! And what for? His name is Pitzela and not Chaim Yankel."

"Thanks."

"You can go anywhere on Maxwell Street and ask anybody you meet do they know Pitzela and they will say: 'Do we know Pitzela? We know Pitzela all right.' So what is there to be gained by calling him Chaim Yankel?"

"Nothing, Feodor. It was a mistake even to think of it."

"It was. Well, as I was telling you before you began this interruption about names, he is exactly 110 years old. Can you imagine a man 110 years old? A man 110 years old is an unusual thing, isn't it?"

"It is, Feodor. But I once knew a man 113 years old."

"Ha! And what kind of a man was he? Did he dance jigs? Did he crack nuts with his teeth? Did he drink like a fish?"

"No, he was an old man and very sad."

"You see! He was sad. So what has he to do with Pitzela? Nothing. Pitzela laughs all day long. And he dances jigs. And he cracks nuts with his teeth. Mind you, a man 110 years old cracks nuts with his teeth! Can you imagine such a thing?"

"No Feodor. It is amazing."

"Amazing? Why amazing? Everything that happens different from what you know is amazing to you! You are very naïve. You know what naïve means? It is French."

"I know what naïve means, Feodor. Go on about Pitzela."

"Naïve means to be childish late in life. In a way you are like Pitzela, despite the difference in your ages. He is naïve. You know what he wants?"

"What?"

"This Pitzela wants to show everybody how young he is. That's his central ambition. He don't talk English much, but when you ask him, 'Pitzela, how do you feel today?' he says to you right back, 'Oi, me? I'm full o' pep.' Then if you ask him, 'How old are you, Pitzela?' he says: 'Old? What does it matter how old I am? I am just beginning to enjoy myself. And when you talk about my dying don't laugh too much. Because, you know, I will attend all your funerals. When I am 300 years old I will be burying your grandchildren.' And he will laugh. Do you like the story?"

"Yes, Feodor. But it isn't long enough. I will have to go out and see Pitzela and describe him and that will make the story long enough."

"It isn't long enough? What do you mean? I just begun. The story ain't about Pitzela at all. So why should you go see Pitzela?"

"But I thought it was about Pitzela."

"You thought! Hm! Well, you see what good it does you to think. For according to your thinking the story is already finished. Whereas according to me the story is only just beginning."

"But you said it was about Pitzela, Feodor. So I believed you."

"I said nothing of the sort. I merely asked you if you knew Pitzela. The story is entirely about Pitzela's son."

"Aha! This Pitzela has a son. That's interesting."

"Of course it is. Pitzela's son is a man 87 years old. Ask anybody on Maxwell street do they know Pitzela's son and they will tell you: 'Do we know Pitzela's son? Hm! It's a scandal."

"The editor, Feodor, forbids me to write about scandals. So be careful."

"This scandal is one you can write about. This Pitzela's son is such a poor old man that he can hardly walk. He has a long white beard and wears a yamulka and he has no teeth and one foot is already deep in the grave. If you saw Pitzela's son you would say: 'Why don't this dying man go home and sit down instead of running around like this?'"

"And why don't he?"

"Why don't he? Such a question! He don't because Pitzela don't let him. Pitzela is his father and he has to mind his father. And Pitzela says: 'What! You want to hang around the house like you were an old man? You are crazy. Look at me, I'm your father. And you a young man, my son, act like you were my father. It's a scandal. Come, we will go to the banquet.'"

"What banquet, Feodor?"

"Oh, any banquet. He drags him. He don't let him rest. And he says: 'You must shave off your beard. For fifteen years you been letting it grow and now it's altogether too long. How does it look for me to go around with a son who not only can't walk, but has a beard that makes him look like Father Abraham himself?'"

"And what does Pitzela's son say?"

"What can he say? Nothing. The doctor comes and tells him: 'You got to stay in the house. You are going out too much. How old are you?' And Pitzela's son shakes his tired head and says: "Eighty-seven years old, doctor.' And the doctor gives strict orders. But Pitzela comes in and laughs. Imagine."

"Yes, it's a good story, Feodor."

271

"A good story! How do you know? I ain't come to the point yet. But never mind, if you like it so much you don't need any point."

"The point, Feodor. Excuse me."

"Well, the point is that Pitzela and the way he treats his son is a scandal. You know why? Because he uses his son as an advertisement. Pitzela's son, mind you, is so weak and old that he can hardly walk and he carries a heavy cane and his hands shake like leaves. And Pitzela drags him around all over. To banquets. To political meetings. To the Yiddish theater. All over. He holds him by the arm and brings him into the hall and sits him down in a chair. And Pitzela's son sits so tired and almost dead he can't move. And then Pitzela jumps up and gets excited and says: 'Look at him. A fine son, for you! Look, he's almost dead. Tell me if you wouldn't think he was my father and I was his son? Instead of the other way around? I ask you.' "

"And what does Pitzela's son say, Feodor?"

"Say? What can he say? He looks up and shakes his head some more. He can hardly see. And when the banquet talking begins he falls asleep and Pitzela has to hold him up from falling out of the chair. And when the food is done and the dessert comes Pitzela leans over and says to his son: 'Listen. I got a treat for you. Here.' And he reaches into his pocket and brings out a handful of hickory nuts. 'Crack them with your teeth,' he says, 'like your father.' And when his son looks at him and strokes his white beard and sighs, Pitzela jumps up and laughs so you can hear him all over the banquet hall. But the point of the story is that two weeks ago Pitzela went to his grandson's funeral. It was Pitzela's son's son and he was a man almost 70 years old. And it was a scandal at the funeral. Why? Because Pitzela laughed and coming back from the grave he said: 'Look at me, my grandson dies and I go to his funeral and if he had a son I would go to his, too, and I would dance jigs both times.' "

PANDORA'S BOX

A dark afternoon with summer thunder in the sky. The fan-shaped skyscrapers spread a checkerboard of window lights through the gloom. It rains. People seem to grow vaguely elate on the dark wet pavements. They hurry along, their eyes saying to one another, "We have something in common. We are all getting wet in the rain." The crowd is no longer quite so enigmatic a stranger to itself. An errand boy from Market Street advances with leaps through the downpour, a high chant on his lips, "It's raining. . . . it's raining." The rain mutters and the pavements, like darkened mirrors, grow alive with impressionistic cartoons of the city.

Inside the Washington Street book store of Covici-McGee the electric lights gleam cozily. New books and old books—the high shelves stuffed with books vanish in the ceiling shadows. On a rainy day the dusty army of books peers coaxingly from the shelves. Old tales, old myths, old wars, old dreams begin to chatter softly in the shadows—or it may be the chatter of the rain on the pavement outside. The Great Philosophers unbend, the Bearded Classics sigh, the Pontifical Critics of Life murmur "ahem." Yes, even the forbidding works of Standard Authors grow lonely on the high shelves on a rainy day. As for the rag-tag, ruffle-snuffle crowd in motley—the bulged, spavined, sniffling crew of mountebanks, troubadours, swashbucklers, bleary philosophers, phantasts and adventurers—they set up a veritable witches' chorus. Or it may be the rain again lashing against the streaming windows of the book store.

People come in out of the rain. A girl without an umbrella, her face wet. Who? Perhaps a stenographer hunting a job and halted by the rain. And then a matron with an old-fashioned knitted shopping bag. And a spinster with a keen, kindly face. Others, too. They stand nervously idle,

feeling that they are taking up valuable space in an industrial establishment and should perhaps make a purchase. So they permit their eyes to drift politely toward the wares. And then the chatter of the books has them. Old books, new books, live books, dead books—but they move carelessly away and toward the bargain tables—"All Books 30 Cents." Broken down best sellers here—pausing in their gavotte toward oblivion. The next step is the junk man—$1 a hundred. Pembertons, Wrights, Farnols, Websters, Johnstones, Porters, Wards and a hundred other names reminiscent more of a page in the telephone book than a page out of a literary yesterday. The little gavotte is an old dance in the second-hand book store. The $2-shelf. The $1-rack. The 75-cent table. The 30-cent grab counter. And finis. New scribblings crowd for place, old scribblings exeunt.

The girl without an umbrella studies titles. A love story, of course, and only thirty cents. An opened page reads, "he took her in his arms. . . ." Who would not buy such a book on a rainy day?

It rains and other people come in. A middle-aged man in a curious coat, a curious hat and a curious face. Slate-colored skin, slate-colored eyes behind silver spectacles. A scholar in caricature, an Old Clothes Dealer out of Alice in Wonderland. The rain runs from his stringy, slate-colored hair. He approaches the high shelves, thrusts the silver spectacles farther down on his nose. In front of him a curious row of literary gargoyles—"The Astral Light," "What and Where Is God?", "Man" by Dohony of Texas, "The Star of the Magi."

Thin slate-colored fingers fumble nervously over the title backs. A second man, figure short, squat, red-faced, crowds the erratic scholar. A third. The rain is bringing them in in numbers. These are the basement students of the gargoyle philosophies, the gargoyle sciences, the gargoyle religions.

Perpetual motion machine inventors, alchemists with staring, nervous-eyed medieval faces, fourth dimensionists, sun worshippers, cabalistic researchers, voodoo authorities—the old-book store is suddenly alive with them. They move about furtively with no word for one another, lost in their grotesque dreamings.

On a rainy day the city gives them up and they come puttering excitedly into the loop on a quest. The world is a garish unreality to them. The streets and the crowds of automatic-faced men and women, the upward rush of buildings and the horizontal rush of traffic are no more than vague grimacings. Life is something of which the streets are oblivious. But here on the gargoyle shelves, the high, shadowed shelves of the old book store—truth stands in all its terrible reality, wrapped in its authentic habiliments. Dr. Hickson of the psychopathic laboratory would give these curious rainy day phantasts identities as weird as the volumes they caress. But the old book store clerk is more kind. He lets them rummage. Before the rain ends they will buy "The Cradle of the Giants," "The Key to Satanism," Cornelius Agrippa's "Natural Magic," "The Astral Chord," "Occultism and Its Usages." They will buy books by Jacob Boehme, William Law, Sadler, Hyslop, Ramachaska. And they will go hurrying home with their treasures pressed close to them. Stuffy bedrooms lined with hints of Sabbatical horror, strewn with bizarre refuse; musty smelling books out of whose pages fantastic shapes rear themselves against the gaslights, macabre worlds in which unreason rides like a headless D'Artagnan; evenings in the park arguing suddenly with startled strangers on the existence of the philosophers' stone or the astrological causes of influenza—these form a background for the curious men whom the rain has drifted into the old book store and who stand with their eyes haunting the gargoyle titles.

The rain brings in another tribesman—a famed though

somewhat ragged bibliomaniac. His casual gestures hide the sudden fever old books kindle in his thought. Old books— old books, a magical phrase to him. His eyes travel like a lover's back and forth, up and down. He knows them all— the sets, the first editions, the bargains, the riff-raff. A democratic lover is here. But the clerk watches him. For this lover is an antagonist. Yes, this somewhat ragged, gleaming-eyed gentleman with the casual manner is a terrible person to have around in a second-hand book store on a rainy day. Only six months ago one of his horrible tribe pounced upon Sander's "Indian Wars," price 30 cents; value, alas, $150.00. Only two months ago another of his kidney fell upon a copy of Jean Jacques Rosseau's "Emile" with Jean's own dedication on the title page to "His Majesty, the King of France." Price 75 cents; value, gadzooks, $200.

There will be nothing today, however. Merely an hour's caress of old friends on the high shelves while the rain beats outside. Unless—unless this Stevenson happens by any chance to be a "first." A furtive glance at the title page. No. The clerk sighs with relief as the Stevenson goes back on the shelf. It might have been something overlooked.

The rain ends. The old book store slowly empties. A troop of men and women saunter out, pausing to say farewell to the gaudily ragged tomes in the old book store. The sky has grown lighter. The buildings shake the last drops of rain from their spatula tops. There is a different-looking, well-linened gentleman thrusts his head into the old book store and inquires, "Have you a copy of 'The Investors' Guide'?"

ILL-HUMORESQUE

The beggar in the street, sitting on the pavement against the building with his pleading face raised and his arm outstretched—I don't like him. I don't like the way he tucks his one good leg under him in order to convey the impression that he is entirely legless. I don't like the way he thrusts his arm stump at me, the way his eyes plead his weakness and sorrow.

He is a presumptuous and calculating scoundrel, this beggar. He is a diabolical psychologist. Why will people drop coins into his hat? Ah, because when they look at him and his misfortunes, by a common mental ruse they see themselves in his place, and they hurriedly fling a coin to this fugitive image of themselves. And because in back of this beggar has grown up an insidious propaganda that power is wrong, that strength is evil, that riches are vile. A strong, rich and powerful man cannot get into heaven. Thus this beggar becomes for an instant an intimidating symbol of perfections. One feels that one should apologize for the fact that one has two legs, money in one's pocket and hope in one's heart. One flings him a coin, thus buying momentary absolution for not being an unfortunate—i. e., as noble and non-predatory—as the beggar.

I do not like the way this beggar pleads. And yet after I pass him and remember his calculating expression, his mountebank tricks, I grow fond of him—theoretically. My thought warms to him as a creature of intelligence, of straightforward and amusing cynicisms.

For this beggar is aware of me and the innumerable lies to which I lamely submit. I am the public to him—one of a herd of identical faces drifting by. And this beggar has perfected a technique of attack. It is his duty to sit on the pavement and lay for me and hit me with a slapstick labeled plati-

tude and soak me over the head with a bladder labeled in stern white letters: "The Poor Shall Inherit the Kingdom of Heaven."

And this he does, the scoundrel, grinning to himself as the blows fall and slyly concealing his enthusiasm as the coins jingle into his hat. I am one of those who labor proudly at the immemorial task of idealizations. I am the public who passes laws proclaiming things wrong, immoral, contrary to my "best instincts." Thus I have after many centuries succeeded in creating a beautiful conception—a marvelous person. This marvelous person represents what I might be if I had neither ambition nor corpuscles, prejudices nor ecstasties, greeds, lusts, illusions or curiosity. This marvelous person is the beautiful image, the noble and flattering image of itself that the public rapturously beholds when it stares into the mirror of laws, conventions, adages, platitudes and constitutions that it has created.

A charming image to contemplate. Learned men wax full of stern joy when they gaze upon this image. Kind-hearted folk thrill with pride at the thought that life is at last a carefully policed force which flows politely and properly through the catalogued veins of this marvelous person.

But my beggar in the street—ah, my beggar in the street knows better. My beggar in the street, maimed and vicious, sits against the building and wields his bladder and his slapstick on me. Whang! A platitude on the rear. Bam! A bromide on the bean! And I shell out a dime and hurry on. I do not like this beggar.

But I grow warm with fellowship toward him after I have left him behind. There is something comradely about his amazing cynicism. People, thinks this beggar, are ashamed of themselves for being strong, for having two legs, for not being poor, brow-beaten, cheek-turning humble mendicants. People, thinks this beggar, are secretly ashamed of themselves for being part of success. And their shame is inspired by fear. When they see me they suddenly feel uncertain about themselves. When they see me they think that reverses and misfortunes and calamities might overtake them and reduce them to my condition. Thinking this, they grow indignant for an instant with a society that produces beggars. Not because it produced me. But perhaps it might produce them—as beggars. And then remembering that they are responsible for my plight —they being society—they beg my pardon by giving me money and a pleading look. Oho! You should see the pleading looks they give me. Men and women pass and plead with me not to hit them too hard with my slapstick and bladder. They plead with me to spare them, not to look at them. And when they give me a dime it is a gesture intended to annihilate me. The dime obliterates my misfortunes. It annihilates my poverty. For an instant, having annihilated poverty and misfortune with a dime, the man or woman is happy. An instant of security strengthens his wavering spirit.

Thus my beggar whom I have grown quite fond of as I write. I would write more of him and of the marvelous person in me whom he is continually belaboring with his slapstick and bladder. But I remember suddenly a man in a wheel chair. A pale man with drawn features and paralyzed legs. It was at night in North Clark Street. Lights streamed over the pavements. People moved in and out of doorways.

And this man sat in his wheel chair, a board on his lap. The board was laden with wares. Trinkets, pencils, shoestrings, candies, tacks, neckties, socks. And from the front of the board hung a sign reading, "Jim's Store—Stop and Shop."

I remember this creature with a sudden excitement. I passed by and bought nothing. But after five days his fate has caught up with me. A sallow, drawn face, burning eyes, bloodless lips and skinny hands that fumbled among the wares on his board. He was young. Heroic sentences come to me. "Jim's Store——" Good hokum, effective advertising. And a strange pathos, a pathos that my beggar with one leg and a pleading face never had.

I do not like cynics. I like Jim better. I like Jim and his burning eyes, his skinny hands, his dying body—and his store. Fighting—with the lights going out. Sitting in a wheel chair with death at his back and despair crying from his eyes— "Come buy from me—a little while longer—I don't give up . . . . another week. . . . another month. . . . but I don't give up. I'm still on the turf. . . . Never mind my dying body. . . . business as usual. . . . business as usual. . . . Come buy from me. . . . little while longer. . . . a. . . ."

But I never gave a nickel to Jim. I passed up his store. I took him at his word. He was selling wares and I didn't want any. But my beggar with the one leg and the inward grin was selling absolutions. . . . And I patronized him.

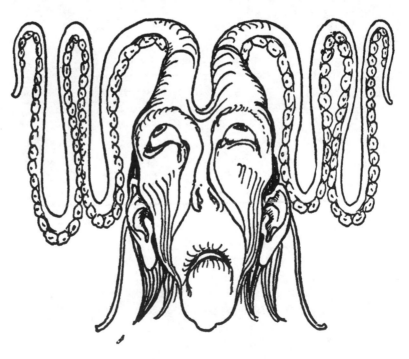

THE MAN WITH A QUESTION

Late afternoon. An hour more and the city will be emptying itself out of the high buildings. Now the shoppers are hurrying home to get dinner on the table.

A man stands on the corner of Michigan Avenue and Adams Street. Unwittingly he invites attention. A poorly dressed man, with a work-heavy face and coarsened hands. But he stands motionless. More than that, he is not looking at anything. His deep-set eyes seem to withhold themselves from the active street.

In the suave spectacle of the avenue his motionless figure is like an awkward faux pas in a parlor conversation. The newspaper man on his way to the I. C. station pauses to light his pipe and his eyes take in the figure of this motionless one.

The newspaper man notices that the man stands like one who is braced against something that may come suddenly and that his deep-set eyes say, "We know what we know." There are other impressions that interest the newspaper man. For a moment the motionless one seems a blurred little unit of the hurrying crowd. Then for a moment he seems to grow large and his figure becomes commanding and it is as if he were surveying the blurred little faces of the hurrying crowd. This is undoubtedly because he is standing still and not looking at anything.

"Can I have a light, please?"

The man's voice is low. A bit hoarse. He has a pipe and the newspaper man gives him a match. Ah, the amiable, meaningless curiosity of newspaper men! This one must ask questions. It is after work, but, like the policeman who goes to the movies with his club still at his side, he is still asking questions.

"Taking in the sights?"

The man, lighting his pipe, nods slowly. Much too slowly, as if his answer were fraught with a vast significance.

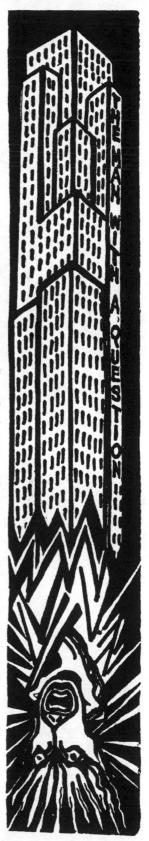

"I like it myself," insinuates the newspaper man. "I was reading Junius Wood's article on Bill Shatov, who is running things now in Siberia. He quotes Bill as saying what he misses most in life now is the music of crowds in Chicago streets. Did you read that?"

This is a brazen lead. But the man looks like a "red." And Bill Shatov would then open the talk. But the man only shakes his head. He says, "No, I don't read the papers much."

Now there is something contradictory about this man and his curtness invites. He seems to have accepted the presence of the newspaper man in an odd way, an uncity way. After a pause he gestures slightly with his pipe in his hand and says:

"Quite a crowd, eh?"

The newspaper man nods. The other goes on:

"Where are they going?"

This is more than a question. There is indignation in it. The deepset eyes gleam.

"I wonder," says the newspaper man. His companion remains staring in his odd, unseeing way. Then he says:

"They don't look at anything, eh? In a terrible hurry, ain't they? Yeah, in a rotten hurry."

The newspaper man nods. "Which way you going?" he asks.

"No way," his companion answers. "No way at all. I'm standin' here, see?"

There is a silence. The motionless one has become something queer in the eyes of the newspaper man. He has become grim, definite, taunting. Here is a man who questions the people of the street with unseeing eyes. Why? Here is one who is going "no way." Yet, look at him closely and there is no sneer in his eyes. His lips hold no contempt.

There you have it. He is a questioning man. He is questioning things that no one questions—buildings, crowds, windows. And there is some sort of answer inside him.

"What you talking to me for?"

The newspaper man smiles disarmingly at this sudden inquiry.

"Oh, I don't know," he says. "Saw you standing still. You looked different. Wondered, you know. Just kind of thought to say hello."

"Funny," says the motionless one.

"I got a hunch you're a stranger in town."

This question the companion answers. "Yeah, a stranger. A stranger. That's what I am, all right. I'm a stranger, all right. You got me right."

Now the motionless one smiles. This makes his face look uncomfortable. This makes it seem as if he had been frowning savagely before.

"What do you think of this town?" pursues the newspaper man.

"Think of this town? Think? Say, I ain't thinking. I don't think anything of it. I'm just looking at it, see? A stranger don't ever think, now, does he? There, that's one for you."

"When'd you come here?"

"When'd I come here? When? Well, I come here this noon. On the noon train. Say, don't make me gabby. I never gab any."

Nothing to be got out of this motionless one. Nothing but a question. A pause, however, and he went on:

"Have you ever seen such a crowd like this? Hurrying? Hm! Some town! There used to be a hotel over here west a bit."

"The Wellington?"

"Yeah. I don't see it when I pass."

"Torn down."

"Hm! The deep-set eyes narrow for an instant. Then the motionless one sighs and his shoulders loosen. His face grows alive and he looks this way and that. He starts to

283

walk and walks quickly, leaving the newspaper man standing alone.

The newspaper man watched him. As he stood looking after him some one tapped him on the shoulder. He turned. "Specs" McLaughlin of the detective bureau. "Specs" rubbed his chin contemplatively and smiled.

"Know that guy?"

"Who?"

"No; just bumped into him. How come?"

"You might have got a story out of him," "Specs" grinned. "That's George Cook. Just let out of the Joliet pen this morning. Served fourteen years. Quite a yarn at the time. For killing a pal in the Wellington hotel over some dame. I guess that was before your time, though. He just landed in town this noon."

The detective rubbered into the moving crowd.

"I'm sort of keeping an eye on him," he said, and hurried on.

GRASS FIGURES

You will sometimes notice when you sit on the back porch after dinner that there are other back porches with people on them. And when you sit on the front steps, that there are other front steps similarly occupied. In the park when you lie down on the grass you will see there are others lying on the grass. And when you look out of your window you can observe other people looking out of their windows.

In the streets when you walk casually and have time to look around you will see others walking casually and looking around, too. And in the theater or church or where you work there are always the inevitable others, always reflecting yourself. You might get to thinking about this as the newspaper reporter did. The newspaper reporter got an idea one day that the city was nothing more nor less than a vast, broken mirror giving him back garbled images of himself.

The newspaper reporter was trying to write fiction stories on the side and he thought: "If I can figure out something for a background, some idea or something that will explain about people, and then have the plot of the story sort of prove this general idea by a specific incident, that would be the way to work it."

Thus, when the reporter had figured it out that the city was a mirror reflecting himself, he grew excited. That was the kind of idea he had always been looking for. But at night in his bedroom when he started to write he hit a snag. He had thought he held in his mind the secret of the city. Yet when he came to write about it the secret slipped away and left him with nothing. He sat looking out of his bedroom window, noticing that the telephone poles in the dark alley looked like huge, inverted music notes. Then he thought: "It doesn't do any good to get an idea that doesn't tell you anything. Just figuring out that the city is a mirror that reflects me all the time doesn't give me the secret of streets and crowds.

GRASS FIGURES

Because the question then arises: "Who am I that the mirror reflects, and what am I?   What in Sam Hill is my motif?"

So the newspaper reporter decided to wait awhile before he wrote his story—wait, at least, until he had found out something.   But the next day, while he was walking in Michigan Avenue, the idea he had had about the mirror trotted along beside him like some homeless Hector pup that he couldn't shake.   He looked up eagerly into the faces of the crowd on the street, searching the many different eyes that moved by him for a "lead."

What the newspaper reporter wanted was to be able to begin his fiction story by saying something like this: "People are so and so.   The city is so and so.   Everybody feels this and this.   No matter who they are or where they live, or what their jobs are they can't escape the mark of the city that is on them."

It was after 7 o'clock and the people in Michigan Avenue were going home or sauntering back and forth, looking into the shop windows, with nothing much to do.   The street was still light, although the sun had gone.   Hidden behind the buildings of the city, the sun flattened itself out on an invisible horizon and spread a vast peacock tail of color across the sky. In Grant Park, opposite the Public Library, men lay on their backs with their hands folded under their heads and stared up into the colors of the sky.   The newspaper reporter stood abstractedly on the corner counting the automobiles that purred by to see if more taxicabs than privately owned cars passed a given point in Michigan Avenue.   Then he walked across the street for no other reason than that there were for the moment no more automobiles to count.   He stopped on the opposite pavement and stood looking at the figures that lay on the grass in Grant Park.

The newspaper reporter had been lying for ten minutes on his back in the grass when he sat up suddenly and muttered:

286

"Here it is. Right in front of me." He sat, looking intently, at the men who were lying on the grass as he had been a moment before. And his idea about the city's being a mirror giving him back images of himself started up again in his mind. But now he could find out what these images of himself were. In fact, what he was. Whereupon he would have his story.

Being a newspaper reporter there was nothing unusual in his mind about walking up to one of the figures and talking to it. For years and years he had done just that for a living—walked up to strangers and asked them questions. So now he would ask the men lying on their backs what they were lying on their backs for. He would ask them why they came to Grant Park, what they were thinking about and how it happened that they all looked alike and lay on their backs like a chorus of figures in a pastoral musical comedy.

The first figure the newspaper reporter approached listened to the questions in surprise. Then he answered: "Well I dunno. I just came into the park and lay down." The second figure looked blank and shook its head. The reporter tried a third. The third figure grinned and answered: "Oh, well, nothing much to do and the grass rests you a bit."

The reporter kept on for a few minutes, asking his questions and getting answers that didn't quite mean anything. Then he grew tired of the job and returned to his original place on the grass and lay down again and stared up into the colors of the sky. After a half-hour, during which he had thought of nothing in particular, he arose, shook his legs free of dirt and grass and walked away. As he walked he looked at the figures that remained. The arc lamps on the park shafts and on the Greek-like fountain were popping on and the avenue was lighting up like a theater with the footlights going on.

"Funny about them," the newspaper reporter thought, eyeing the figures as he moved away; "they lie there on their

287

backs all in the same position, all looking at the same clouds. So they must all be thinking thoughts about the same thing. Let's see; what was I thinking about? Nothing."

An excited light came suddenly into the newspaper reporter's eyes.

"I was just waiting," he muttered to himself. "And so are they."

The newspaper reporter looked eagerly at the street and the people passing. That was it. He had found the word. "Waiting." Everybody was waiting. On the back porches at night, on the front steps, in the parks, in the theaters, churches, streets and stores—men and women waited. Just as the men on the grass in Grant Park were waiting. The only difference between the men lying on their backs and people elsewhere was that the men in the grass had grown tired for the moment of pretending they were doing anything else. So they had stretched themselves out in an attitude of waiting, in a deliberate posture of waiting. And with their eyes on the sky, they waited.

The newspaper reporter felt thrilled as he thought all this. He felt thrilled when he looked closely at the people in Michigan Avenue and saw that they fitted snugly into his theory. He said to himself: "I've discovered a theory about life. A theory that fits them all. That makes the background I'm looking for. Waiting. Yes, the whole pack of them are waiting all the time. That's why we all look alike. That's why one house looks like another and one man walking looks like another man walking, and why figures lying in the grass look like twins—scores of twins."

The newspaper man returned to his bedroom and started to write again. But he had been writing only a few minutes when he stopped. Again, as it had before, the secret had slipped out of his mind. For he had come to a paragraph that was to tell what the people were waiting for and he couldn't think of any answer to that. What were the men in the grass waiting for? In the street? On the porches and stone steps? They were images of himself—all "waiting images" of himself. Therefore the answer lay in the question: "What had he been waiting for?"

The newspaper reporter bit into his pencil. "Nothing, nothing," he muttered. "Yes, that's it. They aren't waiting for anything. That's the secret. Life is a few years of suspended animation. But there's no story in that. Better forget it."

So he looked glumly out of his bedroom window, and, being a sentimentalist, the huge inverted music notes the telephone poles made against the dark played a long, sad tune in his mind.